Entrepreneurship
from Creativity to Innovation

Thinking Skills for a Changing World

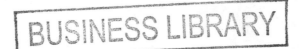
Professor Edward Lumsdaine
Michigan Technological University

Professor Martin Binks
The University of Nottingham

Entrepreneurship from Creativity to Innovation

ISBN 1-4251-0472-X

Previous editions were published as 6x9 inch paperbacks (with blue covers and different titles):

1. *Keep on Moving! Entrepreneurial Creativity and Effective Problem Solving,* © 2003 The McGraw-Hill Companies, Primis Custom Series, ISBN 0-07-284153-2.
2. *Entrepreneurship, Creativity, and Effective Problem Solving: Keep on Moving!* © 2005 Edward Lumsdaine and Martin Binks, published by E&M Lumsdaine Solar Consultants, Inc., Hancock, Michigan, U.S.A., ISBN 0-9761018-0-7.

Cover Design: Casey Cole, Finlandia University, Hancock

1005668885

Copyrights and permissions

The graph on page 4 is used with permission by Gerald Udell, Southwest Missouri State University. The original appeared in *Evaluating Potential New Products: A Manual to Aid in Understanding the Innovation Process and the PIES-VIII Preliminary Innovation Evaluation System,* 1998.

Chapter 4 and Chapter 5 (except for the kitchen lighting example) have been condensed from material in *Creative Problem Solving and Engineering Design* by Edward Lumsdaine, Monika Lumsdaine, and J. William Shelnutt, ©1999 McGraw-Hill Primis, ISBN 0-07-236-058-5.

The Ned Herrmann materials and model are used by permission of Herrmann International, ©2006, ©2003, ©1998 by the Ned Herrmann Group, ©1996 by Ned Herrmann. We gratefully acknowledge the kindness of Herrmann International for generously permitting us to use copyrighted materials from their books and HBDI packets. See www.hbdi.com for more information.

Monika Lumsdaine is a certified HBDI practitioner and management consultant for corporate behavior and has authored Chapter 3 (The Herrmann Thinking Styles Model). She also developed the kitchen lighting example in Chapter 5 as well as the graph of the creative problem solving model superimposed on the Herrmann model of thinking preferences shown in Figure 4.1. This figure and the HBDI graphs from her work in Figure 3.7 and Figure 11.2 are used by permission.

We thank Professor John Pliniussen (course developer) and Professor Peg Tittle (course instructor) for permission to use two exercises (the "Don't Sell Me" game and "The Problem at Algona") from the manual that accompanied the course *ADMN 3917EQ Innovation and Creativity* in the Centre for Continuing Business Education, Nipissing University, North Bay, Ontario, Canada.

Dedication

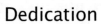

To our entrepreneurial wives and our children:

Monika Lumsdaine
Andrew, Alfred, Anne, Arnold

Alison Binks
Jessica, Laura, Alice

Contents

Figures

Tables

Preface

Entrepreneurship: From Creativity to Innovation is a unique guide for students, potential entrepreneurs and inventors, business managers, team leaders, or anyone seeking to become a more effective problem solver and innovator. It focuses on the creative thinking and problem solving skills needed to succeed in our rapidly changing, high-tech world. This "entrepreneurial" thinking will empower you to cope with uncertainty and behave with greater flexibility in your professional and personal life—these skills are for everyone! Learning is reinforced through application to communication, teamwork and above all to entrepreneurship. You will gain a basic understanding of innovation—a valuable skill in demand by employers who recognize the ability to innovate as a key for remaining competitive in the global marketplace. At a time when traditional jobs are disappearing, you will be able to recognize and profit from new opportunities.

How can this book benefit you?

This revised edition has been substantially enlarged and updated with a strong focus on innovation. As the pace of change in terms of technology and social needs accelerates, the role of successful entrepreneurship becomes even more important. It is for this reason that we have chosen to link the development of effective thinking skills with application to entrepreneurial endeavor, even though it addresses a far wider audience and range of potential applications. In addition, we built in a foundational understanding of the nature of innovation and how it can be encouraged—personally, in a group, and in an organization.

What was our purpose and approach in writing this book?

We have designed the book to be concise and accessible by focusing only on the content that our long experience of teaching in these areas has shown to be most valuable for learners with a wide variety of backgrounds and requirements. It is a practical guide that will be useful for those interested in wanting to learn how to think and solve problems more creatively. Most chapters are accompanied by relevant exercises or activities for individual study or team projects to enhance both explicit and tacit learning. We endeavored to engage different types of learners, but all will be encouraged to value and develop four specific thinking modes or ways of "knowing": analytical-factual-logical, sequential-organized-detailed, interpersonal-symbolic-intuitive, and imaginative-holistic-conceptual. Within this framework, the application to entrepreneurship makes an interesting case study.

How will you learn from this book?

The book is organized into four major parts, with Part 1 providing the thinking tools, Part 2 the application to product development, Part 3 the application to business development, and Part 4 the application to growing a sustainable business through leadership, management, and continuous product and business innovation.

How is this book organized?

Specifically, what are the contents of the four parts?

In particular, **Part One** presents a holistic and historical view of entrepreneurship and its links to creativity and innovation. You will be introduced to the Herrmann thinking styles model, the creative problem solving model and the Pugh method for developing optimized solutions.

In **Part Two**, you will learn to apply these thinking tools to the product development process, from finding a customer or market need to generating and synthesizing creative ideas down to a "best" concept or solution which can be protected with a patent.

Part Three shows how you can apply these tools to business development, from deciding on the legal form to planning your marketing strategies and obtain funding. Other topics include how to make an effective "sales" presentation and how to write a business plan.

Part Four is largely new to this book and discusses strategies for leadership, management and coping with change as related to a startup enterprise. It presents the four crucial pillars needed to sustain organizational innovation for growth and profitability: development of everyone's thinking skills; their application by cross-functional teams at the project level; their integration at the organizational level by management; with open communication linking everyone in the enterprise.

Enjoy this journey of exploration and adventure in life-long learning!

We believe this book is unique in that the underlying thinking skills needed for creative problem solving and for successful entrepreneurial ventures and innovation are purposefully made transparent. This will enable you to apply what you are learning to your work and to your personal life— you can become more creative and innovative. As we state in the close of our book, "The wider application of creative problem solving can make a significant contribution towards the generation of new solutions to the problems of an increasingly complex and precarious world."

Our Thanks

Monika Lumsdaine has done the editing and layout for the digital manuscript. She has been instrumental in integrating text written by two different authors into one synthesized whole—without her efforts, this updated edition would simply not have come into being in time for the 2007 classes and other readers all over the world. We are grateful.

Casey Cole, a graphics design student at Finlandia University in Hancock, Michigan—with the encouragement of her academic advisor, Niki Belkowski—developed the design for the book cover. Thanks for providing a creative vision from a younger generation's point of view. The interaction and synergy of ideas coming from different minds (over time and distance) into the final concept was an amazing process to observe.

We appreciate our entrepreneurial students and colleagues who have given us feedback over the years on how we could improve our teaching materials, delivery, and teamwork. One notable contribution is an application of the Pugh method by one of our Singapore students which we have included in the new edition.

Then we stand in awe at today's print-on-demand technology which is able to produce and print our book in record time. It will allow us to do frequent updates to keep the material current. We are embarking on a new venture by publishing with Trafford, an international company—we believe we have made a good choice to better serve our global market. This is a new business model for us, and we are looking forward to seeing how it will succeed on several levels—from manufacturing and marketing to timely delivery. It has been an opportunity for us to apply what we are teaching.

Edward Lumsdaine
Martin Binks

Authors' Information

Dr. Edward Lumsdaine is currently Professor of Mechanical Engineering at Michigan Technological University and Special Professor of Business, Institute for Enterprise and Innovation, University of Nottingham (England), and for many years was management consultant at Ford Motor Company. In 1994 he received the ASEE Chester F. Carlson award for innovation in engineering education. He has co-authored books and teaches workshops in creative problem solving, engineering design, entrepreneurship and innovation—a synthesis of many years of experience working as engineer in industry as well as serving as dean of engineering and professor at six different universities in the U.S. and four different universities abroad. His engineering specialties are in aero-acoustics, vibration, heat transfer, fluid mechanics, and solar energy, and he has published over 100 papers in these fields.

Each year, Dr. Lumsdaine and Dr. Binks jointly teach a course in entrepreneurship and effective problem solving for MBA students in Singapore—this book has grown out of this cooperative effort. Dr. Lumsdaine is a Fellow of ASME (American Society of Mechanical Engineering) and RSA (the Royal Society of Arts) in the UK.

Dr. Martin Binks is the Director of the Institute for Enterprise and Innovation at the University of Nottingham (UNIEI) and Professor of Entrepreneurial Development at the Nottingham University Business School, specializing in entrepreneurship and the financing of small and medium enterprises (SMEs). He has an established research background in the area of SMEs and their relationship with banks. Among his activities and accomplishments are Visiting Professor to the Claremont Graduate School in California; provision of consultancy to HM Government ministries and member of the Bank of England Governor's Seminar on the Financing of Small Firms; council member of the Small Business Research Trust; and Associate Editor of *The Journal of Small Business Finance*.

Professor Binks developed one of the first university-level courses in entrepreneurship in the UK. His research focus is in entrepreneurship, SME finance, and the development of internet-based survey procedures such as the United Kingdom Business Barometer (www.ukbb.ac). Dr. Binks is a Fellow of the Royal Society of Arts (RSA), and he is also Co-Director of the Center for Integrative Learning at the University of Nottingham.

Part One
Thinking Tools

1   Personal Motivation

> **What you can learn from this chapter:**
> - Why entrepreneurial thinking with an understanding of innovation is for everyone, as integrated in the context of this book.
> - How effective problem solving skills and knowing how to be an entrepreneur can benefit you.
> - What are characteristics and challenges of young entrepreneurs?
> - Tips on how you can best learn from this book.

In today's boisterous entrepreneurial environment, it takes all kinds of people and all kinds of ideas.

Rieva Lesonsky, VP & editorial director, *Entrepreneur Media*

Entrepreneurship—from Creativity to Innovation focuses above all on the thinking and effective problem solving skills needed to succeed in a rapidly changing world. Even if you do not presently see yourself as an entrepreneur and starting your own business, entrepreneurial thinking will enable you to cope with uncertainty and behave with greater flexibility in your professional pursuits as well as in your personal life. The new skills are reinforced as they are applied in exercises, projects and case studies to communication, teamwork, and entrepreneurship; they will enhance your understanding of innovation—a valuable skill sought by many employers today. Also, at a time when companies downsize and jobs disappear, you will be more likely to recognize and profit from new opportunities.

Having an entrepreneurial mindset has become increasingly important in our high-tech information age—this mindset is for everyone! Also, the ability to innovate is a key for remaining competitive in the global marketplace. Table 1.1 compares major issues in the old and new economy.

Table 1.1   A New Economic Paradigm

Issue	**Old Economy**	**New Economy**
Markets	Stable	Dynamic
Scope of competition	Regional and national	Global
Organizational form	Hierarchical	Networked, entrepreneurial
Mobility of business	Low	High
Key factors of production	Capital and labor	Knowledge and INNOVATION
Effect of innovation	Moderate	High
Institutional/firm relations	Self-sufficient	Alliances and collaboration
Business-government relations	Impose requirements	Assist firms; deregulation
Leading research areas	Physical sciences, engineering	Information systems, life sciences

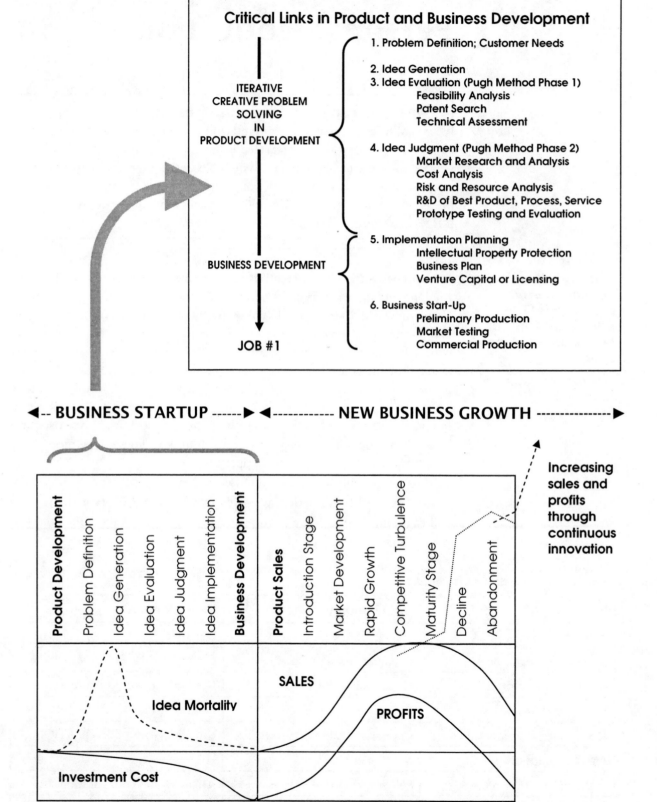

Figure 1.1 *The innovation process in the life cycle of a product or a business, adapted from an original graph by Gerald Udell (Ref. 1.1)*

WHAT YOU CAN LEARN FROM THIS BOOK

Even if you are on the right track, you'll get run over if you just sit there.

Will Rogers

As you study this book, you will gain a holistic view of entrepreneurship and its links with creativity and innovation. You will come to understand and hone the underlying thinking skills. You will learn to use a model for creative problem solving—and these tools will enhance the creativity, teamwork and communication needed to become successful in rapidly changing times. You will be introduced to business startup, from generating viable ideas to product and business development in a globally competitive environment, as shown on the facing page in Figure 1.1. You will be prepared to recognize, use and profit from the opportunities that will come your way.

Part One of this book provides a basic understanding of creativity, entrepreneurship, and innovation, together with the thinking styles model, the creative problem solving model and the Pugh method for developing optimized solutions. **Part Two** shows how these tools are applied to product development. None of the critical links in the product development and creative problem solving process should be skipped or undertaken out of sequence if you want to obtain optimum results. **Part Three** shows how these tools are applied to business development and provides an overview of resources that are available to entrepreneurs for business startup. **Part Four** (new to this edition) discusses the leadership and management roles of entrepreneurs and how they can help people cope with change, as well as the central role of the business model (see Fig. 1.2) and the four pillars needed to sustain profitability and organizational innovation. In brief, this is a unique and practical guide for students, potential entrepreneurs or anyone seeking to become a more effective thinker and problem solver—it is not an in-depth academic study of entrepreneurship or innovation (such as Refs. 1.2 and 1.3).

While creativity is the generation of new ides, which we have in abundance, innovation is the successful exploitation of them.

Sir George Cox

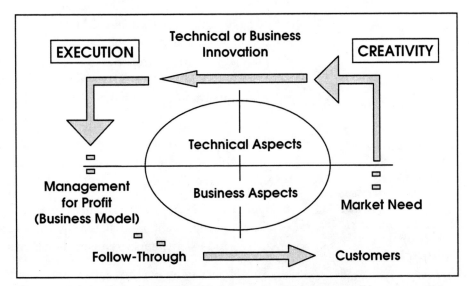

Figure 1.2 *Technical innovation often proceeds from creativity to execution, while business innovation more likely follows a complete cycle from market need to satisfied customers. The four quadrants indicated will be discussed in detail in Chapters 2 and 3. Chapter 12 will expand on the concepts introduced in this figure.*

In the age of technology, the importance of the educated and the creative to the economy is magnified.
USA TODAY,
10 Oct. 2003, p.2A

WHY WE NEED EFFECTIVE PROBLEM SOLVING SKILLS

Effective problem solving skills can benefit society, your organization, and you personally. Personally, you will be better able to cope with change; your thinking, learning, communication and teamwork will be enhanced—all of which can lead to a more enjoyable life. Professionally, you can solve problems and make decisions more effectively, and you are able to create an invigorating work environment leading to a successful career.

In your business or organization, you are will be able to provide a product or service that fully meets the needs of the customer; you can guide or lead the direction of technological development and innovation to gain increased productivity and a favorable competitive position in the global marketplace. Societal benefits are new ideas for solving ecological, technical, economic and social problems. Effective problem solving is all about producing and implementing these solutions, thus creating economic improvement for individuals and communities.

THE BENEFITS OF ENTREPRENEURSHIP STUDY

In general, what is the impact of entrepreneurship education? To find out, the Eller College of Business at the University of Arizona compared MBA alumni who graduated from their entrepreneurship program with alumni from the traditional business program. The study discovered that entrepreneurship graduates reaped the following benefits:

- Three times more likely to start a new business
- Three times more likely to be self employed
- Less likely to work for government
- Annual incomes that are 27% higher and owning 62% more assets
- In large firms, earning about $23,000/year more than their counterparts
- More satisfied with their jobs
- Dramatically increasing sales growth in small firms (by 900%)
- Working for high tech firms in greater numbers
- More involved in product development and R&D activities

When ingenious, creative thoughts result in a new product or process, we have an invention. However, the great majority of inventions never reach the marketplace. Accurate figures are impossible to come by, but one survey by NESTA in the UK suggests that the odds stack up something like this:

- Only 1 in 100 inventions more than covers its costs.
- Only 1 in 300 inventions makes a significant difference to a business.
- Only 1 in 1400 inventions is a world-beater leading to innovation.

Entrepreneurs create new technology, products, processes and services that become the next wave of new industries.

Jeffry A. Timmons
(Ref. 1.2)

This looks like an abysmal failure rate, but it need not be. Most failures are either inevitable because of flaws in the idea, or they are made inevitable by the inventor's mishandling of some aspect of development. Inventors who are able to avoid making mistakes can vastly increase the odds of succeeding, and this is what this book is all about.

WHY YOU MIGHT WANT TO BE AN ENTREPRENEUR

Entrepreneurs form the lifeblood of a healthy economy; they create new jobs, new wealth, new opportunities.

Small entrepreneurs are responsible for 67% of inventions and 95% of radical innovations since World War II.

In the U.S., 700,000 new businesses are started each year; 60% of new jobs are created by 10% of the fastest-growing new companies.

Among Americans born from 1965-1977, 87 percent would like to work for themselves. They want to be their own boss—they want freedom from the 9 to 5 work routine. Autonomy and independence are the main attractions for them. How much respect do you have for your own judgment? If a high regard for your own judgment leads you to disparage the judgment of others, this may present problems, because as an employee, you could be a constant source of disagreement and distraction in your workplace. At the same time, you may feel frustrated and angry, and these negative feelings can prevent you from recognizing positive opportunities. If this is the case, running your own business as an entrepreneur may be a better choice.

Here are some other good reasons for wanting to be an entrepreneur:

- Being bored by your existing job.
- Having an idea that just won't go away and being convinced there is a demand for this product or service.
- Wanting to be more creative and to more fully use abilities, skills and knowledge. Roughly two out of three entrepreneurs start their business for personal satisfaction.
- Has your job disappeared, or are you facing possible layoffs? About 40% go into business for increased job security and other financial reasons.
- Do you want to make lots of money?

Entrepreneurial activities of adults in startups and businesses less than 42 months old are low in Europe and developed Asian economies: Japan, Singapore and France 2%, Germany 5%, India, Italy and the UK 6%. It is higher in Canada 8%, Australia 11%, the U.S. and South Africa 13%. It is highest in developing Asian economies and in South America, with South Korea 14%, Brazil 16%, Thailand 21%, and Venezuela 25%. In every country, most of the entrepreneurial activity is carried out by people 25 to 34 years old. In developed countries, the entrepreneurs tend to be more opportunity driven, in poorer countries more necessity-driven. In poor and rich countries, men and women participate equally in entrepreneurship; in middle-income countries, three quarters of all entrepreneurs are male.

WHAT ARE CHARACTERISTICS OF YOUNG ENTREPRENEURS?

Gerard Darby has examined in a year-long research project the background, behaviors, motivations and qualities of successful young entrepreneurs and has summarized the following key findings (Ref. 1.4):

- Young entrepreneurs often show an inclination for enterprise at an early age, even when the surrounding culture is non-supportive.
- The media by and large have ignored the success of young entrepreneurs and the role models they could be for young people.
- Family members who run their own businesses and other entrepreneurs are the main source of encouragement for young entrepreneurs.

- Young people are also entrepreneurial in financing their fledging businesses, commonly working without compensation for a year or more and using many sources (in small amounts) to get started.
- Young entrepreneurs offer work opportunities that attract other like-minded and talented individuals.
- Young entrepreneurs make up for the lack of experience with drive and extraordinary resourcefulness. Other traits are listed in Table 1.2.

Table 1.2 *Key Characteristics of Young Entrepreneurs (from Ref. 1.4)*

- A sense of integrity, where employees, customers and investors are treated as valuable partners in the business.
- Applying common sense to business.
- An intuitive understanding of what makes a good innovation in a product or service, and the resilience and creativity to turn this into a reality.
- A sense of humor (which is seen in their working environments, marketing and personality).
- Motivated by the challenge of creating something and being in control of their own destiny, not by the desire for large profits.
- Taking a long-term view of the development of their enterprise.

Among major obstacles faced by young entrepreneurs is the lack of education in entrepreneurial skills in public schools. Gerard Darby points out, "In the UK, around 550 businesses are started every week by young people aged under 25, and the failure rate among this age group is particularly high." He counsels, "entrepreneurship would be better fostered if ... entrepreneurial endeavor were celebrated and failure recognized as often being a necessary component of success" (Ref. 1.4). This book aims to fill these gaps by teaching entrepreneurial thinking skills and providing how-to resources. Our desire is simply to show you how to develop and use your innate abilities—to help you become the best "entrepreneur" you can be, whether or not you fit the description of young entrepreneurs given above. This book is above all about personal growth and development.

HOW TO LEARN FROM THIS BOOK

A textbook is a tool to be used, underlined, highlighted, and annotated—not to be preserved in pristine condition.

This "value added" will transform it into a treasure trove and good friend.

Your ultimate goal may be entrepreneurial (starting and running your own business) or intrapreneurial (being an innovator within an organization). In either case, this book can help you accomplish these goals, if you develop the necessary thinking skills and put your learning into action.

This book provides two types of learning: explicit and tacit. By reading, you will learn information or explicit conceptual knowledge about a topic; through reflection, your understanding of models and concepts will grow. As you apply this new knowledge to entrepreneurial projects through specific tasks in appropriate thinking modes and problem solving mindsets, you acquire tacit operational knowledge. Tacit knowledge is reinforced when these experiences are communicated and shared with team members.

Throughout the entrepreneurship process, take every opportunity to sell yourself, your team, and your idea. You can never predict the benefits that such salesmanship will gain for you down the road.

NCIIA

Tips for Enhanced Learning

→ Obtain a notebook for jotting down thoughts and ideas as you read and think about entrepreneurship.

→ Underline or highlight important ideas and concepts as you read.

→ Jot down questions and comments that come to mind as you read, either in the notebook or in textbook margins. We designed the textbook with plenty of white space—use it!

→ Do the activities and exercises inserted in the text or at the end of the chapter.

→ Watch for questions embedded in the text and try to answer them.

→ At the end of a chapter or topic, ask yourself these two questions: "What is the most important thing I have just learned? What is an important question I still have?" Write down your questions—you will be amazed how this technique will sharpen your attention and thereby increase learning and retention.

EXERCISES

1.1 Problem Solving
In a brief paragraph, describe the method you use most often to solve problems. If you are in a class or group, share your answer with one or two people sitting next to you. If you are in a team where the members have similar thinking styles, compare your answers and develop a common definition in twenty-five words or less.

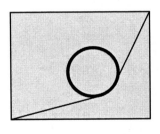

1.2 Diagnostic Question
What do you see in the figure on the left?

1.3 Self-Assessment
In your notebook, quickly write down in three columns (1) your natural talents, (2) your skills—things you have learned to do, and (3) your knowledge of specific fields from your education, work experience, hobbies, or interest. Later, these may help you choose a challenging project topic or team.

1.4 Looking for a Problem to Solve
At work, at home, or at play, watch out for things that annoy you, for a "missing" tool that could make your job easier, or for something that could be redesigned or simplified to improve performance. Jot these down in a notebook to be used later.

1.5 Learning Expectations

Jot down three reasons of why you are reading this book (or why you think it might be a good idea to read it) and what you expect to learn from it.

MOTIVATIONAL RESOURCES

If you have a chance, check out the videotape by Joel Barker: *The New Business of Paradigms* (classic edition, 26 minutes; 21st century edition: 18 minutes. For information see the website www.starthrower.com. These new releases are excellent motivators on the issues of change and innovation. Or check out the related book (Ref. 1.5). Educational groups might be able to borrow the video from a university extension service or a large corporate sponsor, or they may be able to rent instead of purchasing it.

Visit the website of the National Collegiate Inventors and Innovators Alliance (NCIIA) at www.nciia.org. Click on RESOURCES and scroll down to "Student Entrepreneurship Publications."

- Open *Getting Started as an Entrepreneur: A Guide for Students* and click on any of the headings on the cover that might interest you.
- If you and your team want to start a club on campus, *The Entreclub Handbook: An Operating Manual for Student Entrepreneurship Clubs* would be a great resource.

The National Endowment for Science, Technology and the Arts (NESTA) in Great Britain has a website worth exploring, especially by young British entrepreneurs. It can be found at www.nesta.org.uk. Follow the INNOVATION → THINK link and check out some of the articles. Or type in "young entrepreneurs" in the search box and see what pops up.

No longer is it true that having a skill will guarantee a successful career. Technology and markets are so quick to change that the only security or assurance of success people have is their productive capabilities. The implicit rule is, "What value can you add today?"

James S. Pepitone, business building consultant

REFERENCES

1.1 Gerald Udell, *Evaluating Potential New Products: A Manual to Aid in Understanding the Innovation Process and the PIES-VIII Preliminary Innovation Evaluation System*, 1998, page 4. Director, Iowa Small Business Development Center, Southwest Missouri State University.

1.2 Jeffry A. Timmons, *New Venture Creation: Entrepreneurship for the 21st Century*, sixth edition (large paperback), Irwin/McGraw-Hill, 2003. This comprehensive, academic textbook on entrepreneurship is written by the foremost educator and researcher on entrepreneurship in the U.S.

1.3 David Smith, *Exploring Innovation*, McGraw-Hill Education, UK, 2006. This book was mostly written for business undergraduates; each chapter comes with a long list of references and questions which make it suitable for a seminar-style course. It takes primarily an analytical approach for exploring the nature of technology and innovation.

1.4 Gerard Darby, "Encouraging Youthful Enterprise," *RSA Journal*, January 2002, pp. 28-29.

1.5 Joel Barker, *Future Edge: Discovering the New Paradigms of Success*, Morrow, New York, 1992.

2   Entrepreneurship, Creativity and Innovation

> **What you can learn from this chapter:**
> - Discover the historical context of entrepreneurship and its contribution to economic development.
> - Gain an understanding of the role of creativity in the entrepreneurial process and its connection to invention and innovation.
> - How to overcome mental blocks and barriers to creative thinking.
> - How to have some fun with creative thinking exercises.

HISTORICAL CONTEXT OF ENTREPRENEURSHIP

To understand why the creative problem-solving model used in this book is effective, let us briefly explore some key historical routes and theories in terms of entrepreneurship and creativity. In the next chapter, we will examine these relationships from the point of view of a four-quadrant model of thinking preferences.

> **Activity 2.1: Defining Entrepreneurship**
>
> Before we consider the various definitions of entrepreneurship that have evolved over the years, take a moment to jot down in your notebook some of the key characteristics which come to mind when thinking about entrepreneurship. This encourages an easy focus on the subject area. Try to go beyond what you have learned so far about the traits of young entrepreneurs. Discuss your thoughts with two or three other people, if possible outside your own age bracket and background. How did their views differ from yours? Especially watch out for (and jot down) descriptions of stereotypes often associated with the terms.

When attempting to define entrepreneurs and entrepreneurship, we need to choose an appropriate focus. *Entrepreneurs* are people with particular characteristics and traits of behavior whereas *entrepreneurship* is the result of what entrepreneurs do and refers to events and their economic impact. Our concern in this book is mainly with individuals and the development of their entrepreneurial skills and capabilities. Such development is generally regarded as highly positive in its impact on individual effectiveness and, in turn, on society in general. We want to briefly examine how economists in the last 250 years have defined entrepreneurs.

RICHARD CANTILLON (168? – 1734)

The first recorded use of the term entrepreneurship in an economic context was by Richard Cantillon in his *Essai Sur La Nature de Commerce en General*. In this essay first published in 1755, twenty-one years after his death, Cantillon uses the term *entrepreneur* many times to refer to individuals who pursue the profits from buying at a lower price than they expect to sell under conditions of uncertainty. In the case of a farmer as entrepreneur, the uncertainty arises because the farmer knows how much the input costs are to grow the crops but won't know what the market price will be when the harvest is gathered and taken to market.

The individuals first introduced by Cantillon are not necessarily innovative; they simply organize the means of production under conditions of uncertainty and, therefore, are involved in risk taking. In one sense, Cantillon was concerned with establishing a specific category of individual who organized the means of production and received an income in the form of entrepreneurial profit. He clearly perceived a need to differentiate this individual from those who constituted the labor input in the production process. Cantillon may have been referring in part to his own role since he was a banker and also a speculator for whom risk-taking was the norm. As a speculator and as an individual, Cantillon made many enemies. One was the servant whom he sacked in 1734 and who returned a few days later to murder him!

Cantillon's view may fit many people's perception of an entrepreneur, but since we want to focus upon the essential role of entrepreneurial creativity, we will look in more detail on the attributes of entrepreneurs and the way they behave as they start up their enterprises. Some of the earliest observations on entrepreneurial characteristics were made by the great French economist and entrepreneur Jean Baptiste Say.

JEAN BAPTISTE SAY (1767-1832)

Say is well known as a popularizer of the works of Adam Smith (1723-1790) who is often regarded as the father of economics. His *Traité d'économie politique* was translated into English and used as a textbook in England and the United States. Say attributed Britain's success as a growing industrial nation to the "wonderful practical skills of her entrepreneurs" and gave these definitions [from H. G. J. Aitken, "The future of entrepreneurial research" in *Explorations in Entrepreneurial History*, 1963, second series 1(1), pp. 3-9]:

> *The entrepreneur is an economic agent who unites all means of production—the labor of the one, the capital or the land of others and who finds in the value of the products which result from their employment the reconstitution of the entire capital that he utilizes, and the value of wages, the interest, and the rent which he pays, as well as the profits belonging to himself.*
>
> *The entrepreneur has judgment, perseverance and knowledge of the world as well as of business. He is called upon to estimate with tolerable accuracy the importance of the specific product, the probable amount of the demand and the means of its production. At one time, he must employ a great number of hands; at another, buy or order the raw material, collect laborers, find consumers, and give at all times a rigid attention to order and*

Say was one of the first economists to have the insight that the value of a good derived from its utility to the user and not from the labor spent in producing it.

Concise Encyclopedia of Economics

economy—in a word, he must possess the art of superintendence and administration. In the course of such complex operations, there are an abundance of obstacles to be surmounted, of anxieties to be repressed, of misfortunes to be repaired and of expedience to be devised.

Say is much more explicit than Cantillon about the individual characteristics of entrepreneurs. He emphasizes the multiplicity of roles that entrepreneurs must adopt successfully if they are to make profits beyond merely organizing and paying for all inputs and selling the output at a higher price. Entrepreneurs are not simply concerned with the production process or the product market; they must also be able to deal successfully with financial markets and the markets for raw materials, the production plant and equipment, as well as labor and premises.

Say's entrepreneurs must also be aware of relevant legislation as it applies in their area of activity and taxation. Inadequate skills or knowledge in any of these areas will lead to inefficiency and possibly failure. These entrepreneurs have problem-solving abilities to overcome all the challenges and unanticipated problems that confront them. Aside from the slightly unusual English and the absurd assumption that entrepreneurs are necessarily male, it is remarkable how well Say's observations apply in the modern world. But one explicit element is still missing, and that is entrepreneurial creativity—in Say's entrepreneurs, there is still nothing uniquely different, new or innovative about what they produce.

JOSEPH SCHUMPETER (1883-1950)

Whatever the type, everyone is an entrepreneur only when he actually carries out new combinations, and loses that character as soon as he has built up his business.

Joseph Schumpeter

The element of difference, uniqueness, innovation and change that is missing from many perceptions of entrepreneurship is the central feature of entrepreneurs as depicted by Joseph Schumpeter. Despite the awkward translation from the original German, the quote on the left conveys the essence of Schumpeter's view. When we are in the process of combining in a new way the factors of production—people, plant and equipment, raw materials, finance and premises—to generate a new product or process, then we can be called entrepreneurial. But as soon as this combination becomes established as a business and the newness and uniqueness are gone, the term no longer applies. It is an extreme position to insist that only hitherto unknown concepts and ideas are entrepreneurial and this only as they emerge; once they are known and understood, they become part of the status quo and cease to be considered entrepreneurial.

HARVEY LEIBENSTEIN (1922-1994)

Harvey Leibenstein (while teaching at Harvard University) put an alternative view of the role of entrepreneurship forward in 1976 in his book *Beyond Economic Man*. He reiterates Say's emphasis upon the coordination of many inputs in order to produce output, and he refers to the input completion role of entrepreneurs. Leibenstein's definition is also useful for his focus upon what he termed "gap-filling" or the ability to spot opportunities in the market earlier than others and thus make profits by filling these gaps.

THE MAIN ELEMENTS OF THE DEBATE

The differences in opinion reflected in the preceding discussion demonstrate the confusion that surrounds the definition of entrepreneurship and entrepreneur. The debate revolves around three main claims:

1. **Any risk taker or businessperson is an entrepreneur.** The problem with this definition is that it is too general and fails entirely to discriminate between entrepreneurs who administer traditional economic processes and those who are the agents of change.

2. **Entrepreneurs are reactive.** They are associated with change in that they facilitate it in response to the perception of market gaps. Although they are associated with change, they do not cause it but merely enable it—they observe and seize opportunities rather than create them.

3. **Entrepreneurs cause economic development through change.** They are associated with significant changes in economic processes and products and are only entrepreneurial whilst undertaking these changes, ceasing to be so when the changes have become established. The problem with this view is that it is highly restrictive; here entrepreneurs will constitute only a tiny proportion of people running businesses.

To generate a synthesized framework that emphasizes the role of entrepreneurial creativity in economic development, we want to briefly summarize three theoretical positions as well as recent research by Amar Bhidé.

SCHUMPETER'S THEORY OF ECONOMIC DEVELOPMENT

Schumpeter's theories still influence economics today, especially in the area of innovation. The European Union's innovation program and its main development plan, the Lisbon Strategy, are based on his work.

The crucial contribution made by Joseph Schumpeter in *The Theory of Economic Development* (Ref. 2.1) was to highlight the entrepreneur's role as the catalyst for economic development. This contribution connects entrepreneurship, creativity and economic development. To understand the actual and potential impact of entrepreneurship, it is important to consider his analysis.

Schumpeter portrayed any economy as a collection of enterprises and businesses where each represented a particular combination of production factors in the form of people, machines, land, premises, finance, and so on. In some sense every business relied for its market upon the successful activities of all the others. This interdependence through customer demand meant that changes in the nature or level of economic activity would be caused only when a new combination of factors of production was introduced.

The nature of changes as it affected Schumpeter's economy could be either gradual or discrete. Gradual change would do little to alter the nature of economic activity but would simply refer, for example, to alterations in design, new fashions and new ways of presentation. Discrete change was defined by Schumpeter as a fundamental step change in a product or process that could not be traced back to the previous gradual version.

A good example that distinguishes clearly between gradual and discrete change is the movement from long-playing (LP) music recordings to compact discs (CD). The most recent LP record deck can be traced back through gradual steps to the original vertical wax cylinder, needle and sound cone or horn from which it was derived. The CD represents a complete break in the technology of sound reproduction, with no clear technological path backwards to the LP. Similar observations can be applied to many technological developments and the economic progress these innovations created.

DISCRETE CHANGE AND LATERAL THINKING

The importance of Schumpeter's perception of entrepreneurship is the similarity to what has been labeled *lateral thinking* or **thinking out of the box.** Lateral thinking depends on the ability to make associations that are in some sense illogical since they do not result from a clear linear thinking process where the connections are obvious.

Let us illustrate with an example—calculating the number of matches in a singles knockout tennis competition. Given the number of entrants, let us assume 268, the linear thinker will start to calculate the number of matches in each round that will eventually lead to a single champion. The lateral approach would start with the number of losers and would simply observe that 267 must equal the number of games played since each player can only lose once. Methods are available for encouraging a more lateral approach to thinking, particularly when confronted with specific problems. Indeed much of the rest of this book is dedicated to processes for achieving precisely this end. The important point here is the clear association between Schumpeterian entrepreneurship, lateral thinking and economic development.

Schumpeter points out that significant resistance to entrepreneurship may often occur since by definition entrepreneurship involves the unfamiliar. For example, there may be social resistance to a new medical technique. Or, institutional resistance may be encountered in financial institutions considering applications for funding or in businesses where a new technology requires replacement of equipment rendered obsolete yet with years of productive life remaining. Hence, the successful entrepreneur is the individual who breaks down the logjam of resistance and enables a wave of innovation or paradigm shifts to occur that will often cause the replacement of an existing technology with a new one. Schumpeter described this process as one of *creative destruction* that captures brilliantly the notion of dynamic progress and development as opposed to moribund stagnation. The depiction of economic development as the end result of applied creativity through innovation has enormous significance because it implies that an effective increase in applied creativity will accelerate economic development.

Still, this particular view of entrepreneurship is highly restrictive in that it only accepts discrete or catalytic change as entrepreneurship. To capture the full significance of entrepreneurship it is necessary to consider two other views alongside the dramatic catalytic impact described by Schumpeter.

THE ELUSIVE EQUILIBRIUM—AN AUSTRIAN VIEW

The Austrian school of economics sees economies as dynamic and ever changing. Casual observation suggests that this scene of perpetual disequilibria is an accurate portrayal of economies in practice. Process and outputs

They have employed existing means of production differently, more appropriately, more adventurously.

They have "carried out new combinations." They are entrepreneurs.

Joseph Schumpeter

are changing; resources are employed in different ways, and external shocks change trading conditions. Much of this volatility is a result of changes in the underlying conditions of demand and supply. Demand for goods and services depend on tastes and consumer preferences which vary through time. Supply conditions change as new technology arises, creating new production possibilities. But prices and outputs do not move randomly—they reflect the economic adjustment to new conditions in demand or supply or both.

According to the Austrian school, entrepreneurs play a crucial role in this process. Changes to demand or supply create the potential for profit. The first people to notice and respond to an increase in demand for a particular product or service will be able to charge higher prices while costs remain unchanged. When others enter the marketplace to satisfy the rise in demand, the resulting competition may spur pioneers to look for new profit opportunities created by new imbalances in demand and supply in other markets.

Thus entrepreneurs and their alertness to opportunities for profit ensure that resources in the economy are constantly reallocated in line with the changing patterns of supply and demand. Without their alertness and responsiveness, imbalances in markets would occur, with shortages in some areas and surpluses in others.

Although the economy never reaches equilibrium, in a sense entrepreneurial activity is forever pursuing and tracking that stable state. From this view of entrepreneurship, it is clearly vital that entrepreneurs should be able to operate unconstrained and unimpeded if the allocation of factors of production is to best meet the ever changing conditions of demand and supply in order to maximize welfare for the population as a whole.

The *catalytic* entrepreneurs derived from Schumpeter's analysis create new production possibilities, ideas and concepts, but the *allocating* entrepreneurs from the Austrian school of thought observe the changes in conditions and are alert to the opportunities they present—because they realize new ideas and concept through innovation in economic activity. Catalysts are necessary but not sufficient for economic development—allocators are required to put the new concepts into practice.

The activities of catalytic and allocating entrepreneurs put pressure on traditional businesses in the affected markets. The arrival of new firms in a market or new technologies in an industry increases competition, thus putting pressure on existing businesses. To understand the implications of higher levels of competition and the reactions of existing firms, it is useful to consider the concept of X-inefficiency introduced by Harvey Leibenstein.

COMPETITIVE PRESSURE IN EXISTING BUSINESSES

Leibenstein noticed that contrary to the predictions of traditional economics, manufacturing plants that were identical in terms of their plant, equipment and levels of employment produced significantly different levels of output. Production plants differed in terms of their efficiency, and these variations were not explicable through differences in the allocation of plant and equipment and the number of people employed. There was clearly an element of

Entrepreneurs create or carry on an enterprise where not all markets are clearly defined and where relevant parts of the production function are not completely known.

Harvey Leibenstein

efficiency not related to the way productive resources were allocated. Leibenstein termed this efficiency *X-efficiency* and explained variations in levels of X-efficiency in terms of competitive pressure, motivation and the seeking out and use of market information.

More significant for individual competitiveness is the concept of *X-inefficiency*. Viewed in terms of X-inefficiency, lower levels of competitive pressure both outside and inside the firm would lead to lower levels of motivation while higher levels of ignorance as to changing conditions in the market place would reduce management efficiency. Basically there would tend to be more slack in the system in those businesses which confronted lower levels of competitive pressure and which were less aware of external events.

Leibenstein's perceptions are useful for our analysis here since they provide a further motive for entrepreneurial activity. As catalytic events are innovated through allocating entrepreneurs, they put pressure on established businesses, forcing them to refine operations. The resources in these businesses may be allocated in the appropriate proportions but entrepreneurial activity can seek to reduce the levels of X-inefficiency that exist in the organization. In short, the changing competitive pressures brought about by catalytic and allocating entrepreneurship cause entrepreneurial activity in existing businesses as they reduce the amount of slack in their operating systems—this activity is defined as *refining* entrepreneurship.

RECENT CONJECTURES FROM AMAR BHIDÉ'S RESEARCH

In 1988, Amar Bhidé began an in-depth study (spanning a decade) of hundreds of startup businesses. He found that the understanding of entrepreneurship emerging from his data did not fit into the neat economic models of the 1980s and the classical entrepreneurial functions of coordination, arbitrage, innovation, and operating under conditions of uncertainty.

Bhidé distinguishes between three different types of businesses involved in entrepreneurship, with very different characteristics—the startup, a growing long-lived company, and large corporations (Ref. 2.2):

> *Entrepreneurs who effectively adapt to unexpected problems and opportunities and who persuade resource providers to take a chance on their startups can influence their luck.*
>
> Amar Bidhé

1. **Most startups come from eager individuals seeking self-employment.** They start their businesses by copying or slightly modifying someone else's ideas. They do not usually have extensive managerial or industry experience, both of which are barriers to obtaining outside funding. Their modest enterprises are financed from personal assets such as savings and mortgages on their homes. The median start-up capital is around $10,000. The successful new entrepreneurs operate in market niches with a high degree of uncertainty due to changing technology and changing customer wants but with a chance of securing a large payoff. However, they do not have the resources for research or planning. A key characteristic is their high tolerance for ambiguity and for "learning by doing." Bidhé characterized this group as having "personal traits such as open-mindedness, the willingness to make decisions quickly, the ability to cope with setbacks and rejections, and skill in face-to-face selling that help differentiate the winners from the also-rans."

2. **Entrepreneurs growing a long-lived company require different traits** than those needed at startup. Not necessarily the initial founders, these individuals hold a significant economic stake in the business and control its operation. They must have strong ambitions and audacious goals, with a willingness to take personal risks. They must be able to imaginatively make the future conform to their vision and creatively integrate ideas from many sources. They must learn new business and administrative skills few founders possess initially. In addition, they must develop a business strategy and a firm commitment to implement it through inspiring leadership and persuasion. Only a small number of startup entrepreneurs go on to build their business into a significant enterprise. Typically, it takes decades for these companies to develop their assets and organization into a leader in their field.

3. **Entrepreneurial conditions in large corporations are quite different.** Champions of new initiatives must conduct extensive research and set up detailed plans to reduce uncertainty and document the likelihood of profits to obtain approval for their projects. Success then hinges on the cooperation of many individuals and teams. These projects will have much larger funding available but at a loss of flexibility for course changes once the project is launched. Contrary to Schumpeter's view, innovations in large corporations are usually routine and involve many small steps rather than a single catalytic event. New ideas will only gradually replace existing products and processes since the corporations do not want to jeopardize the profits from their current products.

SYNTHESIS

Having considered the three types of entrepreneurial activity—catalytic, allocating, and refining—we can now observe the full implications of a creative leap or inspiration in three terms: (1) the catalytic effect entrepreneurship has upon economic development potential; (2) the actual effect realized through allocating activity, and (3) the efficiency effects from the refinement of traditional business operations.

Entrepreneurship is an unrehearsed combination of economic resources instigated by the uncertain prospect of temporary monopoly profit.

Martin Binks and Philip Vale, 1990

It also helps us to understand how we as individuals might fit into this process, whether as a founder to start up a business, an entrepreneur building a business, or an *intrapreneur* championing innovation in a large corporation. Creativity and effective problem solving are required at all points. Although most clearly observable in the generation of catalytic events, ideas and concepts, creativity, and effective problem solving are also needed by allocating entrepreneurs if the developmental potential of these events is to be realized and by refining entrepreneurs as they confront the new problems facing their business. Individuals may also fall into more that one category. The concept originator may go on to realize its profit-generating potential and thus creates the economic development that it makes possible. The important point here is that creativity and effective problem solving are indelibly linked with entrepreneurial activity in all its forms. The question of what constitutes, enables, and encourages creativity is explored next.

ENTREPRENEURIAL CREATIVITY

Before we proceed any further, we need to stop and consider the definitions of creativity, invention, and innovation and how these concepts relate to entrepreneurship.

WHAT IS CREATIVITY?

The word *creativity* is derived from the Latin *creare* to make and the Greek *kreinein* to fulfill. Creativity can be examined from each of these perspectives. Creativity enables us to make something new and hitherto unimagined. In the context of entrepreneurship, it is creativity that leads to the development of new products and processes which when innovated replace the traditional and previous versions. Creativity leads to greater fulfillment on an individual basis as we use our imagination to create new horizons for what we do in our lives. By imagining what we could be and achieve, we move beyond the boundaries we have previously set for ourselves. Creativity therefore has a novelty and also relevance in terms of changing what we do and what we believe about our potential which is yet to be realized.

WHERE DOES CREATIVITY COME FROM?

An essential quality of creativity is that it involves the unexpected, the new and the surprising. As a result, it has been attributed to a variety of sources.

I must give up everything else to develop and cultivate the germ that God has planted in me.

Tchaikovsky

- **Divine Inspiration** → Creativity is seen as "higher-order" thinking or divination.

- **Serendipity** → Here creativity is seen as the product of a fortuitous coincidence of thoughts and events. For example, saccharin was discovered accidentally by a chemist who happened to eat his lunch in the laboratory. After doing experiments involving the components of the sweetener, he had neglected to wash his hands before eating.

In the fields of observation, chance favors only the mind that is prepared.

Louis Pasteur

- **Contrived Luck** → Here creativity is seen as the natural outcome of a more systematic approach to generate conditions conducive to creativity. This involves a mindset that deliberately explores existing conditions and scans for opportunities. In such a climate, creativity is more likely to occur, and the frequency of those events will be greater. For example, companies such as 3M, Hewlett-Packard and Glaxo have established organizational cultures to ensure that "luck" is a highly probable and frequent occurrence.

- **Determinism** → Under this viewpoint and interpretation, creativity is "forced" via tenacious determination to solve a particular problem. The desired outcome is seen to eventually determine the creative ideas that enable it to happen for the first time.

- **Learning Processes** → In this case it is accepted that high levels of creativity are associated with particular processes that characterize the way we think and behave. Sources of this way of thinking can be identified and lead to the possibility for learning to be more creative. In some

A company cannot expect creative acts in a particular area to come only from the experts in that area.

The problem with expertise lies precisely in those grooved-in patterns and scripts that make people experts in the first place.

Alan Robinson and Sam Stern (Ref. 2.3)

way this view reflects an acceptance of the effectiveness of contrived luck and determinism since it refers to a variety of techniques that can be applied to encourage creative problem solving. This perception underpins much of the approach adopted in this book and constitutes the link between creativity, entrepreneurship and innovation in practice.

HOW ARE CREATIVITY AND INNOVATION RELATED?

Ned Herrmann (1922-1999), the inventor of whole-brain technology and the Herrmann Brain Dominance Instrument (HBDI), saw creativity as a dynamic, whole-brain activity that involves conscious and subconscious mental processing in both generating an idea and making something happen as a result. Creativity rarely occurs in isolation—it needs other people's minds, ideas, and inventions. Thus in the broadest perspective, creativity is expressed in the quality of the solutions we develop in problem solving. Creativity also involves looking beyond the obvious and is a necessary condition for invention or innovation. Because the word creativity carries a value judgment, Edward de Bono created the neutral label of *lateral thinking* to describe the change from one way of looking at things to another (Ref. 2.4).

Innovation can be seen as the practical application of creativity in an organization. Creativity originates in an individual mind (often enhanced by group interaction and synthesis), but innovation usually requires the involvement of a team and subsequently a wider organization. As we shall see in Chapter 12, good communication is central to innovation. Businesses often use the terms creativity and innovation interchangeably, because many managers feel more comfortable with the word innovation.

One key difference between the two processes is timing—creativity is needed in the early stages of product development, whereas innovation occurs much later and usually in the broader context of dissemination and acceptance. Innovation builds on a creative idea, or it can combine creative ideas in novel ways. In general, innovation is much safer; it is incremental; it is building on an already established product or process, and it is far easier to achieve successfully than creating something new where a successful outcome is by no means assured and the possibility of failure must be acknowledged. The two processes are championed by different types of entrepreneurs—the adaptive (or allocating) entrepreneur to shepherd innovation, the inventive (or catalytic) entrepreneur to chart or envision new paths.

WHO ARE THE INVENTORS AND INNOVATORS, AND WHAT ARE THEIR COMMON TRAITS?

Conventional wisdom says that if you want to invent something highly technical, you must have extensive technical knowledge in the subject area. Yet many inventors are outsiders; they learn on their own and create knowledge as they go along. Developing inventions into more useful and more sophisticated products is another story; this usually happens through many successive improvements and innovative steps by people with expertise in the relevant areas of science and engineering. The Wright Brothers invented the first successful airplane, but it took thousands of Boeing engineers to design and build the 747 jumbo jets to fly non-stop across the Pacific.

Chester Carlson invented the Xerox process, but it took years of development at Battelle to produce a practical copier. Whereas Alistair Pilkington thought of the idea of float glass while helping his wife wash dishes, it took a team of six people working in secret for seven years (and a huge research budget) to develop the process into a technical and commercial success. A key ingredient was the optimism maintained by the team while struggling to overcome problem after problem. Art Fry was the inventor of the Post-it note, but it took teams of people at 3M to turn the invention into a line of successful business products. Characteristic common traits of inventors, innovators and many entrepreneurs are listed in Table 2.1.

Table 2.1 *Common Traits of Inventors, Innovators and Entrepreneurs*

- Being curious—looking at the frontiers of knowledge; eager to learn.
- Inventing to satisfy a need or solving problems creatively.
- Looking for new ways and many approaches for doing things.
- Observing trends, looking for opportunities, and then working hard.
- Realizing that most progress is made in small steps through continuous improvement.
- Dedicated and passionate about their projects, with a low need for status and power and a low vulnerability to rejection.
- Having a sense of value, integrity, purpose and humor; being hands-on and flexible.
- Being self-confident, independent, courageous, persistent, reliable, and tenacious.
- Not afraid to take risks and make mistakes; questioning conventional wisdom.
- Having a tolerance for ambiguity; able to deal with contradictory information; imaginative.

Especially in the academic environment, researchers are often more interested in discovery and invention for the sake of new knowledge than in subsequent technology transfer or commercialization. One reason for this phenomenon is that commercialization of a creative idea requires a different mindset, as we shall see in Chapter 3. Governments in many industrialized countries are providing funds in an effort to increase the flow of commercially viable ideas from their academic institutions to spur economic development. Because of increasing global competition, businesses with ability for innovation have a distinct advantage—a lack of innovation can lead to stagnation and imperil the ultimate survival of the business.

OVERCOMING BARRIERS TO CREATIVITY

It is now generally accepted that most people are born with the capacity to think creatively, but that through influences at home, in school, and in their particular culture they bury their natural creativity. We believe that these barriers to creativity can be overcome and that we can learn to be lateral thinkers. We will briefly examine three types of barriers: false assumptions, habits, and emotions.

FALSE ASSUMPTIONS BARRIER

The basic aim of education is not to accumulate knowledge, but rather to learn to think creatively, teach oneself, and "seek answers to questions as yet unexplored."

Jim Killian, former president of MIT

Here are some examples of false assumptions:

The belief that *we are not creative* is a self-fulfilling prophesy. This assumption is false, because we have an astounding potential to be creative and can learn to unlock or hone our creative thinking skills.

Edward de Bono has shown that *an intelligent mind is a good thinker* is a false assumption for a number of reasons, such as mistaking verbal fluency for good thinking, arguing a case for a certain point of view well and thus failing to see the need to explore alternatives, or jumping to quick conclusions from a few data points.

The attitude that *play is frivolous* is a false assumption prevalent in the business world, in schools, and often among parents as well. Yet unstructured play is very important to our cognitive development. Humor is related to play and beneficial to creative thinking because it turns the mind from the usual, expected track to making an unexpected lateral leap (Ref. 2.5).

We can overcome false assumptions by spending time with creative people—we can let them mentor us and find out what it means to express and champion creative ideas. We can play with ideas, analogies and metaphors. We can frequently exercise our imagination by asking what-if questions. We can practice new creative thinking and problem-solving modes!

Activity 2.2: Symbols Problem

Circle the figure below that is different from all the others, then explain the reason for your choice.

a. △   b. ☐   c. ○   d. ∩   e. ✛

LEARNED HABITS BARRIERS

The correct answer to the symbols problem is that *all are different*. Can you find reasons to explain why each of the symbols is different from all the others? Most people stop after finding one answer, because we have not been trained to look for alternatives. This little exercise illustrates that different answers can be correct or appropriate depending on the questions being asked or the criteria being used.

Here are examples of mental barriers that are often learned in school:

- *There is only one right answer* is a serious barrier when we are dealing with other than purely mathematical problems. Looking for alternatives is especially important when dealing with ideas. How do we know our answer is best if we have nothing to compare it with?

- *Looking at a problem in isolation* is a related mental block. When you look at this page, how many rectangles do you see? Most people would say two—the grey frame around the activity and the second symbol inside the box. Some might say three when they the word *rectangles* in the question. Or was your answer five if you also saw the two open pages in front of you or six if you considered the two pages together as an additional rectangle? What if you included other rectangles in your field of vision in the room (and outside): windows, checkered shirts, papers, boxes, shelves, floor or ceiling tiles, and so on? Before we can find answers to a problem, we must find out if the problem is part of a larger problem. The context is never irrelevant! Having a very narrow point of view can be a mental barrier to creative thinking and easily happens when we have become experts in our work.

- *Following the rules* is a mental block that requires wisdom to overcome. Sometimes, before we can come up with truly novel ideas, we must question existing constraints. Also, we have to make sure we do not make up our own rules and barriers. Are the "rules" we put on others or ourselves really necessary or helpful? When we do not question arbitrary criteria, we may miss opportunities for creative thinking and improvements. Sometimes we follow rules when the original reason no longer exists. The classic example is the QWERTY system of arranging the letters on a computer keyboard. It was originally invented to slow down typists because the typewriter keys were jamming when they typed too fast. However, some constraints are necessary. For example, when working with others, following the rules of etiquette for courteous behavior creates a safer, less stressful environment for creativity. As we shall see in Chapter 4, rules and problem solving paradigms are generally useful to function well in our daily routines.

We can overcome habit barriers that have been taught by explicitly looking for a broad context and seeking different alternatives, analyzing the purpose of rules and deciding which should be suspended in the initial stages of problem solving.

ATTITUDE BARRIERS

This group of mental blocks is difficult to deal with because it involves our attitudes and emotions. Let us briefly examine some examples.

- *Negative, pessimistic thinking* (including criticism, sarcasm and put-downs) are mental blocks that not only inhibit creative thinking in the person using them—they have the same effect on all those coming in contact with the negative thinker and are thus doubly destructive. It is so easy to focus on small shortcomings of an idea (or person) rather than recognize the good features. This influence starts at a young age: a typical child may receive a vast number of negative reactions per positive reinforcement. Remember that a judgmental attitude, including our own inner "critical voice" can be powerful barriers against expressing creative thoughts.

- *Risk-avoidance or the fear of failure or rejection* prevents creative thinking as well as action. Examples of the kinds of risks we are talking about here are: speaking out in a group when you have an idea, even though it

To overcome a spirit of criticism and negative thinking, look at things as being different or interesting—not good or bad!

Edward de Bono

might be "hooted" down; learning something new where you will often fail until you become good at it, or standing up against peer pressure. Yes, you have to stick your neck out when you champion a creative idea; you also need a thick shell, and you have to be persistent in getting to your goal. If you do not encounter critics trying to make "turtle soup" out of you, your idea probably was not that creative! The need for "being cool" and being accepted by one's peer group is especially strong among young people who are particularly vulnerable to rejection.

We are becoming increasingly convinced that tomorrow's winners in business will be those who master the challenges of innovation and creativity and can do so continuously. Innovation is an engine for growth and value in business.

Prof. Robert Goffee, London Business School, RSA Lecture, Jan 2000.

We can overcome attitude barriers by encouraging people around us with positive feedback when they share creative ideas. We can take risks with learning and use failure creatively as a stepping-stone to success. We can practice out-of-the-box thinking daily! We can recognize flaws as opportunities for improvement! Similarly to athletes who practice mental toughness to succeed among fierce competitors, we can adopt traits of mental toughness when developing a creative thinking mindset.

CREATIVE THINKING EXERCISES

2.1 Warm-ups

Don't just go with the first or obvious answer—play with possibilities. Make sketches to help you visualize the problem; you will be surprised how fast the answers will come.

a. Recorded on side A of an old 45-rpm LP record is a musical number that lasts three minutes and twenty seconds. How many grooves are there on side A of this old record?

b. In a large box, there are six boxes, each of which contains three small boxes. How many boxes are there in all?

c. Two cities are exactly 100 miles apart. Charley leaves City A driving at 30 mph and Bertha leaves City B 30 minutes later driving 60 mph. Who will be closer to City A when they meet?

d. How do you keep fish from smelling?

e. A woman went into a hardware store and priced certain items. She was told they were 25 cents each. She replied, "I would like one hundred, please." The clerk rung up 75 cents on the register for the entire purchase. What did the woman buy?

f. A boy and a girl born on the same day of the same year with the same parents are not twins. How is this possible?

g. Three friends are on a bike trip. When a severe storm threatens, they decide to rent a room in a lodge instead of camping out. The proprietor quotes a price of £30 for the room, so each bicyclist digs out a ten-pound note. Later, the proprietor finds that he has overcharged the group by £5 and sends the errand boy to their room with the change. The boy—of a practical mindset—thinks that the three guests would have a hard time dividing up £5; thus he helps himself to two pounds (as a tip) and returns three pounds to the guests. This means that each person in essence would have paid £9, with the errand boy having pocketed an additional £2, for a total of £29. Where did the remaining pound disappear?

2.2   Geese and Lambs

A farmer's child received a gift of 8 animals (geese and lambs) with a total of 22 legs. Determine the number of geese in at least three very different ways.

2.3   Mountain Path Problem

Read through the following story. Jot down several ways you are thinking about the problem, even if you are not able to come up with a solution.

> A certain mountain in Nepal has a shrine at its peak and only one narrow path to reach it. A monk leaves his monastery at the base of the mountain at 6 o'clock one morning and ascends the mountain at a steady pace. After some hours, he tires and takes a long rest. Then he resumes his climb, albeit more slowly, and he pauses often to meditate. Finally, at sunset, he reaches the shrine where he spends the night.
>
> At sunrise, he begins his descent, quickly at first, and then more slowly as his knees begin to ache. After a couple of rest stops, he accelerates his pace again—he does not want to miss dinner at the monastery. Prove that there is a point in the path that the monk reached at exactly the same time of day on his way up and on his way down.

The analytical mind may be able to spot the "right" answers, but it takes a very creative mind to ask the right questions.

2.4   The Fastball Problem

The players form teams of 10 to 15 each. Each team is given a ball and players are asked to stand in a circle and count off. The object of this game is to have everybody on the team touch the ball in order. Time starts with the first touch and ends with the last. Each team passes the ball around the circle as fast as possible, like a hyperactive bucket brigade fighting a fire. The typical winning team takes just under 45 seconds. However, one winning team takes just two seconds. Impossible! No, there are at least two ways this can be achieved. Can you come up with a solution? Use a rolled up wad of paper and experiment, then sketch or describe your idea in your notebook.

2.5   Lateral Thinking Exercise

In the following problems, try to identify the problem-solving paradigm that is implied. Then try to side-step it and look at the problem in a different way to come up with an answer.

a.   The butcher at Tony's Meat Market is 41 years old, 6 ft 2 inches tall, wears an extra-large shirt and a size 46 shoe. What does he weigh?

b.   How many times can you take three from 25?

c.   Here is an equation of Roman numerals, made with 10 sticks. It is incorrect. Can you correct the equation without touching the sticks, adding new sticks, or taking away any sticks?

X I + I = X

d.   Shown below is a Roman numeral nine. By adding only a single line, turn it into a six. Find two different ways for solving this problem.

I X

e.   Take two apples from five apples. How many do you have?

f.   A plane with English tourists on board flies from Holland to Spain. It crashes in France. Where should the survivors be buried?

g.   How many letters are in Mississippi?

h.   What do you sit on, sleep on, and brush your teeth with?

2.6   Light Bulb Problem

In one location (say a central office) there are three switches; each switch is connected to a light bulb in another location (say a warehouse). The warehouse cannot be seen from the office. How could you determine—taking only one trip—which switch controls which bulb?

2.7 Geometric Problems

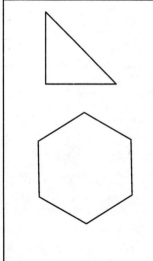

a.   Divide the triangle into four identical pieces.

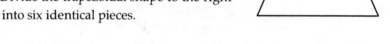

b.   Divide the trapezoidal shape to the right into six identical pieces.

c.   Divide the hexagon to the left into eight symmetrical identical pieces.

d.   Divide the hexagon below into eight asymmetrical but identical pieces.

e.   Divide the parallelogram into nine identical pieces.

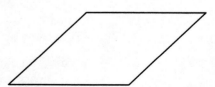

2.8　Sentence Problem

In how many ways can you complete the following sentence to get a true statement? Try to find at least eight different answers.

This statement has ...... "t" letters

INVENTIVE THINKING EXERCISES

2.9　The Missing Baseball Problem

Inventive thinking is not limited to adults but can be done by people of all ages, as illustrated by this problem. A young boy loved to play baseball, and he took his bat and balls everywhere. However, when visiting his grandmother one day, he discovered that he had brought his bat but had forgotten his balls. To prevent this from happening again, he came up with an invention (which he patented and is now sold by Toys-R-Us). What did he invent?

2.10　The Hanging Chain Problem

Imagine being in a totally empty room except for two chains that are hanging from the ceiling. If you grab one by the hand and move toward the other, it is still about a foot too far away for you to reach with your other hand. Yet the assignment is to tie the two chains together. Describe or sketch at least two different solutions to solve the problem. Hint: What is the real problem?

2.11　Moving the Transformer Problem

A transformer weighing two tons sits on a free-standing platform 4 ft above ground. Find two ways for lowering the transformer to the ground without using a crane and without destroying the platform or the transformer. Then discuss which of the solutions you consider to be superior and why.

2.12　The Chocolate Candy Problem

You have brought a big box of chocolate candies to a party. These candies are shaped like small bottles and are filled with thick raspberry syrup. When you pass the box around, one of your friends wonders how the syrup was placed in the candy. Can you think of at least two ways that these candies could be made? If you were the manufacturer, which of your solutions would be the easiest and most economical to produce? Would your solution work if the filling were cherry brandy, or how would you have to change it?

FOLLOW-UP EXERCISES

2.13　Definition of Entrepreneurship

Review your initial definition of "entrepreneurship" from Activity 2.1 at the beginning of this chapter. From what you have learned in this chapter, re-write your definition, if possible in thirty words or less.

2.14　Reminder to Encourage Creative Thinking

Place your watch on the opposite arm from where you usually wear it. Each time you look at it, let it serve as a reminder to check if you can incorporate creative thinking into your current activity.

Imagination is more important than knowledge. For while knowledge defines all we currently know and understand, imagination points the all we might yet discover and create.

Albert Einstein

2.15 Play!

Schedule a one-hour "playing with ideas" time into your weekly calendar. Then keep your appointment! Jot down your most creative ideas in your notebook. Be flexible, not perfect!

2.16 Encourage Other People's Creativity

Make a conscious effort to praise the creative thinking of another person, even if the occurrence annoys you. Example: A seven-year old youngster used a tea strainer for cleaning the cat's litter box when she couldn't find the regular tool to do the assigned chore.

2.17 Logic Puzzle

Turn the six squares in the figure on the left into five squares by moving just two lines to another location.

2.18 Lateral Thinking, One More Time

Imagine using six toothpicks to form a hexagon shape, like the one shown on the left. Now rearrange the toothpicks to form four identical triangles. To visualize this, play with some real toothpicks on a soft surface.

2.19 The Soup Spoon Problem

How could you feed one hundred people at the same time with one spoon?

> If you want to check how your lateral thinking skills are developing, you can find possible answers at the back of the book.

REFERENCES

Entrepreneurship is the process of creating something different with value by devoting the necessary time and effort, assuming the accompanying financial, psychic, and social risks, and receiving the resulting rewards of monetary and personal satisfaction.

Robert Hisrich and Michael Peters (Ref. 2.6)

2.1 Joseph Schumpeter's book, *The Theory of Economic Development*, was first published in 1911. It was reprinted by Transaction Publishers as a paperback in 1982 and is still available from several online booksellers.

2.2 Amar V. Bhidé, *The Origin and Evolution of New Businesses*, Oxford University Press, 2000. New insights from ten years of intensive research!

2.3 A. Robinson and S. Stern, *Corporate Creativity: How Innovation and Improvements Actually Happen*, Berrett-Koehler Publishers, San Francisco, 1998. This is a practical guide with many interesting examples.

2.4 Edward de Bono, *Lateral Thinking*, Harper and Row, 1970. Also by the same author, *Serious Creativity*, Harper Business, New York, 1992 (paperback). These older books give a good introduction to lateral thinking.

2.5 James L. Adams, *Conceptual Blockbusting—A Guide to Better Ideas*, paperback, fourth edition, Basic Books, 2001. This book discusses mental languages and the mental blocks that keep us from thinking creatively.

2.6 Robert D. Hisrich and Michael P. Peters, *Entrepreneurship: Starting, Developing, and Managing a New Enterprise*, sixth edition, Irwin/McGraw-Hill, 2004. This 641-page, very thorough textbook is built on the definition of entrepreneurship given on the left.

3 The Herrmann Thinking Styles Model

> **What you can learn from this chapter:**
> - How thinking styles influence our approach to problem solving.
> - How the Herrmann four-quadrant model was developed.
> - An understanding of analytical, logical quadrant A thinking.
> - An understanding of detailed, organized quadrant B thinking.
> - An understanding of interpersonal, symbolic quadrant C thinking.
> - An understanding of imaginative, conceptual quadrant D thinking.
> - The implications of thinking styles on communication, teamwork and entrepreneurship.

Why are some people so smart and dull at the same time? How can they be so capable of certain mental activities and at the same time be so incapable of others?

Henry Mintzberg, Harvard Business Review, July 1976

It has long been recognized that people vary significantly in their thinking styles, and models have been put forth in an attempt to capture these differences. The most familiar distinction (known since antiquity) is left-brain and right-brain thinking, where the left brain is considered to be analytical, systematic and logical, while the right brain is perceived as creative, artistic and intuitive. We want to go beyond this simple two-sided approach by adopting a *four-quadrant model of thinking* which enables a much clearer understanding of the creative problem solving process (described in the next chapter) for generating and developing entrepreneurial ideas from "brain to market." This *creative problem solving model* can be applied to a wide variety of situations, but the focus on entrepreneurship and innovation provides a powerful vehicle to convey the nature and effectiveness of the two models.

The way people approach problem solving is strongly influenced by their preferred ways of thinking and "knowing." For example, one person may carefully analyze a situation before making a rational decision based on the available data; another may see the same situation in a broader context and will look for alternatives. One person will use a very detailed, cautious, step-by-step procedure; another has a need to talk the problem over with people and will solve the problem intuitively. All use their particular approaches based on successful experiences. We will now explore a model of thinking preferences that will help you learn to become a more effective thinker, problem solver, and entrepreneur.

DEVELOPMENT OF THE HERRMANN MODEL

Ned Herrmann earned a degree in physics and was hired by General Electric, where he soon worked in human resource development. In years of research into the creativity of the human brain, he came to recognize that the human

Strong as well as low preferences (akin to avoidances) are expressed in clues that can be observed in a person's behavior.

brain is specialized in the way it functions. These specialized modes can be modeled and organized into four distinct quadrants, each with its own language, values, and "ways of knowing" (see Fig. 3.1). Each person is a unique mix of these thinking preferences and has one or more strong dominances. Dominance has advantages: quick response time and higher skill level. We use our dominant mode for learning and problem solving.

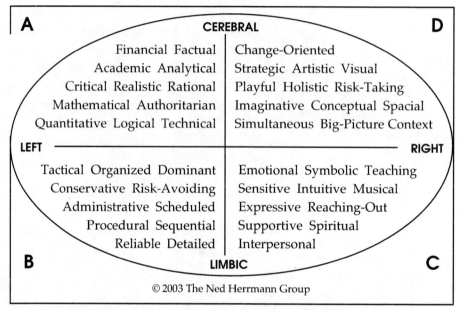

Figure 3.1   *Thinking characteristics and behavioral clues of the four-quadrant Herrmann model of brain dominance*

The stronger our preference for one way of thinking, the stronger is our discomfort for the opposite mode. "Opposite" people have great difficulty communicating and understanding each other because they see the world through very different filters. Is there a best way? Ned Herrmann found that each brain mode is best for the tasks it was designed to perform. All thinking modes and brain dominance profiles are valuable—there is no right or wrong. We can learn how to use and integrate these modes for whole-brain thinking and problem solving.

The HBDI is an assessment or a survey for personal development, <u>not</u> a test.

When Ned Herrmann looked around for a method to diagnose thinking preferences based on brain specialization, he could not find any existing tools suitable for his purposes (since many tools such as the Myers-Briggs Type Indicator (MBTI) are based on psychological constructs). So he developed his own assessment, now known as the Herrmann Brain Dominance Instrument (HBDI™) which has been validated by scores of studies over many years. When the answers to 120 questions on the HBDI are scored by a computer at Herrmann International headquarters in North Carolina, the numerical results are also shown as a graphical profile. Recent advances in brain research support the validity of the descriptive model that divides the brain into left and right halves and into the cerebral and limbic hemispheres, resulting in four distinct quadrants.

> ### Activity 3.1: Carte Blanche Video
> Take a few minutes to watch a brief video on-line—it will give you a visual and interpersonal introduction to the HBDI and what it can do. This video shows an excerpt of a South African news program called "Carte Blanche" and you can access it through the following links:
>
> www.hbdi.com → Resources → Video → Carte Blanche : Watch video !
>
> In your notebook, jot down your initial guess at what your thinking profile might be and how knowing your HBDI might benefit you.

Although the four-quadrant model was organized based on the divisions in the physical brain, it is a *metaphorical* model, as shown in Figure 3.2. The newest imaging techniques show the brain's complexity, subtlety, and versatility involved in even the easiest thinking tasks. Yet, this simple model is useful for clarifying how we think, and it allows for the varied interrelationship of the different thinking abilities associated with each quadrant.

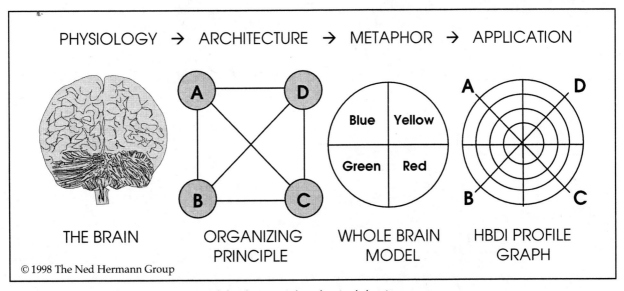

Figure 3.2   *How the Herrmann model relates to the physical brain*

The following sections illustrate the characteristics of each quadrant, together with activities that can strengthen these thinking modes. Typical average HBDI profiles of different occupational groups are also given. In general, it is easier to develop competencies in areas of strong preference.

CHARACTERISTICS OF QUADRANT A THINKING

Quadrant A thinking is analytical, quantitative, technical, precise, logical, rational, and critical. Thus it deals with data analysis, risk assessment, statistics, financial budgets and computation, as well as with analytical problem solving, technical hardware, and making decisions based on logic. Quadrant

Figure 3.3 *Typical average HBDI profile for chemical engineers (Ref. 3.3)*

Quadrant A cultures are materialistic, academic, and authoritarian; they are achievement-oriented and performance-driven. Examples of quadrant A thinkers are *Star Trek's* Mr. Spock, George Gallup the pollster, and Marilyn Vos Savant (a person with one of the highest IQ scores in the world). Mathematicians, accountants, actuaries, computer analysts, and engineers as well as surgeons and pathologists generally show strong preferences for quadrant A thinking (as shown in Fig. 3.3). Quadrant A thinkers talk about "the bottom line" or "getting the facts" or "critical analysis," and their preferred learning activities are listed in Table 3.1.

Table 3.1   *Quadrant A Learning Activities and Behaviors*

- Looking for data and information; searching libraries and the web.
- Listening to informational lectures; reading technical textbooks.
- Analyzing and studying example problems and solutions.
- Doing research using the scientific method.
- Judging ideas based on facts, criteria, and logical reasoning.
- Doing technical and financial case studies.
- Knowing how things work and how much they cost.
- Dealing with hardware; answering "what" questions.
- Joining an investment club; financially planning for retirement.

CHARACTERISTICS OF QUADRANT B THINKING

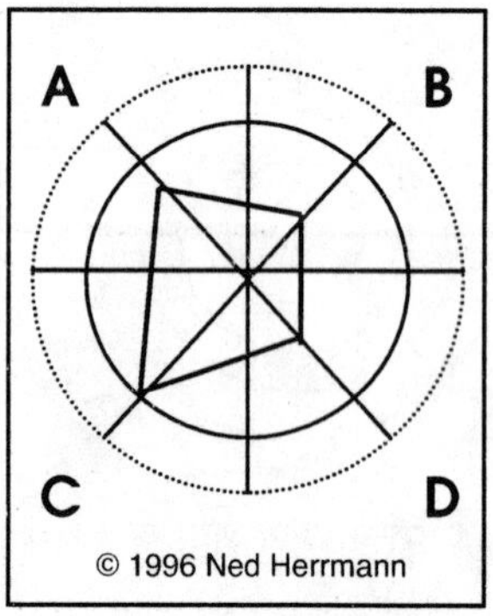

Quadrant B thinking is organized, sequential, detailed, controlled, conservative, planned, structured, and scheduled. It deals with administration, tactical planning, procedures, organizational form, maintaining the status quo, the "tried-and-true," and solution implementation. The culture is reliable, traditional, and bureaucratic. It is production-oriented and task-driven. Edgar Hoover (past FBI Director), Prince Otto von Bismarck (Prussian Chancellor of Germany, 1871-1900), and Native American Indian Chief Geronimo exemplify quadrant B thinkers. Quadrant B thinkers such as planners, bookkeepers, bureaucrats, administrators and clerks (see Fig. 3.4) want their jobs to be structured and sequentially organized. They talk about "we have always done it this way" or "law and order" or "self-discipline" or "playing it safe." Quadrant B learning activities are listed in Table 3.2.

Figure 3.4 *Typical average HBDI profile for manufacturing foremen (Ref. 3.3)*

Table 3.2   *Quadrant B Learning Activities and Behaviors*

- Doing detailed written work neatly and conscientiously.
- Doing lab work, step by step and then writing a sequential report.
- Using computers with tutorial software. Asking "how" questions.
- Organizing a collection (or a closet or drawer).
- Planning an elaborate project, then executing it according to plan.
- Practicing new skills through frequent repetition and drill.
- Assembling an object according to detailed instructions.
- Setting up a detailed budget and keeping track of expenditures.
- Setting up a filing system and then using it regularly.

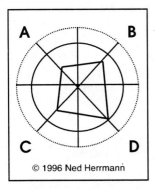

Figure 3.5 *Typical average HBDI profile for rehab counselors (Ref. 3.3)*

CHARACTERISTICS OF QUADRANT C THINKING

Quadrant C thinking is sensory, kinesthetic, emotional, people-oriented, and symbolic. It deals with awareness of feelings, body sensations, spiritual values, music, personal relationships, teamwork, nurturing, and communication. Quadrant C cultures are humanistic, cooperative, and spiritual; they are feelings-oriented and value-driven. Dr. Martin Luther King, Jr., Mahatma Gandhi (Hindu social reformer) and Princess Diana typify strong quadrant C people. Quadrant C thinkers (see Fig. 3.5) like the social sciences, music, dance, and highly skilled sports; they love to talk and prefer group projects to working alone. Elementary school and foreign language teachers, trainers, counselors, dental assistants, nurses, social workers, and musicians generally have strong preferences for interpersonal quadrant C thinking. These folks talk about "the family" or "the team" or "personal growth" and "values." Table 3.3 lists some quadrant C learning activities.

Table 3.3 *Quadrant C Learning Activities and Behaviors*

- Listening to others; sharing idea and having group discussions.
- Self-motivation by asking "why" and seeking personal meaning.
- Learning through sensory input—moving, smelling, tasting, etc.
- Hands-on learning by touching and using tools and objects.
- Keeping a journal to record feelings and spiritual values, not details.
- Studying with background music.
- Making up a rap song as a memory aid and to express feelings.
- Learning by teaching others; using people-oriented case studies.
- Playing with small children they way they want to play.

CHARACTERISTICS OF QUADRANT D THINKING

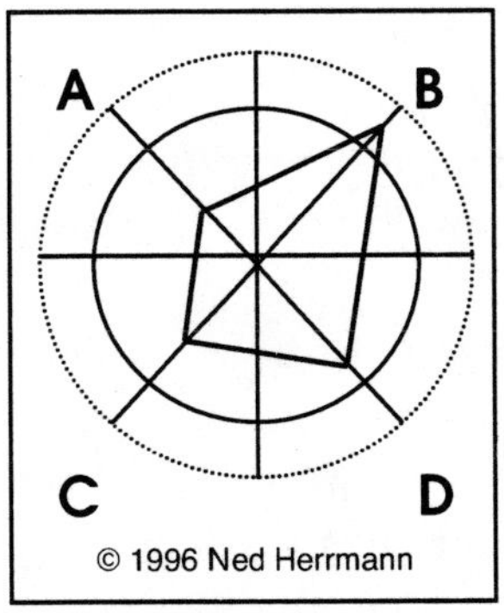

Quadrant D thinking is visual, holistic, metaphorical, imaginative, creative, integrative, spatial, conceptual, flexible, and intuitive. It deals with futures, possibilities, synthesis, play, dreams, vision, strategic planning, the broader context, and change. A quadrant D culture is explorative, entrepreneurial, inventive, and future-oriented. It is playful, risk-driven, and independent. Leonardo da Vinci (the Renaissance painter, sculptor, architect and scientist), Pablo Picasso (the modern painter), Albert Einstein (physicist) and Amelia Earhart (aviation pioneer) exemplify strong quadrant D thinkers. Quadrant D thinkers enjoy design, architecture, art, geometry, and poetry. Explorers, artists, playwrights and entrepreneurs (see Fig. 3.6) typically have strong quadrant D thinking preferences, as do many scientists doing research and development in engineering, medicine, and physics. Quadrant D thinkers talk about "playing with an idea" or "the big picture" or "the cutting edge." Table 3.4 lists some quadrant D learning activities.

   If we want to strengthen a particular quadrant, we must use our brain more frequently for tasks requiring those modes. When we use our brain in new ways, it will build new structures and new connections—in essence, we will expand our brain. Ned Herrmann told everyone, "Claim your space!"

Figure 3.6 *Typical average HBDI profile for female entrepreneurs (Ref. 3.3)*

© 1996 Ned Herrmann

Table 3.4 Quadrant D Learning Activities and Behaviors

- Looking for the big picture and context, not the details, of a topic.
- Doing simulations and asking what-if questions; brainstorming.
- Making use of visual aids; preferring pictures to words.
- Doing open-ended problems and finding several solutions.
- Experimenting and playing with ideas and possibilities.
- Thinking about the future; imagining different scenarios.
- Synthesizing ideas to come up with something new.
- Trying a different way (not the prescribed procedure) to do something, just for the fun of it.
- Making sketches to visualize a problem or solution; doodling.

WHOLE-BRAIN THINKING, TEAMWORK, AND COMMUNICATION

We have examined the characteristics of four distinct "ways of knowing." However, only five percent of people have a single strong dominance; 58 percent have a double dominance, 34 percent have a triple dominance, and only three percent have equally strong dominances in all four quadrants. Each person represents a unique coalition of thinking preferences. Imagine having a team of players inside your brain. You send out specialists for specific tasks: you send out one, two or maybe even three star players more often than the others, but to function well, the whole team is needed.

This is particularly true for the creative problem solving process. We need to systematically apply all four thinking styles if we want to successfully generate and implement new ideas. No matter what our dominance patterns are, we can effectively use any of the four distinct styles when required. Although most people will naturally find certain thinking styles more comfortable than others—depending on their strong preferences—this should not be a surprise or a matter of concern when proceeding with creative problem solving. The important point is to recognize and accept this virtually inevitable experience and avoid the temptation to reject those styles that come least naturally.

Many of these tensions and difficulties can be more easily overcome if the stages of the creative problem solving process are faced by a team rather than solo. In his work on whole brain thinking, Ned Herrmann placed considerable emphasis on its application to the more effective performance of teams. For our purposes here, two key points emerge:

The brain is designed to be whole, but at the same time we can and must learn to appreciate our brain's uniqueness and that of others. A balanced view between wholeness and specialization is the key.

Ned Herrmann

1. Whole brain teams with all four thinking styles are more effective than teams where only one or two dominances are present. Research shows improvements of 30 to 100 percent can be achieved. This is significant, because teams that are self-selected usually have members with similar thinking styles—because "similar" people tend to gravitate towards each other. Such homogeneous teams may miss important viewpoints and problem solving strategies, unless they make a strong effort to use the modes that are not represented in the team's dominant thinking profile.

A high level of conversation during an unstructured task alone was not a good predictor of team performance.

Having someone in the group who contributes a lot of ideas was needed.

Successful teams have individuals who can verbally contribute and support their ideas and position.

Marla R. Hacker, Engineering Professor, *ASQ Quality Progress,* Jan 1999

2. The implications of the HBDI profile for communication are equally important. Tensions can arise within teams when different problem solving approaches are taken by people with different brain dominance. Without an understanding of different thinking styles, the effectiveness of a team can be drastically reduced because individuals with different styles communicate almost as if speaking different languages. Numerous examples exist where a raised awareness and appreciation of different thinking styles has greatly improved the functionality of teams within organizations and family groups (see Refs. 3.1, 3.2, and 3.6).

Figure 3.7 shows the preference map (profile "tilt" distribution) of a team in the auto industry charged with developing high-tech training materials (Ref. 3.4). This dysfunctional team had three quadrant D members who were ready to quit—the two left-brain "tribes" derogatorily called them "the oddballs." The team members received their HBDI results as part of a one-hour workshop. Two months later, the team leader reported on the benefits of the HBDI—the difference was "like day and night." Now the Quadrant D members were energized; they felt they were valued and their creative ideas were welcomed. The quadrant A thinkers improved these ideas and made them more practical (and cost-effective), while the quadrant B people worked out the implementation. As a result, the entire team became more successful!

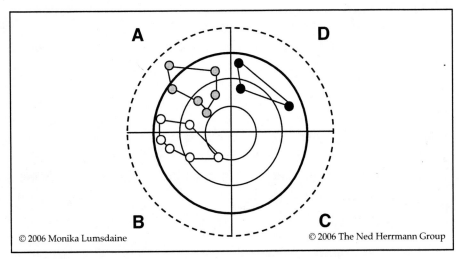

© 2006 Monika Lumsdaine   © 2006 The Ned Herrmann Group

Figure 3.7   *HBDI profile "tilt" pattern for a high-tech development group*

Teams of engineers (and other predominantly left-brain thinkers) need to watch out for two habits that can be detrimental when working in heterogeneous (whole-brain) teams:

1. **Automatically discounting emotional arguments.** Value the input of quadrant C people—they may often have important insights about customers and team dynamics that might otherwise be missed.

2. **Ignoring people who have unorthodox ideas.** Learn to appreciate the ideas of creative thinkers. These ideas—when improved and implemented—may be crucial for the survival and success of the team and the company, as seen in the example shown in Figure 3.7.

> ## Activity 3.2: Barriers to Effective Communication
> For good communication with people with strong thinking preferences in a particular quadrant, avoid the barriers listed for that quadrant. In the list in Table 3.5, check the barriers in each quadrant that annoy you and make communication with you less effective. For example, does excessive chatter bother you? If yes, you may have a strong preference for quadrant A thinking. Does repetition bother you? In that case, you may have a brain dominance in quadrant D.

Table 3.5 Diagnosing Our Communication Barriers (use with Activities 3.2 and 3.3)

Barriers to communicating with Quadrant A:	Barriers to communicating with Quadrant D:
__ Inarticulate, "off the track" talking.	__ Repetition.
__ Excessive chatter.	__ Too slow paced.
__ Vague, ambiguous instructions.	__ "Playing it safe" or "by the book."
__ Illogical comments.	__ Overly structured, predictable.
__ Inefficient use of time.	__ Absence of humor and fun.
__ Lack of facts or data.	__ Lack of flexibility; too rigid.
__ Inappropriate informality.	__ Not "getting" concepts/metaphors.
__ Overt sharing of personal feelings.	__ Drowning in detail.
__ Not knowing the "right" answer.	__ Too many numbers.
__ Fear of challenge or debate.	__ "Can't see the forest for the trees."
__ Lack of factual "proof" for ideas.	__ Inability to talk about intangibles.
__ Lack of clarity and precision.	__ Narrow focus.
__ Excessive use of hands or gestures.	__ Resistance to new approaches.
__ Unrealistic touchy/feely approach.	__ Dry, boring topic or style.
Barriers to communicating with Quadrant B:	**Barriers to communicating with Quadrant C:**
__ Absence of clear agenda.	__ Lack of interaction.
__ Disorganized.	__ No eye contact (in Western culture).
__ Hopping from topic to topic.	__ Impersonal approach or examples.
__ On and on and on and on.	__ Dry, stiff, or "cold" interaction.
__ Unpredictable.	__ Insensitive comments.
__ Too fast paced.	__ No time for personal sharing.
__ Unclear instructions or language.	__ Low recognition or praise.
__ Too much beating around the bush.	__ Lack of respect for feelings.
__ Incomplete sentences.	__ Overly direct or brusque dialogue.
__ Lack of closure.	__ Critical, judgmental attitude/voice.
__ Not letting a person finish thinking.	__ Being cut off or ignored.
__ Lack of practicality.	__ Lack of empathy for others.
__ Too many ideas at once.	__ Avoidance of face-to-face meeting.
__ Unexpected "off the wall" speech.	__ All data, no nonsense.

THE HERRMANN MODEL AND ENTREPRENEURSHIP

As we have seen in Chapter 2, an entrepreneur is a person who organizes and manages a business and assumes the risk for the sake of profit. Adaptive entrepreneurs are involved in businesses with comparatively low risk; they solve problems in tried and understood ways by "doing things better." They manage change incrementally, work within the system, and when collaborating with inventors, supply stability and organization. These people implement inventions and thus institute innovation—the term from entrepreneurship theory most closely associated with them is *allocating entrepreneur.* Their strongest thinking preferences would tend to be in quadrants A and B.

Inventive entrepreneurs discover problems and originate creative ideas and creative solutions; they question assumptions and take risks; they do things "differently." They provide strategic vision and create the dynamics for radical change--they are *catalytic entrepreneurs* who originate breakthrough ideas. They are typically impatient with routine and detail and are seen as chaotic and abrasive, with little respect for rules—all characteristics of quadrant D thinkers. These entrepreneurs are compared in Figure 3.8.

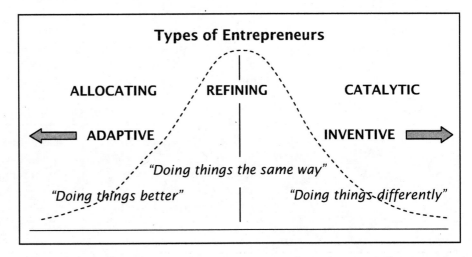

Figure 3.8 *Different types of entrepreneurs and entrepreneurial managers*

When the intended communication is significant, it is necessary to design and deliver it in ways that allow for understanding to take place in all four quadrants.

My experience clearly demonstrates that the use of illustrations, graphics, stories, examples, and metaphors greatly enhances the likelihood that the intended meaning is conveyed to a wide range of people.

Ned Herrmann,
The Whole Brain Business Book, p.119

Figure 3.8 compares Michael Kirton's model of adaption-innovation theory (Ref. 3.5) with the definitions for entrepreneurs synthesized in Chapter 2. The Kirton Adaption-Innovation scale is along the horizontal axis and only indicates comparative degrees of preference for adaptive or inventive thinking and problem solving. Art Fry, the inventor of the Post-it notes, has superimposed a bell-shaped curve on the Kirton scale to indicate a somewhat quantitative measure of the different types of entrepreneurs, since only a comparatively few individuals would be found at the extreme range, whereas many are found in refining-type enterprises. According to Art Fry, the CEOs and managers of established businesses typically want to keep the status quo and "do things the same way"—with little change. However, to remain competitive and survive in a changing environment, they are forced to either become adaptive or inventive to some degree to make their businesses more efficient. Inventive entrepreneurs need adaptive managers or colleagues to help them implement creative concepts and achieve innovation.

We will take another look at different types of management (based on thinking style) in Chapter 12 in the context of managing for innovation.

EXERCISES

3.1 Analysis of a Sales Advertisement
Obtain a selection of sales advertisements for cars from magazines. Then in a heterogeneous group, select one and analyze what you like and dislike about the ad. How could the ad be improved by using all thinking quadrants?

3.2 Whole-Brain Communication
Use a memo you have recently written or received. Do a "four-quadrant walk-around" to identify areas where the memo could have been improved for better communication, using the scheme in Figure 3.9. Then rewrite it.

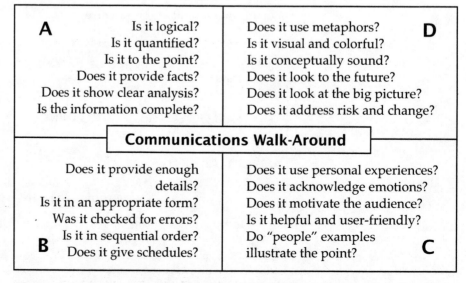

Figure 3.9 Communications checklist (©1998 The Ned Herrmann Group)

3.3 Team Analysis

As a team, write up an analysis of your collective strengths and weaknesses. Which thinking preferences make it easy to communicate within the team? Which areas will need special attention when doing your team project? Discuss how you could increase the mental diversity of your team.

3.4 Working with "Opposite" People

a. As a manager or team leader, you must be able to overcome the effect of your own thinking preferences when giving assignments to your staff or team members, or when involved in a difficult negotiation. Write down a typical assignment and explain it in terms of each thinking quadrant.

b. Think over a recent conflict situation and try to analyze it from the point of view of different thinking preferences. Can you identify where the differing parties may have been coming from? See Reference 3.6 for a discussion of "creative abrasion" for enhancing teamwork.

3.5 Turn-on Work

In Table 3.5 (from Ref. 3.3, page 26), circle the eight elements that most turn you on. Turn-on items are usually strongly aligned with your thinking preferences. Underline the two elements that turn you off the most. These are usually found in the diagonally opposite quadrant of your strongest preference. This analysis is more difficult to do when your thinking preferences are evenly distributed over all four quadrants. Only the HBDI can give an accurate indication of your thinking preferences.

***Table 3.5** Turn-On Work*

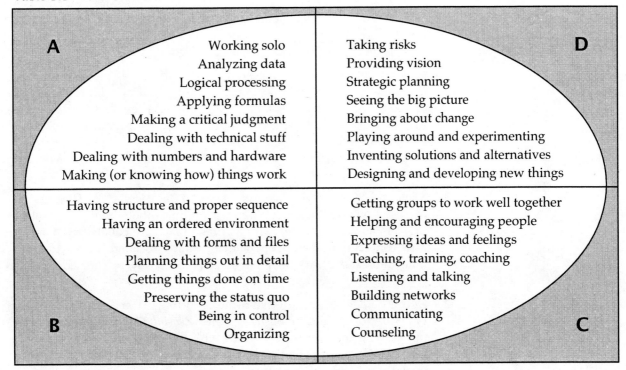

3.6 Mission Statement

Obtain the mission statement of an organization you are associated with or know well. Look for clues in the vocabulary and "world view" for the dominant thinking quadrant(s). Is the mission statement in line with the day-to-day operation and values of the organization?

3.7 Definition of Entrepreneurship

From what you have learned about the four thinking styles and "clues" in the Herrmann model, do a pro-forma analysis of the definition on the left. Which words or phrases are clues to a specific thinking preference? Which thinking quadrants are addressed? How balanced is the definition between left-brain and right-brain thinking? Which quadrants (if any) are missing?

REFERENCES AND RESOURCES

3.1 For case studies on HBDI applications, visit www.hbdi.com. Click on RESOURCES, then open the case studies ("View All") and select those that may interest you.

3.2 Ned Herrmann, *The Creative Brain,* Herrmann International, Lake Lure, North Carolina, 1990. This "whole-brain" book explains the theory and development of the four-quadrant model of brain dominance and contains applications to many different areas of life. See especially pages 111-113 for the story of "Weird John." It also exemplifies a whole-brain approach in its writing and lay-out.

3.3 Ned Herrmann, *The Whole Brain Business Book: Unlocking the Power of Whole Brain Thinking in Organizations and Individuals,* McGraw-Hill, New York, 1996. This book contains much insight and practical advice on how to use whole-brain thinking to enhance leadership, teamwork, and creativity in an organization to increase productivity.

3.4 Edward Lumsdaine, Monika Lumsdaine, and J. William Shelnutt, *Creative Problem Solving and Engineering Design,* McGraw-Hill, 1999, ISBN 0-07-236-058l-5. Chapters 3, 4, and 5 (pp. 49-152) provide additional information, tools, exercises and examples on the Herrmann model and its application to communication and teamwork. See pages 67 through 79 for a description of the knowledge-creation model and how it maps onto the Herrmann model.

3.5 Michael J. Kirton, *Adaption-Innovation in the Context of Diversity and Change,* Taylor & Francis, 2003. Adaption-Innovation theory is a model of problem solving and creativity. It aims to increase collaboration and reduce conflict within groups. The theory and associated Kirton Adaption-Innovation (KAI) inventory have been extensively researched (see also www.kaicentre.com).

3.6 Dorothy Leonard and Susaan Straus, "Putting Your Company's Whole Brain to Work," *Harvard Business Review Reprint 97407,* July-August 1997, pp. 110-121. It compares the HBDI with the MBTI and presents helpful hints on how to use team conflict (termed *creative abrasion*) in a constructive way to enhance team effectiveness.

Entrepreneurship is the process of identifying, developing and bringing a vision to life.

The vision may be an innovative idea, an opportunity, or simply a better way to do something.

The end result of this process is the creation of a new venture, formed under conditions of risk and considerable uncertainty.

Entrepreneurship Center, Miami University, Ohio

4

The Creative Problem Solving Model

What you can learn from this chapter:
- Gain an understanding of the creative problem solving model and the associated metaphorical mindsets and thinking quadrants.
- Learn about right-brain problem exploration and left-brain problem analysis and definition, with associated tools.
- Learn about idea generation, especially as done by brainstorming with a team.
- Learn about creative idea evaluation and critical idea judgment.
- Learn about the two phases of solution implementation: "selling" the idea and carrying out the implementation.

COMMON PROBLEM SOLVING SCHEMES

People have always had distinct preferences in their approaches to problem solving.

Today's pace of change demands that these individuals quickly develop the ability to work together.

Rightly harnessed, the energy released by the intersection of different thought processes will propel innovation.

Dorothy Leonard and Susaan Straus (Ref. 3.6)

Let us begin with a brief survey of commonly used problem solving schemes. A problem is not only something that is not working right or an assignment teachers give to students—a problem is anything that could be fixed or improved through some change. A problem is finding the best birthday gift ever for someone you love. A problem is inventing something (a product or service) that fills a specific need. Schools heavily emphasize the teaching of analytical problem solving. Yet it has been estimated that about eighty percent of all problems in life need to be approached with creative thinking. Problem-solving approaches that are taught in various fields are compared in Table 4.1. In addition, some people use unguided experimentation, trial and error, or guessing. But because these commonly have unreliable outcomes, they are not included here. Creative problem solving is a structured model that uses exploratory, analytical, creative, critical, organized and interpersonal thinking in the most effective sequence to obtain optimum outcomes. Effective problem solving is applying this whole-brain model iteratively to achieve a desired goal, such as starting a successful business enterprise.

The field-specific problem solving schemes in Table 4.1 have limitations. The scientific method is taught and reported as a sequential procedure, whereas the actual process includes many detours—with intuition and idea synthesis—that are rarely recognized and acknowledged. Creative thinking adopts the first idea that comes to mind and may not necessarily lead to a superior solution, since better alternatives are not sought. Analytical problem solving is taught well in mathematics and engineering courses but cannot be applied to other types of problems because it discourages contextual, holistic, and intuitive thinking. Large companies have developed their own problem solving methods based on a team approach, but because few people on these teams have training in creative thinking, analytical thinking predominates and innovative design concepts or solutions are rare.

Table 4.1   *Problem Solving Schemes of Various Fields*

Method	Phase 1	Phase 2	Phase 3	Phase 4
Science *Scientific method*	Inductive data analysis and hypothesis.	Deduct possible solutions.	Test alternate solutions.	Implement best solution.
Psychology *Creative thinking*	Exploration of resources.	Incubation— possibilities.	Illumination— definite decision on solution.	Verification and modifications.
Math *Polya's method*	What is the problem?	Plan the solution.	Look at alternatives.	Carry out the plan; check the results.
Engineering *Analytical thinking*	Define and sketch system; identify unknowns.	Model the problem.	Conduct analysis and experiments.	Evaluate the final results.
Industry *Team problem solving*	1. Use a team approach. 2. Collect data; define the problem.	3. Deal with emergencies. 4. Find the root cause.	5. Test corrective action; devise action plan. 6. Implement the plan.	7. Prevent problem recurrence. 8. Congratulate team.
Many Areas *Creative problem solving*	1. Define the problem: explore the context; analyze data.	2. Generate many ideas. 3. Develop and synthesize better ideas.	4. Judge the ideas: establish criteria; decide on the best solution.	5. Implement the solution; do a follow-up. What have you learned?

CREATIVE PROBLEM SOLVING METAPHORS

Creative problem solving as outlined in Table 4.1 and Figure 4.1 can be effectively used in all but routine problems. It will prevent superficial solutions to deep-seated strategic and operational problems and long-term solutions to short-term tactical problems. It is a key for addressing unstructured, elusive, and ambiguous problems. Creative problem solving has five steps that are specifically related to six different *metaphorical mindsets* with distinct ways of thinking as shown superimposed on the Herrmann model in Figure 4.1. For each mindset, a tool box of different techniques is available to carry out the particular problem solving step. The choice depends on the goals, type and context of the problem, the time and resources available, the capability of the team members, and the organizational culture.

Edward Lumsdaine and his wife Monika first learned about different problem-solving mindsets from Roger Von Oech (Ref. 4.1). They added the "detective" for data analysis to the "explorer" to indicate that both left-brain and right-brain thinking are required for complete problem definition. To emphasize a key step in creative problem solving—idea synthesis and optimization—they invented an idealized "engineer." This mindset is placed between the right-brain "artist" and the left-brain "judge" and iterates rapidly between creative and analytical thinking. And they changed the "warrior" into the "producer" in response to requests from students and teachers for a more positive image. These metaphors make it easier to remember the type of thinking that we need to use at each creative problem-solving step.

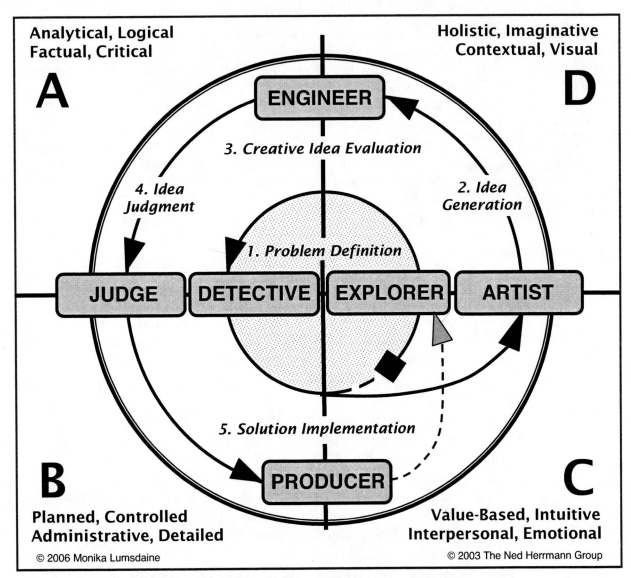

Figure 4.1   *How creative problem solving relates to the Herrmann model*

But why do the iterative cycles move in a counter-clockwise direction? When the Lumsdaines analyzed the knowledge-creation cycle developed by Nonaka and Takeuchi (Ref. 4.2) in terms of the Herrmann model, they found that it moved in sequence through the following quadrants and processes:

1. **Quadrant C:** Motivation through personal experiences; interface with customers, as well as the shared beliefs and values held by the team.

2. **Quadrant D:** Vision and new concepts developed through brainstorming, metaphors, models, and divergent thinking.
3. **Quadrant A:** Information flow and explicit systemic knowledge through data collection, analysis, documentation, and dissemination.
4. **Quadrant B:** Implementation to solve problems and do the job well—which involves mastery "learning by doing," prototyping products or piloting new processes, with on-the-job training to gain tacit, operational knowledge.

Metaphor is the use of one subject to clarify understanding of another.

A product of the right brain, it can be thought of as a translation from one mental language to another, from the literal to the analogical.

Its power is the instant understanding it brings by reason of the translation.

Ned Herrmann

The knowledge creation cycle moves through all four quadrants at the team level (often more than once). Then it can spiral up to different organizational levels (as will be explained further in Chapter 12). The Lumsdaines found a striking correspondence between the knowledge-creation cycle and their creative problem solving model when they placed the "explorer" ahead of the "detective" in problem definition by starting the process in quadrant C at the black square as shown in Figure 4.1. (Their early work did not yet incorporate this optimum sequence.) Also, this governs the direction of the flow diagram shown in Figure 1.2 for technical and business innovation.

OUTLINE OF THE CREATIVE PROBLEM SOLVING STEPS

1. Problem definition

To look at the big picture or context of a problem or to discover its opportunity and future-oriented aspects, we use the mindset of an **EXPLORER**, primarily using quadrant C and D thinking. To find the root causes of problems, we need to think like a **DETECTIVE**—we look for clues and ask questions using quadrant A and B thinking. Problem definition ends with a summary briefing and a positive problem definition statement based on an analysis of the collected information.

2. Idea generation

Here we brainstorm a multitude of creative ideas based on the problem definition in the imaginative, intuitive mindset of an **ARTIST**, using thinking quadrants C and D.

3. Idea synthesis

In the creative idea evaluation phase, we play around with the brainstormed ideas to obtain fewer but more practical, optimized, synthesized solutions in the mindset of an **ENGINEER** using thinking quadrants D and A.

4. Idea judgment

In the critical idea evaluation phase, we must use relevant criteria to determine which ideas and solutions are best and should be implemented, in the mindset of a **JUDGE** and primarily using thinking quadrants A and B.

5. Solution implementation

Putting a solution into action requires a new round of creative problem solving in the mindset of the **PRODUCER** where the focus is primarily on quadrant B planning and quadrant C communication to carry the project to a successful conclusion.

Let's play with the six mindsets and look at some common problem-solving scenarios:

- What would happen if we left out the "explorer" or "detective"? We can still come up with ideas and find a solution, except that the solution may not solve the real problem.

- What would happen if we left out the "artist" and "engineer"? This happens when we take the first idea that comes to mind and rush to implement it without looking for alternatives. It happens when the "judge" appears too soon in the process—when we tell ourselves, "This is a dumb idea," or when we ridicule the creative ideas of others. Most analytical problem solving approaches skip these two mindsets.

- What happens when we leave out the "judge"? Without the "judge" we will not be able to select the best idea nor find the flaws (which can then be overcome with additional creative problem solving).

- What would happen if we only had the "producer"? This might work in rare cases, when a solution out of the blue actually works by sheer luck. But to create conditions for developing an optimum solution to a problem, it is best to follow the creative problem solving process in the most effective sequence, whether we work alone or in a team.

As we have seen in Chapter 3, we can expect better solutions when we use all four brain quadrants or thinking styles. The brain has direct connections between adjacent quadrants; thus we can move easily between quadrant A and quadrant B thinking and between quadrant C and quadrant D thinking. Alternating quickly between quadrants A and D and quadrants B and C can be learned and becomes easier with practice. However, switching between diagonally opposite quadrants is difficult and takes longer because the brain does not have nerve fibers that connect these quadrants directly—the brain has to "translate" via an intermediate quadrant to accomplish such a switch. Through practice, we can strengthen the intermediate quadrants, and the creative problem solving model has these intermediate steps built in!

危
机

Wei ji.
The modern
Chinese characters
for crisis are made
up of
two words:
DANGER
+
OPPORTUNITY

PROBLEM DEFINITION
OVERVIEW AND OBJECTIVES

A problem has two aspects—danger and opportunity—although one may be more apparent than the other. It is easy to overlook the opportunity aspect when dealing with an emergency. Yet once the crisis has been dealt with, we can introduce a policy of continuous improvement or creatively make a fundamental change leading to innovation. The two aspects of problem definition require two different mindsets: the "detective" to address the crisis and the "explorer" to exploit the opportunity, as contrasted in Table 4.2. To identify the real problem and its context, we need to use the whole brain or both mindsets. In Figure 4.1, this is shown in the inner circle, with the black square marking the starting point. Always begin by considering the quadrant C aspects, including your own motivation.

Table 4.2 Whole-Brain Problem Definition

Type of problem

| Explorer: | Finding or identifying a "mess." Discovering a problem, need or opportunity. |
| Detective: | Assigned a problem or crisis. Something is not working right. |

People involved

| Explorer: | Cooperative teamwork; include people from other fields, not experts. |
| Detective: | Autocratic chain-of-command. Who is responsible? Who is the expert? |

Viewpoint/scope

| Explorer: | What would be nice if it could be done? Systems thinking; explore change. |
| Detective: | What is terrible about a particular situation? Narrow scope, with focus on task. |

Information

| Explorer: | Look into context and trends; set goals. Imagine the future or ideal situation. |
| Detective: | List known facts. Determine what data are needed. Look for causes and clues. |

Boundaries

| Explorer: | Keep limits in the back of the mind; seek to overcome the boundaries. |
| Detective: | Determine constraints and limits on time, budget, staff, and resources. |

Paradigm/approach

| Explorer: | Look for new approaches or alternatives; divergent, intuitive, flexible thinking. |
| Detective: | Use existing tools and methods; traditional, analytical, convergent thinking. |

For example, middle-school students wanted to creatively solve the problem of bicycle theft. As "detectives" they tested chain and cables with hacksaws and bolt cutters. To their surprise, a customer survey found that the biggest problem with bike locks was that the owners forgot how to open them. The "explorers" saw the larger picture and changed the real problem to bike security, where bike design, parking, and registration schemes would be considered and where the solution might be applied to other uses.

THE "EXPLORER" FOR DIVERGENT THINKING

The main goal of "explorers" is to discover the larger context of a problem. They must have a sense of adventure and an eye for the far view, as visualized by the picture. "Explorers" use quadrant D thinking to speculate about possibilities, opportunities, and futures that may be related to the problem. They use quadrant C thinking to investigate how the problem impacts people. The explorer's mindset provides a divergent, positive, long-term perspective to balance the narrower, convergent, and often negative thinking of the "detective" who may be overwhelmed by a data swamp.

Trend watching, or how to anticipate the future

Studying trends can help us see the development of problems in a wider context and time frame. With this information, we may be better able to devise appropriate solutions. Studying trends lets us identify actions, markets, and future products or services—it is a valuable skill for inventors and innovators. In an article on "How to Think Like an Innovator" (May-June 1988, *The Futurist* magazine), Denis E. Waitley and Robert B. Tucker, two California consultants on personal and executive development, offer ideas on how to become a good trend watcher, as summarized in Table 4.3.

Table 4.3   *Tips on How to Become a Good Trend Spotter*

Audit your information intake; make your reading time count

Cut down on mental "junk" food—make informed choices about what you currently read and seek to expand your worldview. Take notes. Look for developing trends and ideas that are different, exciting, incongruous, worrisome, or unexpected. Many innovators read for several hours a day.

Develop your front-line observational skills; ask questions

Become a people watcher. Listen in on conversations to find out how people think and feel. How do the main topics of conversation change over time? What perspectives do you pick up from the popular culture (movies, MTV, blogs, and chat rooms)? Ask questions to find what the customers *really* want?

Find opportunities

Search for solutions to negative trends and offer a means of prevention. Watch for patterns that can tip you off to new opportunities. Even when a present trend is against you, it might be used to come up with a breakthrough idea to counteract it. Watch what the competition is doing and do it better.

Other tools and techniques for "explorers"

In addition to observing trends, "explorers" can use a number of tools for problem exploration, from the personal, introspective level to group brainstorming activities such as *Synectics* (Ref. 4.3) and *Morphological Creativity* (Ref. 4.4)—both are advanced techniques that require special training. Or you can network with experts in the problem area and its context. As an entrepreneur, you will benefit from using the following resources:

Where the telescope ends, the microscope begins. Which of the two has the grander view?

Victor Hugo,
Les Misérables

1. **Searching the Web.** Use a search engine to surf the Internet for information, not just in the specific problem area but also at its fringes and related areas. If you are inventing or improving a product, it is crucial that you conduct a preliminary patent search (see Chapter 7).

2. **Enhancing Your Intuitive Insight.** Alone or in a team, try to model the problem using a wide range of artistic materials and props. Or play the "Don't Sell Me" game in Chapter 6 or do other brainstorming activities in the problem area which exclude non-judgmental thinking.

3. **Mind Mapping.** This visual technique combines aspects of brainstorming, sketching, and diagramming in the process of thinking through a subject and organizing the available information. Tony Buzan, a British brain researcher, invented this method in the 1970s as a note-taking technique that can display the relationships between facts and ideas. Reference 4.5 lists tools and information on mindmapping.

THE "DETECTIVE" FOR CONVERGENT THINKING

"Detectives" deal with crisis and danger—their job is to look for the root causes of problems. They do not assume that they already know what the *real* problem is. Therefore, they look for information that is hidden. To find it, they must be persistent; they must think logically about where and how to

find the desired detailed information and clues; they must use the right "lens" as illustrated in the figure. A methodical, careful quadrant B approach combined with quadrant A analytical thinking is needed. For example, Scotland Yard is doing amazing detective work in sifting clues and questioning many people as they track down terrorists, in cooperation with other intelligence bureaus and law enforcement agencies all over the world.

Tools and techniques for "detectives"

"Detectives" have a virtual toolbox of techniques for identifying the root causes of problems. The choice is guided by problem type, the organization's problem-solving culture, and the available time, budget, and expertise. Special training is needed to learn to use the specialized analytical tools.

1. **Asking questions (Kepner-Tregoe approach).** Detectives ask questions about who, what, where, when, why, and how much. Long lists of questions have been published to help in this process of data collection. In the Kepner-Tregoe method, the problem is defined as the extent of change from a former satisfactory state to the present unsatisfactory state. Finding the causes of the deviation should help solve the problem. It also helps to describe the problem in terms of what it is not (Ref. 4.6).

2. **Surveys.** Manufacturing and service companies depend on surveys to collect data on "the voice of the customer." When this data is analyzed (and visualized with a Pareto diagram), it often yields insight into the real problem that is surprisingly different from the original perception and can change the direction of problem solving.

3. **Introspection.** When time is too short to do in-depth data collection and analysis, we can engage in a few minutes of quiet introspection. We dig into our memories to bring up and share any information that we already have about the problem, before the team collectively works out a problem definition statement.

4. **Statistical process control (SPC).** Manufacturing companies frequently use SPC, which includes seven different tools: check sheets, histograms, cause-and-effect (fishbone) diagrams, Pareto diagrams, scatter diagrams, process control charts, and additional documentation. These are methods for finding the causes of problems by making graphs of the data and then analyzing the results.

5. **Force field analysis.** The problem is analyzed in terms of supporting and hindering forces and their strengths on the way toward achieving a satisfactory state or solution. This is not to be confused with *SWOT analysis*, which is a whole-brain tool looking at strengths, weaknesses, opportunities and threats surrounding a problem.

6. **Other methods.** Ford Motor Company, for example, uses two specific methods to analyze causes of failures. *Failure mode and effects analysis (FMEA)* explores all possible failure modes for a product or a process, and *fault tree analysis (FTA)* is restricted to the identification of the system elements and events that could lead to or have led to a single, particular

The form of made things is always subject to change in response to their real or perceived shortcomings, their failure to function properly.

This principle governs invention, innovation, and ingenuity; it is what drives all inventors, innovators, and engineers.

Henry Petroski (Ref. 4.7)

A problem in an imbalance between what should be and what actually is.

Paraphrased from the Kepner-Tregoe definition

failure. Some specialized methods for "detectives" are very challenging and time consuming. Carefully *designed experiments based on statistical methods* are conducted to get the data needed to answer the list of questions and define the problem accurately. In *Weibull analysis*, the results of testing products to failure are plotted on a log-log paper. When warranty claims about a product need to be analyzed, or products and services are evaluated against the competition, *benchmarking techniques* are employed. *Quality function deployment (QFD)* is used to improve the quality of a product's components above that of the best competing product.

How to complete the problem definition phase

Detectives are responsible for bringing problem definition to a close by completing four tasks: assessing available resources, writing the briefing document, stating the problem definition, and collecting solution ideas that pop up during the incubation period.

1. **Resource assessment.** Consider the following relevant factors: Is the problem an emergency? How much time is available for problem solving? Who is available to help you solve the problem, as a team member or expert? What about finances? What is your budget for the problem solving process and for implementing the solution? If no money is available, you must either concentrate on ways that do not cost much or include fund raising as a separate problem.

2. **Briefing document.** Whether a team or individual is involved in problem solving, the information collected about the problem should be assembled in a briefing document (see Table 4.4) for distribution to the problem-solving team or other stakeholders. Although the data collection file may be substantial, the briefing document should be brief—at most a page or two for all but very complex problems.

Table 4.4   Contents of the Briefing Document

1. Background and context of the problem, including trends.
2. Specific data collected about the problem, with data analysis.
3. Summary of things that were tried but did not work.
4. Thoughts on possible solutions that have come to mind (attached).
5. Conclusion: What is the real problem?
6. The problem definition statement expressed as a positive goal.

3. **Problem definition statement.** This statement, in positive terms, will direct your thoughts or the thoughts of the brainstorming team toward solutions. This goal can be quite specific or an "impossible" big dream. "How can we serve our customers better" most likely will result in mundane ideas, but "How can we provide instant service" will force the mind to seek unusual or innovative ways to reach the goal. Play around with several versions of the statement before selecting the best one; use a thesaurus to find synonyms. See Table 4.5 for an example of a reworked

statement. If a team is involved, brief the members ahead of the scheduled brainstorming. Team members can ask questions and share insight to make sure they understand the problem and the solution goals.

Table 4.5 *Improving a Problem Definition (Example)*

1. **"Secondary school students have a hard time understanding the concept of centripetal force."**
   The spotlight is on the problem; thus this is not a positive statement looking to solutions.

2. **"Design a mini merry-go-round that will let students experience centripetal force."**
   This definition is too narrowly focused on a particular solution. The idea should be jotted down, however, as a possible solution to start the brainstorming, but the definition needs to be broader.

3. **"Teachers need an inexpensive device (presently unavailable) to use in the classroom to enable student to experience and experiment with rotational motion and the forces involved."**
   This definition invites other solutions (besides a merry-go-round) that might solve the problem; also, it provides some criteria.

4. **Incubation and collective notebook.** The mind needs "soak time" so it will be prepared to generate innovative ideas. An overnight period makes a good time-out, or a week may be most convenient for your schedule. At the least, organize a refreshment break with some relaxing activities. Both Albert Einstein and Thomas Edison played a musical instrument or went for a walk when they needed creative ideas. During this incubation, all solution ideas that come to mind must be quickly jotted down, or they will be forgotten. Our mind often has to be cleared of the well-known solutions before we can come up with truly novel ideas. The notes are collected and a summary of the results is prepared, with the most interesting ideas used for further exploration or to start the brainstorming session in the next creative problem solving stage.

IDEA GENERATION

Visualize being in a thunderstorm. You see and feel the awesome power of wind and lightning. Wouldn't it be wonderful if this energy could be harnessed and put to good use? In a way, when we brainstorm, we want to provoke a storm of ideas—a gentle breeze just won't have the same result. Brainstorming procedures are like a harness for directing and optimizing the energy in idea generation. We will first present classic brainstorming and then summarize some variations that have been developed to accommodate special conditions. Brainstorming can be done by individuals (especially when using a visual method such as mind mapping). However, when dealing with complex situations, we should try to bring a team together (including some people not too close to the problem) to increase the probability that novel ideas will be generated.

The verbal method known as classic brainstorming was developed in 1938 by Alex Osborn in his advertising business (Ref. 4.8). It then came into widespread use in the 1950's as a group method for creative idea generation.

The best number of people for verbal brainstorming is from three to ten. Brainstorming does not work for all types of problems all the time, but its successes have made it a valuable problem-solving tool. It is easy to learn, and it gets more productive with practice. People frequently mistake random, routine, critical discussion in meetings as brainstorming. As you will see, brainstorming requires careful mental preparation. Although it is a creative, freewheeling activity, definite procedures and rules are followed.

THE ROLE OF THE "ARTIST"

Generating and igniting imaginative ideas is at the heart of the creative problem solving process. "Artists" create something new, something that first existed only in their minds. As "artists," our task in creative problem solving is to transform information into new ideas. We can and must break out of our usual mold—we can go to town with our quadrant D imagination and our quadrant C feelings! Welcome eccentric, wild, weird, crazy, off-the-wall, out-of-the-box ideas and "lightning storms"—your own and those of your team! The figure on the left will help you remember this metaphor. In brainstorming, the mental activity of using the imagination is called "freewheeling." This means we impose few restrictions on ourselves or our team members on the types of ideas that can be expressed.

The four rules of brainstorming

Brainstorming is easy to learn because it only has four rules. These four rules are important principles, so fix them firmly in your mind!

1. Generate as many solutions as possible—quantity counts.
2. Wild ideas are welcome—be as creative as you can be.
3. "Hitchhiking" is encouraged—build on the ideas of others.
4. No criticism is allowed—defer judgment until the evaluation phase.

The more ideas you generate, the better the chance that you will come up with an innovative solution. The wilder the ideas, the greater the odds of generating a truly original concept! But avoid using words and sharing ideas that are hurtful or offensive to your team members, because the resulting stress would inhibit creative thinking and undermine the team's spirit. Do not put down ideas or the people who express them (including yourself). Humor, laughter, and applause are valued responses. In brainstorming, there are no dumb ideas or wrong answers. Ideas do not have to be entirely new—you *should* hitchhike on other people's ideas. Idea pinching is allowed!

Freedom versus control

Strongly left-brain thinkers may feel uncomfortable with sharing ideas involving quadrant C emotions or "impractical" quadrant D thinking. If you have such reactions, give yourself explicit permission to play with and express all kinds of ideas. Brainstorming is fun! Be surprised by the freedom of the "storm." The interaction that occurs between the minds of collaborating team members is important; ideas can be used as igniters or stepping-stones to new ideas, or they can be combined or synthesized in new and unexpected ways. Wild ideas are valuable and needed at this stage—the normal forces of life will make them more practical later. Maintaining a safe, uncritical climate for expressing creative ideas is important here because these ideas can be very fragile.

Strongly right-brained people may find it difficult to follow "rules." Procedures can ensure that brainstorming will be as efficient and productive as possible. Constraints can both help and hinder brainstorming. They attempt to contain the "storm" within a specific goal or problem area. If they are too rigid, a vigorous "storm" cannot develop. But a limited number of carefully thought-out constraints will not significantly affect creativity. The problem definition statement is a useful constraint: it provides direction and a target for idea generation, as well as boundaries. However, team members should also have permission to push the boundaries—this is when breakthrough ideas may appear.

PROCEDURE FOR VERBAL BRAINSTORMING

The step-by-step procedure for conducting a brainstorming session is presented from the facilitator's point of view, with the preparations summarized in Table 4.6. Since you are now learning about brainstorming, it is likely that you will be leading sessions in the future.

Table 4.6 Preparation for Verbal Brainstorming

Team members: If possible, some of the stakeholders affected by the problem and solution should be among the brainstorming team, and some members should have quadrant D thinking preferences. All should receive the briefing document ahead of the brainstorming session if possible.

Location: People are able to think more creatively if they are in an unfamiliar location. Thus, find a place with beautiful, relaxing surroundings. At the least, select a room that is different—not one regularly used for meetings. Seat people in a circle or horse-shoe. If you must use a conference room with a long table and facing chairs, enhance the atmosphere with classical background music, colored posters, and a fragrant snack.

Schedule: Brainstorming is exhausting; thus do not plan to cover more than two topics or exceed a three-hour period. Pick a time and day that shields people from the stress of pressing business, perhaps by using a "camp" theme.

Materials: Obtain and set up the necessary equipment: easels, flip charts, markers, note cards, and visual aids or props to stimulate creative thinking. For long sessions, have light refreshments, including coffee or tea. A tape recorder can capture comments that do not get written down during the session. For a large team, an assistant can help record ideas, perhaps by using a laptop computer.

Step 1—Briefing: Give the team members a few minutes for social interaction and comfortably seating themselves. Turn on the tape recorder, open with a review of the briefing, and invite team members to share new insights about the problem. Prominently post the problem definition statement and amend it if desired. Make sure that distractions on people's minds or in the room's environment are taken care of before the actual brainstorming starts.

Step 2—Review the rules and required mindset: Review the four brainstorming rules. Explain that anyone offering more than two negative remarks will be asked to leave the session—this is the "three strikes and you're out" policy for preventing a negative atmosphere. Review the characteristics of the artist's mindset to be used for the brainstorming session.

Step 3—Explain the procedure: Explain that all ideas and combinations of ideas will be numbered and recorded. In a small team, ideas can be called out as fast as they can be written down on the flip chart. In large teams, members have to take turns speaking. The other participants must jot down all ideas that flash into their minds, so they won't forget them while they await their turn. Ask for brief statements only; the "engineer" will have an opportunity later for elaboration. Set an initial time limit of 20-30 minutes. Adding a quota is often helpful to increase the number of ideas generated, such as, "Let's see if we can come up with 50 ideas in 20 minutes."

Step 4—Warm-up exercise: Conduct a 5-minute creative thinking warm-up using a familiar object: brick, pencil, popcorn, ruler, coffee cup, CD—an example is given in Table 7.1. Turn on the classical background music now to encourage right-brain thinking modes. Jot down the called-out ideas on a flip chart. Usually, mundane ideas will be expressed at first. When more humorous ideas come forth and the team members relax with laughter, their minds are "primed" and you can start to brainstorm the defined problem.

Problems cannot be solved by thinking within the framework in which the problems were created.

Albert Einstein

Step 5—Brainstorming: Teams usually begin by "dumping" well-known, obvious ideas—these have to be purged from the mind before it can bring out really new, creative ideas. Write down all ideas; when a sheet is full, post it on the wall. If the flow of ideas is very slow or stuck, encourage the process by throwing out a wild idea to serve as a stepping-stone (or use a thought-starter technique—see Chapter 7). But don't rush into this; quiet periods to allow reflection and synthesis in the subconscious mind can be beneficial.

Step 6—Close: Once the flow of ideas has slowed down to a trickle and the announced time is up, give an extra three minutes. Some of the best ideas are often generated during this time. Or challenge the team to come up with five to ten additional ideas before stopping.

Step 7—Dismissal: Thank the team members for their participation and let them know what will happen next. Collect all ideas that were written down, as well as the tape recording, for later processing and evaluation. Encourage the team members to e-mail you additional ideas that might come to them in the next few days.

Other brainstorming methods

What if you have shy or domineering team members? What if you have a group of a hundred or more people you want to involve in brainstorming? What if there is open conflict among people who must participate? To address special circumstances, other brainstorming techniques have been developed—a few of the easier, low-tech approaches are listed in Table 4.7. Many books are available with information on alternate methods for idea generation (such as Ref. 4.9). *Morphological Creativity, Synectics* and *TRIZ* are complicated techniques that require special training. Many engineers prefer to use TRIZ (Ref. 4.10) because it depends on a basic knowledge of science. Table 4.8 lists techniques that can be used to get idea generation going.

Table 4.7 *Some Simple Brainstorming Alternatives*

1. Pin card method: Written technique for a small group of shy or confrontational people.
2. Crawford slip writing: For large groups, with each person submitting 20-30 ideas.
3. "Ringgi" process: People sequentially modify a proposed idea; this avoids face-to-face conflict.
4. Panel method: Seven volunteers out of 30-40 people brainstorm; all others jot down ideas.
5. Story board: Ideas are brainstormed and posted on note cards for different categories.
6. Electronic brainstorming/bulletin board: Ideas are collected on a posted problem.
7. Idea trigger: Individual lists are shared in a group and trigger additional creative ideas.
8. Gallery method: People work silently on flip charts, inspect other's ideas, add modifications.
9. Mind mapping: "Visual" method especially useful for individual brainstorming.

Table 4.8 *What to Do When You Are "Stuck"*

1. Imagine success: Imagine the ideal situation; mentally remove all constraints.
2. Imagine the worst: Imagine the most absurd things to do to solve the problem.
3. Force-fitting ideas: Force two wild, unrelated ideas together to generate solutions; purposefully search for wild options.
4. Free association: Start this "game" with a symbol; continue a chain to good ideas.
5. Big dream: Think of a far-out dream solution and what-if wishful scenarios.
6. Thought-starter tools: Osborn's Nine Questions and commercial tools based on the nine (or similar) questions—see Table 7.2.
7. Attribute listing: Consider all parts/features under consideration. What would happen if each were changed in different ways?
8. Bionics: Ask, "How is the problem solved in nature?"

High-tech (electronic) brainstorming

Computers can be used for brainstorming, and a number of software packages are available. *IdeaFisher* is probably one of the best known and has survived the test of time. Others are *MindManager Pro 6* and *Imagination 8* (see Ref. 4.5). Computer programs can inject out-of-the-box ideas and are thus beneficial when a homogeneous workgroup is brainstorming—especially a group that is stuck in routine problem-solving habits. In this case, only one computer is required. Similarly, the program can also enhance brainstorming by individuals. If everyone on the team has access to a networked computer, the members can brainstorm from their own desks in a "virtual" meeting. Research seems to indicate that the productivity (quantity as well as quality) of ideas generated by electronic brainstorming is not significantly different from that obtained by traditional techniques.

CREATIVE IDEA EVALUATION

Idea evaluation is a two-step process, where each step uses a different mindset. We begin with creative idea evaluation in the engineer's mindset, followed by critical evaluation as a "judge." The two steps are used iteratively in the Pugh method, a structured process of creative concept evaluation for synthesizing an optimum solution described in detail in Chapter 5.

THE ROLE OF THE "ENGINEER"

Creative idea evaluation is basically a second, focused round of brainstorming that builds on the ideas generated the first time around. The required mindset is symbolized in the figure. The goal is to arrive at practical ideas that have the potential for solving the original problem. "Engineers" categorize, mesh, develop and improve the "artist's" ideas; they combine, synthesize, force-fit, and generate additional creative ideas. Each wild idea is questioned: How can it be used as a stepping stone to a better idea? What is useful or valuable about it? "Engineers" move quickly between quadrant D and quadrant A thinking with a nonjudgmental, positive attitude.

The four rules of creative idea evaluation

Like brainstorming, creative idea evaluation also has four rules.

> 1. Look for quality and "better" ideas.
> 2. Make wild ideas more practical.
> 3. Synthesize ideas to obtain more complete, optimized solutions.
> 4. Maintain a positive attitude; continue to defer critical judgment.

Instead of quantity, we are now aiming for quality. Look for the good in each idea and try to make it even better. Use wild ideas as stepping-stones or thought-starters to generate more practical solutions. This requires iteration between creative and analytical thinking. Instead of hitchhiking on ideas, we will now try to integrate, synthesize, force-fit, or meld different ideas to develop optimal solutions. We will continue to abstain from quick judgments and negative comments; instead, we try to overcome obvious flaws in ideas with additional creative thinking.

Timing and preparation

If possible, wait at least one day after the original brainstorming—creative idea evaluation will be more productive if done with fresh minds. This time lag will also give the facilitator, team leader, or the entire team a chance to do some preliminary organizing work with the pool of brainstormed ideas.

To prepare for idea evaluation, each brainstormed idea is written on a separate note card. Some teams may prefer to use Post-it notes instead. Use a heavy pen and print legibly; start writing at the top of the card to leave some blank space for notes at the bottom, and include the identification number. When new ideas come to mind during this process (as is quite likely), they are written down on cards, too, and added to the stack.

Many ideas grow better when transplanted into another mind than in the one where they sprang up.

Oliver Wendell Holmes

The facilitator needs to bring the following materials to the evaluation session: the completed idea cards, blank cards, and pens in different colors for writing on the cards, paper clips, rubber bands, a flip chart, markers, and masking tape. The meeting room should have a large table and empty wall space where flip chart pages (or the Post-it notes) can be posted. To save time, the facilitator can do Task 1 ahead of the meeting. Keep in mind that creative evaluation may take much longer than the original brainstorming.

THE CREATIVE IDEA EVALUATION PROCESS

This is an open-ended activity involving brainstorming—the results are not entirely predictable, even though a structured, three-step approach is used.

Task 1—sorting related ideas into categories

The idea cards are randomly spread out over the table. Ponder the ideas in silence for a few minutes. Some ideas seem to naturally want to be together. For these similar ideas, make up a *title card* in a different color—any idea that seems to fit can be placed in this category. Do not make these categories too broad—it is quite all right to have many different categories. Team members can have brief discussions about where the ideas should go; if an idea fits into more than one category, make a duplicate and enter the idea in both.

Again, jot down any new ideas that come to mind on new cards and add them to the pool. This sorting process is accomplished quickly—our brain naturally likes to group and categorize ideas. Ideas that do not fit into any obvious category can be placed under "odd ideas." With the title card on top, the idea cards in each category are bundled together with a rubber band. If more than seven categories are present, repeat the process by combining two or more into a larger category. For some topics, it may be difficult to come up with category headings. In this case, sort ideas according to well-known ideas, novel ideas, and wild ideas, or according to the degree of difficulty of implementation—simple (inexpensive) ideas, "meaty" (more challenging) ideas, and difficult ideas (requiring major resources and innovation).

Task 2—developing quality ideas within a category

Each category is now worked on separately. If the team is large, categories may be assigned to balanced subgroups of three to five members. At the start of Task 2, conduct a brief creative thinking warm-up. The objective here is to "engineer" the many ideas or idea fragments within the category down to fewer, but more completely developed, practical, and higher-quality ideas. The team members can discuss and elaborate on the ideas in the category and creatively add more detail. Primarily, idea synthesis—combining several concepts or ideas into a new whole—is the key mental process used.

To save time, changes and additions to ideas are made directly on the cards. Use paper clips to fasten cards together that have been combined into one idea, with the most developed, synthesized idea placed on top of the stack. Do not be in a hurry to discard wild ideas or ideas that do not seem to fit; try to use them as idea triggers—the most useful and innovative solution to the original problem may originate here. Attempt to make well-known

You can be wrong, you can commit errors in logic, even record inconsistencies, but I won't care if you can help me to useful new combinations.

J.W. Haefele
Procter & Gamble

ideas better. Examine novel ideas closely but do not get carried away with any of these—continue to look for ways to improve and synthesize all ideas in the category to come up with fewer, but higher-quality solutions. When the team has gone through all ideas in a category, the "improved" ideas are written on a flipchart and posted on the wall to facilitate the next step.

Task 3—force-fitting unrelated ideas between categories

The teams now try to combine the "improved" ideas from all categories to come up with superior solutions. This is truly a force-fitting activity because these ideas are usually very dissimilar. Mentally try out different combinations of final ideas. Entirely new and interesting ideas and high-quality solutions may be generated through this process. Again, post these "synthesized" ideas. However, for some types of problems, it is impossible to distill a large number of original ideas down to a few comprehensive solutions; creative idea evaluation instead results in a list of valuable ideas or design criteria that, when implemented together, will solve the problem. In this case, the entire list is carried forward to idea judgment.

Then the "engineers" need to STOP! Quadrant B people may feel uncomfortable with unfinished business; they want to immediately adopt one of the "synthesized" ideas as the solution to the problem. Others want to keep working to exhaustion to find a perfect solution or they may begin criticizing ideas. Critical idea evaluation requires a different mindset and techniques and is the next step in the creative problem solving process.

CRITICAL IDEA EVALUATION

Solutions to problems can be the direct causes of failures, if our judgment is flawed. In this step of the creative problem solving process, we use critical thinking to detect and eliminate shortcomings in the proposed solutions, as well as to evaluate the risks and consequences involved, all with the purpose of finding the best solution to pass on to the "producer" to implement.

THE ROLE OF "JUDGE" IN CRITICAL IDEA EVALUATION

At first glance, the judge's mindset seems to be a natural for most of us since it is easier to criticize than to explore new options or take action. However, being a "judge" can be difficult because we must weigh different alternatives to determine a "best" solution, as symbolized in Figure 4.6. "Judges" need to make wise decisions based on evidence and principles, primarily using quadrant A thinking. They need a sense of timing to figure out if decisions can be made quickly or only after long, careful study, and they must also discern if the time is right for a new idea. "Judges" must detect bias and flaws (using safe-keeping quadrant B thinking) and then devise ways of overcoming the flaws with a new round of creative problem solving in quadrant C and quadrant D mode. Also, they must look ahead and consider the risks and impact of the solution. "Judges" must be able to imagine all the things that could possibly go wrong with the solutions under consideration. This is very difficult to do for people with strong left-brain dominances. In "The Road to September 11" (*Newsweek*, October 1, 2001, page 41) we read, "The inability of the government to even guess that nineteen suicidal terrorists might turn four jetliners into guided missiles aimed at national icons was more than a failure of intelligence. It was a failure of imagination."

What is good judgment?

Good judgment comes from experience. Experience comes from poor judgment.

Ziggy

On the warranty statement of a product we saw this warning: "We cannot be responsible for the product used in situations which simply make no sense." With increased use of technology, good judgment becomes critically important. The precision of the computer's numerical output can give a false sense of security as to the validity of the calculations (which may have ignored factors critical to a particular situation or human interface). Good judgment also involves an awareness of bias and ethics, underlying values and the presuppositions that can influence decisions. It has been said that our technological development and achievements have far outstripped moral and ethical development. Can you support this opinion with concrete evidence? Can you cite evidence supporting an opposing view?

TECHNIQUES FOR IDEA JUDGMENT

Having a list of evaluation criteria is crucial—judgment techniques work best when they are supported with a good list of criteria. We will briefly summarize some judgment techniques including the Pugh method—a team-based idea evaluation tool for developing an optimum solution.

The list of criteria

A good list of criteria includes all factors that influence a problem or decision. It takes time to make up a valid list of criteria. The list can be developed through regular brainstorming—the more criteria, the better! Through creative evaluation, the criteria are further refined, and the most useful and important criteria are selected. Make sure the evaluation is balanced between analytical and intuitive criteria, as well as between quantitative and qualitative factors. Some people like to use a weighting system. It can simply be based on rank, for instance from 1 to 5, with the highest number assigned to the most important criteria.

Criteria can be thought of as the boundaries, limits, or specifications that the solution must fit to solve the problem. For example, applicable government laws and regulations must be observed, or the product is constrained by physical parameters. But if time permits, limits should be questioned. Think of specifications not as chains but as challenges! Pay attention to intuition—what attributes do you *feel* the ideal solution should have? We need to look to the future and consider factors that will make implementation easier and more successful, including people, their motivation and values, cost, support and resources, time, and consequences. Basically, criteria help us evaluate the capability of proposed ideas for solving the original problem. But rarely will an idea emerge as a clear winner that will satisfy all criteria. Consequently, evaluation techniques are employed to sift and rank ideas.

Quick procedures

When we do not have time to develop a good list of criteria that will allow us to rank ideas, we can use some type of *judgment by vote*. A major disadvantage of quick voting is a lack of explicit criteria since each person makes the decision based on his or her own values or prejudices. Quick votes tend to discourage the discussion of flaws. While a large number of ideas can be quickly reduced to a more manageable level through a *single criterion*, such as cost, a hasty decision here could eliminate good potential solutions.

Advantage/disadvantage techniques

The simplest approach with this type of tool is to make a separate *listing of advantages and disadvantages* for each idea, with one column for all its advantages (positive marks or pros) and one column for all its disadvantages (negative marks or cons). The idea with the most advantages and least disadvantages "wins." This method has a major weakness because one negative can be so important that it could outweigh all positives. When we add a third column to this evaluation to take the long-range potential of each idea into account, we have the *advantages, limitations, and potential (ALP) method*. This method makes it somewhat easier to give a fair evaluation to untried, creative ideas that depend on their potential benefits for acceptance.

If we construct an advantage-disadvantage matrix with the list of criteria in a column to the left and the ideas to be evaluated across the top toward the right, we have a method that compares each idea with all the others for each criterion, as illustrated in Table 4.9. Each of the five job options has advantages (+) and disadvantages (0) when evaluated against the list of brainstormed criteria. So, which option should you choose? For Job 1, the salary offer is very good, and this advantage receives a plus mark. For Job 2, the pay is low (a disadvantage) and this is scored a zero, and so on. When the matrix is completed, the scores are added separately for both marks.

It is impossible to go through life without making judgments about people.

How well you make those judgments is critical to the quality of your life.

Before you judge someone else, you should judge yourself.

M. Scott Peck, M.D., psychiatrist and author

Table 4.9 Advantage/Disadvantage Matrix

List of Criteria	Job Options				
	1	2	3	4	5
Pay	+	0	0	0	+
Other benefits	+	+	0	0	+
Personal growth	0	+	+	0	0
Good for the family	+	+	0	+	0
Independence	0	+	+	+	0
Status	0	+	0	0	+
Excitement/adventure	+	+	+	0	0
Quality coworkers	+	0	+	+	+
Supportive boss	+	+	0	+	0
Fits with life goals	+	+	0	0	+
TOTAL +	7	8	4	4	5
0	3	2	6	6	5

In this example, Options 1 and 2 are fairly close, with the next three ranking quite a bit lower. Small differences in points are not important; thus the two top options must be considered further. Can the negatives be removed through negotiation, such as the salary offer in Job 2? When weighting factors are used, the final results may have a larger spread, and it will be easier to select the best solution. The advantage-disadvantage matrix is useful for ranking ideas and making decisions, because people working out the matrix will understand *why* ideas are ranked high, since they have an opportunity to discuss and modify the criteria.

The **QFD House of Quality** is an example of a matrix employing weighting factors. When the advantage-disadvantage matrix employs an existing idea or a benchmark product, process, or service as the standard against which the new concepts are compared on a three-way scale, the technique is known as the **Pugh method**. It will be discussed in more detail in Chapter 5, since it is a crucial idea evaluation and decision making tool throughout the product and business development and innovation process. As you will see, the Pugh method is an iterative technique that goes through many rounds until it results in a "best" or superior idea, concept or solution.

Other judgment techniques

When we have only a small number of ideas, the **advocacy method** can be used. Serious weaknesses may be overlooked, but the procedure generates excitement about innovative ideas. **Reverse brainstorming** is the opposite of advocacy since the weaknesses and flaws of each idea are pointed out. This approach must be coupled with a strong effort of overcoming the weaknesses. Sometimes, experimentation is needed to supply more data. If only a few solutions have to be tested, Edison's **trial-and-error method** might suit. Techniques based on statistics, such as the **Taguchi method of designed experiments**, can be used for evaluating many parameters and design options.

DECISION MAKING

The methods we have just discussed result in ranked ideas. Criteria clarify priorities—they do not make the final decision. Decision making has been defined as selecting a course of action to achieve a desired purpose. As a "judge," how can we be sure to make good decisions? We will need to appraise the situation and decide which form of decision making is most appropriate for the problem at hand. A summary of different techniques is given in Table 4.10. Important decisions with long-term effects and strong organizational impact require more thought, care and time, whereas decisions on minor issues can be made quickly and routinely. Established procedures and policies in an organization are useful since they form a framework for decision making that can reduce time and error. We must realize that it is impossible to please everyone. However, as individuals, we can make better decisions when we get into the habit of routinely using the whole-brain decision-making walk-around shown in Table 4.11.

Table 4.12 is a simple and quick checklist for a "judge" that you can apply when evaluating ideas as an individual. Keep a copy in your wallet!

The only tyrant I accept in this world is the "still small voice" within me.

Mahatma Gandhi

Table 4.10 Forms of Decision Making

Coin toss: When two options are equally good, a coin toss can help us decide quickly, since either choice will give an acceptable result.

Easy way out: When several ideas are judged equally good (including the long-term consequences), the easy way out will lead to the quickest and least painful solution.

Checklist: We can make up a checklist (list of criteria) that needs to be satisfied by the best solution. The quality of the solution will depend on the quality of the criteria.

Advantage/disadvantage matrix: We can make the decision to select the highest-ranking option (after disadvantages have been removed if possible).

Common consensus: This is the lowest level of group decision making. A decision that is reached quickly by common consensus is usually mediocre because only what the majority likes and agrees with is being incorporated into the solution. When a quick decision has to be made, people tend to disregard creative ideas. Common consensus may be expedient to quickly solve an urgent problem when delay has serious consequences. For the long run, a better-quality solution should be sought.

Compromise: People with widely differing views may work out a solution through compromise—a second level of group decision making. Good parts are given up by both parties to gain acceptance of other parts. This approach is regularly used in government but may not be the best result for the community because good features were traded off.

Compound team decision: This process—the highest level of group decision making—can result in a superior solution because the team concentrates on making the solution incorporate the best features of several ideas, to where everyone agrees that no further improvement is possible. This is the approach used in the Pugh method. In this process, what people don't like gets improved, not thrown out, to obtain a win-win outcome.

Delay or "no" decision: Delay may give you time to get more data and find a better solution, especially if circumstances have changed. Or a "no-go" decision may be the best decision. Alternatively, you may want to avoid making a decision for political reasons. By delaying the decision past a specified deadline, you can exercise the "pocket veto."

Intuitive decision: Some people make decisions intuitively, without consciously reasoning through the process or working out an explicit set of criteria. Then, to explain their decision, they may "invent" rational reasons for their choice. This right-brain approach works quite well with people who have learned to trust their intuition and its reliability in making good judgments in particular situations.

Table 4.11 Decision-Making Walk-Around © 1998, Ned Herrmann

A *Analytical, logical, fact-based, rational, bottom-line view*	*Intuitive, visual, conceptual, future-oriented, big-picture view* D
Does my proposed decision stand up to a rational analysis of the facts? Have I considered possible bias and filters?	Is my proposed decision aligned with my vision of the future? Can I live with the risks and consequences?
Do the planned actions based on my proposed decision leave me with enough control? *Organized, chronological, safe-keeping, control-oriented, detailed view* B	Are the effects on people of my proposed decision consistent with my values? *People-oriented, sensing, value-based, caring view* C

Table 4.12   Idea Judgment in a Nutshell

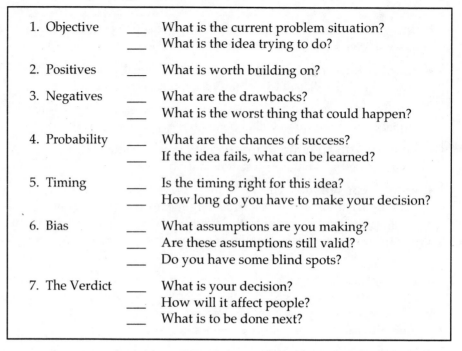

1. Objective	___	What is the current problem situation?
	___	What is the idea trying to do?
2. Positives	___	What is worth building on?
3. Negatives	___	What are the drawbacks?
	___	What is the worst thing that could happen?
4. Probability	___	What are the chances of success?
	___	If the idea fails, what can be learned?
5. Timing	___	Is the timing right for this idea?
	___	How long do you have to make your decision?
6. Bias	___	What assumptions are you making?
	___	Are these assumptions still valid?
	___	Do you have some blind spots?
7. The Verdict	___	What is your decision?
	___	How will it affect people?
	___	What is to be done next?

Special implications of decision making for entrepreneurs

Even though strong quadrant D thinking is a primary characteristic of entrepreneurs, they also need good judgment and decision-making skills. Entrepreneurs are in charge; they are ultimately responsible for their own fortunes and often those of others, to the extent that these are under their control. This is a lonely and exposed position that requires a high level of self-confidence in terms of individual judgment and awareness. Self-confidence without good judgment can have disastrous consequences—it is possible to confidently make a decision that is completely wrong!

Good judgment is usually deliberate, not impulsive. For specific decisions, it can be purchased, for example by obtaining the advice of an expert consultant. Ultimately, however, the turbulence and uncertainty caused by rapidly changing economic, technological and social conditions in the twenty-first century mean that successful entrepreneurs are responsible for making decisions marginally more quickly and accurately than their competitors. Those in the process of deciding whether to start a career as an entrepreneur need to make a careful and honest assessment of their strengths and weaknesses and how these affect their ability to make rapid decisions under pressure and conditions of uncertainty. As we have seen in Chapter 2, Bhidé found that fast decision making is crucial when growing a business.

Leadership is both isolating and lonely. You make the best decisions you can based on the advice and counsel that you have, but ultimately it's all going to come back to you.

Renetta McCann, CEO, Starcom MediaVest Group

SOLUTION IMPLEMENTATION

Solution implementation has two aspects, and creative problem solvers may only be involved in the first one—selling their "best" idea to someone else for implementation that would then be in charge of putting the idea into action.

THE ROLE OF THE "PRODUCER"

In the mindset of the producer we take action. "Producers" are managers; they have something to fight for; they are courageous, optimistic, and do not give up. They are good communicators. Implementation is time-consuming and involves several key steps. Although quadrant B planning and quadrant C interpersonal skills are emphasized, "producers" use the entire creative problem-solving process—the whole brain—since implementation is a new, unstructured problem. Much effort, organization and attention to detail is required. Entrepreneurs as "producers" shoulder the risks involved in doing something new; they need persistence when "selling" their innovative ideas to others, when obtaining support and to overcome resistance. What picture comes to mind when you think of the role of the producer?

The story of Art Fry and his Post-it™ notes provides an excellent illustration as the implementation went through several phases.

How Post-it Notes Became Successful

The 3M Company encourages creativity in its employees, and its researchers are allowed to spend about fifteen percent of their time exploring creative projects. Art Fry decided to use this time to deal with a small irritation in his life. He sang in the church choir and used small bits of paper to mark his pages in the hymnal. Invariably, these bits of paper would fall out. He remembered that a colleague, Spence Silver, had developed an adhesive everyone thought was a failure because it did not stick well. Art Fry played around with this and found it made not only a good bookmark but was great for writing notes because they would stay in place as long as needed, yet could be removed without damage. The resulting product's trade name is Post-it. Here are the major steps it took to get the notes produced and into the marketplace.

First, Art Fry sold the idea to his skeptical boss who agreed that the product was worth testing. The two of them distributed samples throughout the company. Soon, the 3M people using them were sold on the idea.

The next problem was how to produce these pads, since 3M manufactured products in rolls only. Art Fry invented and constructed an assembly machine in the basement of his home. It took a team three years to perfect the product before 3M was ready to test-market it in four cities with eye-catching displays and large newspaper ads. The tests were an absolute failure—and the company decided to kill the product.

But Art Fry and his boss persuaded the 3M commercial office supply people to try another approach—they needed to talk to the customers. They found that people who used the product loved it and wanted more, but the others had no idea what the notes were—this product had to be experienced before it would be bought.

Thus in the next marketing test, thousands of samples were given away. Normally, a 50-percent repurchase indicates a wild success—this test resulted in an astonishing 94-percent repurchase, and sales took off. In two years, distribution was nationwide and across Canada; the following year the product was marketed throughout Europe. Post-it notes became one of 3M's most successful office products.

The first task as "producers" is to plan your strategy. Will you have to convince others of the benefits of your idea, so they will buy and implement it, or will you and your team be in charge of the entire implementation process? You must also plan for a final evaluation of the creative problem solving process and the lessons learned.

SELLING YOUR IDEA

Gaining acceptance for your idea involves careful planning. Analyze your targeted audience; prepare a list of benefits; develop a strategy on how to make an effective sales presentation. Use the whole brain, but concentrate on quadrant C as you develop your selling strategy. The results of the Pugh method will supply much of this information.

Who is your target?

Do you need to sell your idea to managers in your organization? As an inventor, do you need venture funding or help to get a patent? Determine who your audience is and what these people may want from you. Chapter 10 will provide tips and techniques for crafting an effective 30-second "sales pitch."

Why do you need a selling plan?

The selling plan will prepare you to make a sale. You can have the best idea in the world, but if it is poorly presented, the result could be "no sale." You need to know some selling strategies, and you must employ techniques that make for an effective presentation.

What are some principles of selling?

Selling is not a one-shot deal—consider it in the whole context of gaining acceptance and overcoming opposition. Your success also depends on the kind of person you are—your character, your reputation, your integrity. Never jeopardize these to get a quick sale. Do not look at "making the sale" as winning a battle of wits; think of it in terms of building long-term relationships. Learn good presentation techniques—watch your timing; be brief and to the point, use visual aids, make your ideas easy to accept by emphasizing the benefits, and avoid confrontation.

How do you deal with opposition?

You can expect opposition, especially if you are working with a very creative idea! A person opposing your idea can have any number of reasons, such as lack of understanding or different priorities or loyalties to your competitors. Or they are put off because you are not "following the rules," or they fear change. Do not take opposition personally. Realize that people may take your idea as implied criticism that their way of doing something is inadequate. Dealing with opposition requires great sensitivity and diplomacy. Recruit a champion or team for extra support.

How can you make new ideas easier to accept?

Demonstrate the benefits with a small pilot program or in a test market. Having a concrete prototype that can be seen and tacitly experienced with tangible results is very important. Also, if the idea doesn't work, is it possible to

People seldom hit what they do not aim at.

Henry David Thoreau, writer, engineer and naturalist

go back to the way things were done before, without a lot of hassle? Or can you implement the idea in easy steps requiring only small changes each time? Can you build on what is already there—in a process of continuous improvement? Does your idea fit into the culture and long-term goals of the organization? How to deal with change will be discussed in Chapter 11.

In a well-organized system, all the components work together to support each other.

W. Edwards Deming, quality expert

THE WORK PLAN AND IMPLEMENTATION

For preparing a work plan, the predominant thinking preference is quadrant B, because the work plan maps out the exact steps needed for implementation—who does what, when, where, and why. You prepare time schedules and cost budgets and, as a "producer," you need to also address the prevention of possible failure. Since implementation is an unstructured problem, you must be prepared to use the other five creative problem solving mindsets to consider alternative ideas, the context, and the people interface.

The purpose of a work plan is to make sure that the idea or solution will be put to work—that it will work right and be on time as well as within budget. Different procedures are available for the work plan—some are summarized in Table 4.13. The complexity of the problem will determine which approach should be taken. Also consider the resources available to help make implementation successful.

Table 4.13   Work Plans—Tools for Solution Implementation

Copycat: If your idea is similar to one that has been successfully implemented before, just copy the procedure, maybe with some minor adjustments, to save time and trouble.

The 5-W method: Answer the questions "who, what, where, when, and why" for every task in the implementation process. Note that the "how" is not specified. People usually perform better when they can make their own decisions on how they will do their assigned tasks, but specify where certain critical procedures must be followed and explain why.

Flow charts: They visually present all activities that must be performed sequentially and thus are useful for showing simultaneous activities and prerequisites.

PERT (program evaluation and review technique): This method is a planning and a progress monitoring tool for large and very complicated engineering projects. The chart depicts a network of interconnected activities and identifies bottlenecks and critical paths. Complex networks are handled with computer programs tracking thousands of activities. Although this detailed planning takes much effort, it leads to routine implementation.

Time/task analysis (Gantt chart): This is one of the simplest work plan formats. It shows the time requirements of each implementation task. Every task is listed in the left-hand column of a lined chart, with the time scale across the top. For each task, a time line is drawn from starting date to the projected completion date. The chart clearly shows simultaneous or overlapping activities.

Risk analysis: Potential problem analysis for risk assessment is used for very important projects where major obstacles to implementation are anticipated, but it is not cost-effective on a routine basis. Develop appropriate measures and incorporate them in your work plan for dealing with any potential risks that were identified during the critical evaluation phase.

Information from the work plan is useful for preparing the implementation cost budget, since you will know who does what for how long. Use a standard format and work with a person who has the required accounting information. If you have an entrepreneurial mindset tilted toward quadrant D, make sure you present the budget in a quadrant A "voice" with sufficient quadrant B detail—those who will need to approve it for go-ahead will most likely be left-brain administrators.

Implementation monitoring and evaluation

After the solution has been implemented, the last remaining responsibility for "producers" is to make sure that the solution actually works. In a small project, you may be able to personally check up on the success of the implementation. Plan a first review after two weeks, followed by a second six to twelve months later. If your project was starting a new business, plan how you will regularly track your success, not just by the bottom line but also by monitoring trends and interacting with your customers and employees. Plan to give your team positive feedback.

If you kept a journal or notes during the creative problem solving process, it will be easy to write a brief summary of your results when your project has been completed. Then sit back and review what the process has done for you. What have you learned? Did it help you grow? Can you use this idea somewhere else? Did you achieve your goals? How did the process help you communicate with people? Did it open future opportunities for you? If the solution did not work out right, what can be learned from the experience? Keep your summary and conclusions in a file. As you complete more creative problem solving projects, this file will grow into a valuable data base.

You need to develop a careful balance between making judgments based on past experiences and keeping your mind open to new possibilities.

Mark Von Wodtke,
<u>Mind Over Media</u>

BUSINESS DEVELOPMENT AND THE METAPHORICAL MINDSETS

In order to gain a deeper understanding of the transition from original "brainwave" to establishing a business and market, it is helpful to consider the three distinct phases in the framework of the creative problem solving mindsets, since they identify the predominant thinking involved.

The creative phase

This stage refers to the emergence and development of the new concept that is to be commercialized. The concept is in itself a product of creative thinking, and its assessment, evaluation, improvement and refinement also require creativity to be effective. In essence, this phase calls for the "explorer" and "detective" at the outset, followed by the crucial "artist" with the assistance of the "engineer" and "judge" when the Pugh method evaluation tool is employed. This will be discussed in detail in Part 2 of this book.

The technical phase

The progression from concept to feasibility demands appropriate technical expertise and knowledge in order to incorporate logistical requirements into the assessment and evaluation process. Thus in this phase the "engineer" predominates, assisted as needed by the "artist" and "judge." As seen in Figure 1.1 and Chapter 8, this phase occurs during the Pugh method evaluation process. This phase helps deepen our understanding of the product (or service) that constitutes the core of a new venture.

Business development and market phase

With the creativity realized in terms of a technically viable concept, it is necessary to initiate at least two new rounds of creative problem solving to determine the most effective strategies for market entry and business operation as guided by the business model. All mindsets are employed, but the emphasis is on the "producer" to bring the process to a successful conclusion with sufficient attention to detailed planning and developing a customer base. More information is provided in Chapters 9 and 10 (Part 3) and Chapters 11 and 12 (Part 4). A visual overview is provided in Figures 1.1 and 12.1.

EXERCISES FOR "EXPLORERS AND DETECTIVES"

4.1   Technical Knowledge

Predictions are that all the technological knowledge today will represent only about one percent of the knowledge that will be available by the Year 2050. What are the implications of this (a) for education and schools, (b) for the workplace, (c) for libraries, (d) for book publishers, (e) for authors, (f) for business, or (g) for the Internet? Brainstorm one of these topics and see if you can come up with a business idea.

4.2   The Greenhouse Effect

Many scientists are predicting global warming. Brainstorm some positive outcomes or opportunities. For example, more air conditioners will be in demand (and will require substitutes for Freon). Also, new cosmetics providing better protection from ultraviolet radiation will be needed. Come up with ten ideas on new products and markets.

4.3   Time Use Analysis and Exploration

(a) As a detective, complete a detailed log on how you are using your time (in 15-minute chunks, over three days). Then do an analysis to determine which activities waste the most time. Make a Pareto diagram to find "the 20 percent that cause 80 percent of the trouble." Make a plan to eliminate the top three time wasters (one at a time).

(b) To practice the mindset of an explorer, take an afternoon off to look around in a subject you don't know anything about, by reading, speaking to people, visiting exhibits, or attending lectures. Repeat once a month.

4.4   Briefing Document Samples

Obtain samples of briefing documents from three different organizations. How was the data collected and presented? As a team, play around with ways of improving the problem definition statement.

Recipe for a mini-adventure:

Go on an occasional wild goose chase. That's what wild geese are for.

EXERCISES FOR "ARTISTS AND ENGINEERS"

4.5   Warm-Up Exercise for Brainstorming Session

Find different uses for one of the following "fun" objects: a worn sock or sneaker, a feather, a bucket of sawdust, a Frisbee, or a pumpkin.

4.6   What-if Creative Thinking Warm-Up

Brainstorming sessions should "bubble" with laughter.

Funny ideas are often stepping stones to the best solutions.

Pose a what-if question and play around with it for a while, preferably in a group. The exercise is especially valuable if you do it with an impossible, wild and crazy idea.

Examples: (a) What if gravity were suspended for 10 minutes each day—how would bedrooms and bathrooms have to be redesigned? (b) What if people all looked identical—how would one be identified as an individual? (c) What if insects worldwide suddenly quadrupled in size—would this mean a new food supply or a disaster? (d) What if you were stranded on a desert island with the three people you most dislike—what would you do to make this a pleasant experience?

4.7   Disaster—So What?

Suppose that while on a vacation trip, your car with all your money and luggage is stolen. Find ten ways to turn this apparent disaster into a positive experience. Then do a creative idea evaluation—integrate these ideas into one or two practical solutions.

4.8   Sensory Experiences and Sales Ad

First, buy a fruit or a vegetable that you have never eaten before. Note the shape, color, textures, flavor, sound-producing aspects, and fragrance—use all your senses to describe and appreciate this new experience. Write each statement on a separate note card. Use analogies and images. Be wildly poetic! Next, sort the statements using creative idea evaluation. Combine ideas within categories and then between categories. Use one of these improved ideas and write a sales ad for this fruit or vegetable. Test your ad on several of your friends—would they want to buy?

4.9   Paradigm Shift Question

Once a month, alone or with others, brainstorm answers to the paradigm shift question (Ref. 1.3): "What is impossible to do in my field or organization today, but if it could be done, would fundamentally change what I do?" Jot down the ideas in a notebook.

EXERCISES FOR "JUDGES AND PRODUCERS"

4.10   Check Your Assumptions

Anthony and Cleopatra are found dead on the library floor in the middle of a pool of water and broken glass. Write a story of what happened. Then try to identify the hidden assumptions in your story.

4.11   How to Criticize

a.   Make up a scenario in which you have to criticize someone. Write it in such a way that you start out with two positive statements. Then make a wishful statement about the item you want to change, followed by another positive statement about the other person. Then conclude with a hopeful, cooperative, positive statement.

b.   When you are tempted to criticize someone's idea, try to use the imperfect idea as a stepping-stone and generate at least three "better" ideas. Or come up with your own idea and then work with the other person to integrate both ideas into one solution.

4.12   Authoritarian Environment

If you live in an authoritarian environment (strict parents, teachers, boss, or political system) think about what steps you can take to be more creative and overcome the "follow the rules" mindset, yet live at peace with the authorities. Then divide into two groups of three people each, with one group representing authority, the other the creative problem solvers. Make up a scenario where a creative idea is "sold" through negotiation and compromise. Note that "breaking the rules" does not mean breaking the law. The new idea must be legal, moral, and ethical—it simply does not follow the traditional way of doing things.

4.13   Evaluation of Conflicting Opinions

Find newspaper or journal articles that give two opposing points of view on a certain subject. For example, *USA TODAY* carries a daily feature that presents two views on a current issue. Give a brief summary of each; then indicate your agreement or disagreement with the expressed views. Support your viewpoint with additional facts or point out where the writers should have supplied more information.

4.14   Analysis of "wrong" decision

Analyze a case in the past where you made what you feel was a "wrong" decision. What aspect of the judgment process would you need to improve to prevent this from happening again?

4.15   Selling Technique Analysis

a.   From the marketplace or business world, identify some selling techniques, for example, from a printed or televised advertisement. What makes them effective or not effective? What are the objectives? How well do they address customer needs? Write a brief essay.

b.   Find effective advertisements aimed at particular thinking quadrants.

c.   Observe your junk mail for several weeks and collect the letters from organizations asking for support. Then analyze the content. What approaches do you find appealing and persuasive, and what approaches do you find distasteful and negative? Select the best and the worst and prepare a 2-minute presentation.

d.   Analyze a recent resume for signs of effective selling.

There seems to be no invention, no matter how sophisticated, that can equal the power, flexibility and user-friendliness of the whole human mind.

We all possess the world's finest multisensory decision-making machine right in our heads.

All we have to do is learn how to use it.

H. B. Gelatt

REFERENCES AND RESOURCES

4.1   Roger Von Oech, *A Kick in the Seat of the Pants,* second edition, Warner Books, New York, 1998. Four roles of the creative process are presented, together with interesting stories and exercises. Optionally, the book comes with the **Creative Whack Pack**, a deck of topical cards to encourage people to think and play with ideas in new ways as they solve problems.

4.2   Ikujiro Nonaka and Hirotaka Takeuchi, *The Knowledge-Creating Company: How Japanese Companies Create the Dynamics of Innovation,* Oxford University Press, New York, 1995. Through a theoretical model and many case studies (including organizations in the U.S.), the authors show how Japanese companies create new knowledge and use it to manufacture successful products and develop innovative technologies.

4.3   George M. Prince, *Practice of Creativity, Macmillan,* New York, 1970. The main topic is *Synectics,* but the book includes a discussion of the importance of the briefing document.

4.4   Myron S. Allen, *Morphological Creativity: The Miracle of your Hidden Brain Power,* Prentice-Hall, 1962. This book presents the principles of morphological creativity; the technique is demonstrated by the organization of the material in the book.

4.5   Joyce Wycoff's paperback, *Mindmapping: Your Guide to Explaining Creativity and Problem Solving,* Berkley, New York, 1991, is a paperback that expands on Tony Buzan's whole-brain technique by presenting many applications the author has taught in workshops for creative problem solving, decision making and organizational skills. The following are software programs for mindmapping: (a) www.mindjet.com offers *MindManager Pro 6*—a commercial package for mindmapping and organizing ideas, reputedly used by sixty percent of the Fortune top 100 companies; (b) www.inspiration.com sells *Inspiration 8*—which can brainstorm and organize, as well as plan and create for all ages.

4.6   Charles H. Kepner and Benjamin B. Tregoe, *The Rational Manager,* McGraw-Hill, New York, 1965. This book thoroughly explains the Kepner-Tregoe method of problem solving.

4.7   Henry Petroski, *The Evolution of Useful Things,* Knopf, 1992 (hardback), Vintage (paperback, 1994). The stories of the invention and development of simple items such as the fork, zipper, and paper clip are told in the cultural context.

4.8   Alex F. Osborn, *Applied Imagination: The Principles and Problems of Creative Problem-Solving,* third revised edition, Scribner's, New York, 1963. This book by the inventor of brainstorming is well worth reading, especially by team leaders; it explains the technique and its applications.

4.9   Arthur B. Van Gundy, Jr., *Techniques of Structured Problem Solving,* second edition, Van Nostrand Reinhold, New York, 1988. Over 100 proven problem-solving methods are explained and evaluated.

4.10 Genrich Altshuller (translated by Lev Shulyak), *And Suddenly the Inventor Appeared: TRIZ, the Theory of Inventive Problem Solving,* Technical Innovation Center, Inc., Worcester, Massachusetts, 1992.

TRIZ uses three tools to encourage inventive thinking based on science and technical knowledge:

1. A patent search reveals the evolution of technical systems.

2. Contradictory needs must be accommodated with problem solving, not trade-offs.

3. An ideal, imaginary system models how all functions can be met.

Although engineers in general like this method because of its emphasis on science, they need training in the creative aspects of Steps 2 and 3.

The method is taught in the former USSR and other European countries from fifth grade on up

5 The Pugh Method

What you can learn from this chapter:
- Gain an introduction from facts about the origin, "definition" and benefits of the Pugh method.
- Learn about the two phases and steps in the Pugh method and how the evaluation matrix works.
- Learn more details about the process by studying some examples.

First, an overview of the Pugh method of creative concept evaluation is presented. Although this evaluation method had its origins in engineering design, it can be used to evaluate many different types of concepts, alternatives, proposals, bids, options, choices, and ideas, as will be illustrated with two different case studies. Another detailed "teaching" example can be accessed from a website.

OVERVIEW OF THE PUGH METHOD

Why was the Pugh method developed?

The Pugh method of creative design concept evaluation was developed by Stuart Pugh, a design and project engineer with many years of practice in industry. He later became professor and head of the design division at the University of Strathclyde in Scotland. He came to see that designs done purely by analysis were "somewhat less than adequate" because it took a long cycle of modifications to completely satisfy the customers. He realized that engineers need to recognize the whole picture in product design and development; they need an integrated approach to be competitive. Although the Pugh method has its most direct application in product design, the thinking skills and procedure can be applied to many situations where different options have to be evaluated to find the best solution. For example, the outcome of the Pugh method in evaluating business concepts will feed directly into the business plan.

What is the Pugh method?

It is a creative concept evaluation technique that uses criteria (usually derived from "the voice of the customer") in an advantage-disadvantage matrix. The best existing concept (which in a business enterprise can be a product, process or service) is used as datum against which the new concepts are compared. In the process of completing the evaluation matrix, new ideas and concepts are generated and added to the matrix. This process is repeated several times until a superior concept emerges which will have all negatives removed. Because the concepts are evaluated side-by-side in the matrix, the process encourages force-fitting and synthesis on the conscious as well as the subconscious level. The exploration of many different alternatives on how to satisfy the criteria is encouraged before beginning the evaluation process.

What are the benefits of the Pugh method?

1. All participants (an individual, a small team, or several different teams) gain insight into the problem and a clear understanding of the criteria which are becoming increasingly better defined.
2. The Pugh method is an effective communications tool.
3. All customers (manufacturing, sales, service, the impact on individuals and society as a whole) are considered, not just the purchaser or end user of the concept.
4. When teams are involved, the discussion can lead to creative leaps between different concepts and subsequent idea synthesis, as flaws are attacked together and the teams experience synergy.
5. The resulting new concepts are better than the original ideas. No flaws are overlooked; invulnerable products or services are developed that will succeed in a competitive market.
6. The participants develop consensus regarding the best solution; they understand its strength and champion the concept.
7. It prevents a business from making costly mistakes in the choice of products and leads to many other cost savings and applications.
8. In the case of complete concepts (such as submitted proposals or bids), the Pugh method is used for a single round to identify the best among the competing proposals. The evaluation will reveal areas of weaknesses in the best proposal, where the proposers may be asked to overcome weaknesses before receiving funding or go-ahead—thus potentially resulting in a better project outcome.
9. As a decision-making tool, the Pugh method has helped improve course syllabi with new content while keeping the most relevant core.

Optimization only happens if you want it that way.
It takes extra effort to get that extra plus.

Sidney F. Love

What are the steps in the Pugh method?

The Pugh method has two phases, where each phase differs in emphasis. In Phase 1, the focus is on generating creative concepts in several rounds of increasing quality. In Phase 2, the iterative process converges to an optimum solution.

Phase 1 steps:

1. The list of evaluation criteria is developed and the datum (benchmark) is selected, usually the best existing product. When no existing product is available, one of the new concepts is chosen at random to be the datum.
2. Original concepts are brainstormed, sketched and described.
3. Each concept is discussed and evaluated against the datum for each criterion. New concepts that emerge are added to the matrix. When an individual uses the method, the process must still be written down and the thinking and decisions documented.

4. The first-round results are evaluated; the top-ranked concept becomes the new datum, and all designs or concepts are improved for the next round and then evaluated.

5. This evaluation and improvement process is continued for additional rounds, each time using the highest-scoring concept as the new datum—depending on the complexity of the problem and the time available.

Phase 2 steps:

6. Weaker concepts are now dropped. The evaluation is continued with increasingly stronger concepts (which are "engineered" or developed to more detail). Criteria are expanded and refined. The participants continue to gain valuable insight into the problem and proposed solutions.

7. The process converges to a strong consensus solution that cannot be improved further. The participants are committed to this superior concept.

Is there a "fast-track" version for simple problems?

Phase 1 is conducted using Steps 1-4 above. Then the highest scoring concept of Round 2 is closely examined. If possible, any identified weaknesses are eliminated with features from other concepts or additional creative ideas—this then becomes the final concept. Example 3 illustrates this approach.

What are "concepts"?

Concepts can be ideas or solutions to any problem, not just engineering designs. They are usually worked out in sufficient detail to allow a rough estimate of cost and feasibility and a determination of major features. Whenever a team is involved, a sketch or description of each concept is prepared on a large sheet of paper, to be visible to everyone in the room when posted on a wall above the evaluation matrix.

How does the evaluation matrix work?

It is highly recommended that a heterogeneous team be used for conducting the Pugh evaluation. The evaluation meeting is held ideally in an ample conference room with a large board covering an entire wall. An evaluation matrix is set up on the board, with the design criteria listed in the left-hand column of the matrix. The large sketches or brief descriptions of the concepts are posted across the top of the matrix, with the datum entered first. The main features of each concept (including the datum) are explained by its champions. Right after each presentation, the concept is evaluated against the datum, using the three-way rating scale given in the box. The three-way evaluation may appear rather primitive, but it is easy to do with a team. The results are effective, because the goal is not quantitative, precise information but a movement toward increasing quality and superior satisfaction of all criteria. Inexperienced teams may be very defensive of their concept and will argue about every minus mark. They need to remember that this evaluation serves to point out weaknesses or potential problems in the concept that must be overcome for it to be viable (and help the business to prosper). The judgment only determines as objectively as possible if the concept is better or

Pugh Method Evaluation Scale

+ means clearly better

– means clearly worse

S means more or less the same

worse than the datum or benchmark for each criterion. However, if the evaluation continues to get sidetracked in an unusually argumentative team, it can be performed by each member independently on a sheet of paper. The results are then compiled by the leader.

What if an individual does the evaluation?
When we are the sole evaluator of our own ideas, we must be careful to analyze possible bias and blind spots. We also must guard against falling in love with a particular concept before generating and developing several viable alternatives. All concepts must be evaluated fairly and critically.

What do you do with the Round 1 result?
The first-round matrix is critically examined. Is there a criterion that received no plus signs all across the matrix? This indicates that none of the new concepts addressed an important customer need or solution requirement—a critical omission. If a criterion received all positives, it must be made more specific for subsequent rounds. Criteria that are least important can be dropped; new criteria that clarify an ambiguity or address newly discovered concerns are added. Typically, customers become identified more precisely. The scores in each column are added separately for the positives and the negatives. The ultimate goal of the process is to obtain concepts whose flaws have all been eliminated through creative thinking.

The concepts are taken back to the "drawing board" and improvements are targeted at the identified weaknesses. The Round 1 concept with the highest number of positives is chosen as the datum for Round 2. Its creators will try to improve this design by borrowing good ideas from other concepts. All concepts now have to beat a higher standard to remain in the running. Phase 1 evaluations are continued for at least one more round for simple concepts—complicated designs may require two or three additional rounds.

What happens in Phase 2?
Here, the emphasis changes from conceiving additional creative concepts to synthesizing higher-quality solutions by combining ideas and dropping the weaker concepts. During the process, the strong, surviving concepts are "engineered" or developed to more detail; the criteria are expanded and further refined. Cost, market, feasibility and engineering analyses are conducted as applicable (see Chapter 8). The process converges to a strong consensus concept that cannot be overturned by a better idea—all good points have been defended and all negatives eliminated. Everyone is committed to this concept which is now ready for prototyping to demonstrate the concept and for developing into a commercial product.

What if a negative cannot be eliminated?
Costs that are higher than the datum are often a negative criterion that cannot be eliminated. If a competitive price is very important, other concepts that do not have this "flaw" will have to be pursued. This could be an area where new technology may be deployed. For a manufactured product,

Synergy is a key ingredient in the creative mental process.

By synergy, I mean the mental result of interaction between different specialized parts of the inter-connected brain—the creative ideas that can result from the interaction between the different modes of analysis and synthesis, between rational processing and intuitive thought, between facts and feelings, between linear processing modes and global thinking.

Ned Herrmann

Taguchi methods can be used to reduce cost while increasing quality. Or innovative marketing may have to be invented to convince the customers that the value added by the new product is worth the increased price. Examples are the Post-it notes or the Federal Express package delivery system. It must be remembered that the Pugh method does not make the final decisions—it is a judgment tool, and the responsibility for making the final decision rests with the individual or team using the tool. If the problem is very complex, additional resources must be employed which can range from experts to analytical tools such as QFD or FMEA.

The difficulty in concept evaluation is that we must choose which concepts to spend time developing when we still have very limited data on which to base the selection.

David G. Ullman

PUGH METHOD EXAMPLES

EXAMPLE 1—DESIGN OF AN IMPROVED LAMP

A class of high school students in an engineering summer program chose the problem of inconvenient lamp switches to be solved with new lamp designs. They conducted a customer survey, did a Pareto analysis, then brainstormed concepts and a list of design and evaluation criteria. The teams came up with three different types of design concepts: improvements over existing table lamps; innovative—completely new—concepts, and novelty lamps. The novelty lamps did not score well in the first-round evaluation.

For the second round, a traditional lamp with many improvements (built-in timer switch in the base, flexible shade, retractable cord, and fluorescent bulb) was the datum. An innovative design scored very high in this round. It could be used as a table or a pole lamp, and its shade could be fixed for up-down indirect or task lighting or expanded to expose a lighted column for room lighting. The novelty lamp received mostly negative marks, yet the team remained steadfast in not wanting to change its concept; it had "fallen in love" with its design—the Pugh method identified this fatal flaw in this design. Lack of time and resources prevented the high-scoring team from pursuing its invention which had the potential to be patented.

EXAMPLE 2—CAR HORN DESIGN

A detailed "teaching" example for the design of a car horn has been developed by Professor Pugh. Edward Lumsdaine and Monika Lumsdaine adapted and simplified it in their earlier work to bring out different points. This Round 1 car horn example with discussion can now be found at www.InnovationToday.biz under PUBLICATIONS, TEACHING AIDS.

EXAMPLE 3—IMPROVED HANDLING FOR MOISTURE BARRIER BAG

The following example is taken from an application of creative problem solving by Sie Chye Soon, a student in the entrepreneurship course taught by the authors in Singapore through the University of Nottingham in November 2004. The writing has been condensed and edited.

Introduction: Electronic manufacturing companies must continuously improve their processes and products to remain competitive. Starting in August 2002, one company discovered cases of damaged moisture barrier bags during final quality inspection. Their plastic surface-mount devices must be kept from absorbing atmospheric moisture to prevent problems during board mounting. A team was formed to solve this issue.

Problem briefing: The team investigated data from August 2002 through November 2004 and compiled the following data:

- An average of 2 cases of damaged barrier bags reported per month.
- The damage was mostly rips made from the outside.
- Most of the damage originated during the night shift.
- Most of the damage happened on Machine No. 3.
- Most of the damage occurred on the bottom side of the bag.

COMMENT:
The statement could have been in more positive terms.

Problem definition statement: Eliminate damage to barrier bags to avoid delivering defective parts to customers.

Pugh method Round 1: The team developed solution concepts for the Pugh evaluation. These are listed in Table 5.1. Table 5.2 shows the Round 1 evaluation matrix.

Table 5.1   *Concepts for Round 1—Barrier Bag Handling*

1 Change all operators	4 Stop operating the night shift
2 Retrain all operators	5 Revise the method of packing
3 Change to a better quality barrier bag	6 Replace Machine No. 3

Table 5.2   *Round 1 Evaluation for Barrier Bag Handling*

	Criteria *Concepts*	*Now*	*1*	*2*	*3*	*4*	*5*	*6*
1	Ease of implementation		–	+	–	–	+	–
2	Sustainable long-term solution	D	S	+	+	–	+	S
3	Effective	A	+	+	+	+	S	+
4	No re-qualification needed	T	–	+	–	S	S	–
5	Low cost	U	S	S	–	S	+	–
6	Minimum changes	M	S	+	–	–	+	–
7	Able to meet production output		+	+	+	–	+	+
	Total positives (+)		**2**	**6**	**3**	**1**	**5**	**2**
	Total negatives (–)		**2**	**0**	**4**	**4**	**0**	**4**

Pugh method Round 2: The aim in Round 2 was to try and combine concepts (see Table 5.3) to eliminate negatives and supply more detail. For this round, Concept #2—*Retrain all operators*—became the new datum in Table 5.4 since it had the highest number of positives (in Table 5.2). Concept 4—*Stop operating the night shift*—was eliminated at this point as not feasible.

Table 5.3 *Improved Concepts for Round 2—Barrier Bag Handling*

7	Change all night operators
8	Change to a thicker, better quality airbag
9	Retrain all night operators
10	Simplify the method of packing, so it is better understood by operators
11	Replace Machine No. 3 with one that has no sharp edges

Table 5.4 *Round 2 Evaluation for Barrier Bag Handling*

	Criteria Concepts	2	7	8	9	10	11
1	Ease of implementation		–	–	S	+	–
2	Sustainable long-term solution	D	S	+	–	+	S
3	Effective	A	+	+	–	S	+
4	No re-qualification needed	T	–	–	S	+	–
5	Low cost	U	S	–	+	+	–
6	Minimum changes	M	S	–	S	+	–
7	Able to meet production output		+	+	–	+	+
	Total positives (+)		**2**	**3**	**1**	**6**	**2**
	Total negatives (–)		**2**	**4**	**3**	**0**	**4**

"Best" solution and concluding remarks: It would appear that Concept 10—*Simplify the method of packing*—from Round 2 was the "best" solution for solving the problem. However, the team felt that Concept 10 could be improved further by combining it with Concept 2—*Retrain all operators*. Both of these concepts scored high, and they offered hassle-free, no-cost implementation, thus optimizing the benefits. When the outcome of the combined solution was monitored after one month, two positive results were noted: no recurrence of any damage to moisture barrier bags, and a boost in operator morale as they felt the team (and company) cared about their work.

Final comments: It was not necessary to do a Round 3 evaluation, since a "best" solution was easily identified. This example shows that team members need to pay attention not only to the analytical results, but also to their feelings which may indicate the criteria did not incorporate all important angles of the problem and solution. Certainly, the Pugh method guided this team towards finding a good solution to a very narrowly defined problem.

EXAMPLE 4—IMPROVED KITCHEN LIGHTING

Problem Briefing: A large kitchen (15 ft long and 9-1/2 ft wide) in a house built in the late 1940s is quite dark at night, especially at the sink and the chopping board in front of the centrally located window. The slightly sloped cherry-paneled ceiling has an average height of 10 ft 9 in. and is traversed by a 14 in. by 6-in. wood-laminate beam supporting the flat roof immediately above. The walls are painted beige; the cabinets are metal—beige above the counter, brick red below. The countertop is beige, and the vinyl floor has a

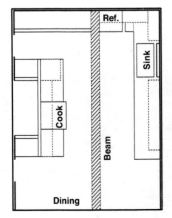

brown brick pattern. Table 5.5 lists the existing lighting fixtures. The fluorescent tubes lying on top of the cabinets are plugged into outlets above the cabinets (all on the same circuit) with switch at the kitchen entrances. All other fixtures are on individual switches. The spotlights over the sink are ugly and off target. The chrome triangular under-cabinet fixtures are quaint but have only a dim light output. All five plugged-in fluorescent tubes look cheap and are hard to clean, and the 2-ft tube is rarely if ever used.

Table 5.5 *Existing Kitchen Light Fixture Schedule*

I.D.	Quantity	Rating	Type Fixture	Location
A	4	20 watt	2-ft fluorescent triangular	Under wall cabinets
B	4	40 watt	4-ft fluorescent tubes	On top of cabinets
C	2	75 watt	Incandescent spot in can	5 ft above sink
D	1	20 watt	2-ft fluorescent tube	Under microwave

Problem definition statement: Improve the general and task lighting in the kitchen shown on the sketch, while upgrading the lamp quality and matching or complementing the style of the lighting fixtures in the adjacent dining and living rooms, at reasonable cost and without remodeling the kitchen or covering up the beauty of the existing paneled ceiling.

Round 1 concepts, performance criteria and evaluation: The concepts for improving the lighting in this kitchen are listed in Table 5.6. The criteria are listed in the Round 1 matrix shown in Table 5.7. The current lighting is taken as the datum. None of the options provide a standout solution for solving the problem. However, the evaluation makes it clear that a second meeting with the lighting supplier is necessary to explore further options and get more information. In addition, some of the criteria will need to be expanded and made more specific.

Table 5.6 *Options for Round 1 of the Kitchen Lighting Evaluation*

1. **Track Lighting**—Install an 8-ft long track with 4 movable spots (250 watts each, black), to match existing track light in adjacent living room. Plug into outlet over cabinet near sink.

2. **Sink Task Lighting**—Replace the two spotlights over the sink with nicer-looking, more efficient, practical lamps.

3. **Over-Cabinet Strip Lighting**—Replace fluorescent tubes B with lighted strip along top of all wall cabinets.

4. **Fluorescent Hanging Fixtures**—Install two 4-ft fluorescent fixtures with efficient diffusers at 8-ft level (on chains, with wood surrounds) to replace tubes B; wire to main switch. Option explored with supplier.

5. **Halogen Fixtures**—Install two hanging halogen down-lights; wire to main switch; match chrome style of under-cabinet triangular fixtures. Option explored with supplier.

6. **Brighter Surfaces**—Paint walls white; install white vinyl flooring; install new white countertops; paint cherry panels in ceiling white.

Table 5.7 *Round 1 Evaluation of Kitchen Lighting Options*

Criteria	Concepts:	Now	1	2	3	4	5	6
1. Adequate sink task light			S	+	—	+	+	—
2. Other countertop lighting			—	S	—	+	+	—
3. General lighting		D	S	S	S	+	+	+
4. Light to ceiling		A	—	S	+	—	—	+
5. Energy efficient		T	—	+	—	+	+	+
6. Easy to clean		U	+	S	S	S	+	—
7. Easy bulb replacement		M	+	S	—	S	+	S
8. Allow deletion of tubes			—	—	+	—	—	—
9. Matching room styles			+	+	—	—	—	S
10. Attractive high-tech look			+	+	+	+	+	S
11. Low labor cost			—	+	+	—	—	—
12. Low materials cost			—	—	—	—	—	—
TOTAL POSITIVES (+)			4	5	4	5	7	3
TOTAL NEGATIVES (—)			6	2	6	5	5	6

Round 2 concepts and evaluation: Option #5—the halogen fixture—becomes the new datum for Round 2 since it had the highest number of positives. The aim for Round 2 is to try and combine concepts to eliminate negatives and supply more detail. These concepts are listed in Table 5.8. The painting option is deleted as too costly, time-consuming and not easily reversible. The Round 2 matrix is shown in Table 5.9. Note that in this table, S is also used to indicate neutral or not applicable.

Table 5.8 *Options for Round 2 of the Kitchen Lighting Evaluation*

7. **Fluorescent Track Lighting**—Install a black 8-ft long, 2-circuit track with 3 movable cans (150 watts incandescent bulbs or fluorescent bulb option) and one 2-ft fluorescent, 40-watt movable parabolic louvered diffuser ("wall washer") to match existing track light in adjacent living room. Mount to bottom of beam; connect to main switches with conduit along beam and ceiling edge.

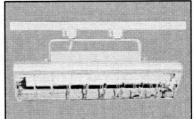

8. **Sink Task Lighting**—Replace the two spotlights over the sink with black cans matching the track light of Option #1. Use fluorescent bulbs.

9. **Over-Cabinet Strip Lighting**—Replace the fluorescent tubes with a rope light along the top of all wall cabinets.

10. **Fluorescent Hanging Fixtures**—Install two 4-ft fluorescent fixtures with efficient diffusers at 8-ft level (sleek high-tech design); hang from ceiling, centered between counters.

11. **Halogen Fixtures**—Install two hanging halogen down lights; wire to main switch; match style of dining room chandelier if possible.

Table 5.9　Round 2 Evaluation of Kitchen Lighting Options

Criteria	Concepts:	5	7	8	9	10	11
1. Adequate sink task light			S	+	—	S	S
2. Countertop lighting (window wall)			+	+	—	S	S
3. Countertop lighting (cook-top wall)		D	—	—	—	S	S
4. Light to ceiling		A	S	S	+	S	S
5. Low-energy night lighting		T	S	+	+	S	S
6. Low glare		U	+	+	+	+	S
7. Flexible (direction, additions, lumens)		M	+	+	—	S	S
8. Easy bulb replacement			S	S	—	—	S
9. Energy efficient			S	S	—	S	S
10. Easy to clean			S	S	—	S	S
11. Preserves view of ceiling/open space			S	+	+	—	S
12. Allow deletion of tubes			+	—	+	S	S
13. Matching room styles			+	+	S	—	+
14. Attractive to future owners			+	+	—	—	S
15. Low labor cost			S	+	+	S	S
16. Low materials cost			—	+	—	+	S
TOTAL POSITIVES (+)			6	10	6	2	1
TOTAL NEGATIVES (—)			2	2	9	4	0

Since Concept #11 has no negatives, does this mean it is the optimum solution? No—as you will see, it will rank very differently when evaluated against the new datum. The over-the-counter strip-lighting option is now eliminated as not being cost effective; the fluorescent hanging fixture is eliminated because it is too intrusive.

Round 3 concepts and evaluation: Concept #8 had the highest number of positives and is chosen as the datum for Round 3. Concepts #7 and #8 are combined as Concept #12 (see Table 5.10). This allows for even lighting of both kitchen sidewalls with an additional "wall washer." Concept #11 is carried forward unchanged. The Round 3 matrix is shown in Table 5.11.

Table 5.10　Options for Round 3 of the Kitchen Lighting Evaluation

11. **Two Halogen Fixtures**—Install two hanging halogen down lights; wire to main switch. Match the style of the glass shades with the style of the dining room chandelier if possible.

12. **Fluorescent Track Lighting System**—Install a black 8-ft long, 2-circuit track with *two* movable cans with fluorescent bulbs and *two* 2-ft fluorescent, 40-watt movable parabolic louvered diffusers (wall washers). Mount to bottom of beam; connect to main switches with conduit along beam/ceiling edge. Replace the two spotlights over the sink with matching cans and fluorescent bulbs to achieve a flexible, attractive, and easily modified, adjustable lighting system—matching the track lighting in the adjacent living room.

Table 5.11 *Round 3 Evaluation of Kitchen Lighting Options*

	Criteria	Concepts:	8	11	12
1.	Adequate sink task light			—	+
2.	Countertop lighting (along window wall)			—	+
3.	Countertop lighting (along cook-top wall)			—	+
4.	Indirect light to ceiling (eliminate "cave" look)		D	S	+
5.	Low-energy night lighting		A	—	+
6.	Low glare, especially for eyeglass wearers		T	—	+
7.	Flexibility in direction, light level, future additions		U	—	+
8.	Easy bulb replacement (with step stool, not ladder)		M	S	S
9.	Energy efficient, cool burning			—	S
10.	Sun-type light quality			+	+
11.	Easy to clean off kitchen grease buildup			S	S
12.	Preserves view of beautiful paneled ceiling			—	S
13.	Allows deletion of all existing plugged-in tubes			—	+
14.	Matching adjoining dining and living room fixtures			S	S
15.	Attractive to future owners; good "selling point"			—	+
16.	Reasonable installation costs			S	S
17.	Material cost in line with "value added"			S	S
	TOTAL POSITIVES (+)			1	10
	TOTAL NEGATIVES (—)			10	0

Best solution and concluding comments on the process: The concept that ultimately was incorporated into the best solution was generated for Round 2 by combining the track lighting and fluorescent bulb concept. The supplier suggested this option, and the owner was able to see such an installation in a store nearby. Combining the track lighting and the over-the-sink fixture into a matching system optimized the solution, and the merits of this solution are confirmed by the Round 3 evaluation.

This solution solves the original problem, with added value. A strong selling point is the built-in flexibility which easily allows future modifications as well as on-site adjustments after installation, depending on changing needs. With this solution, the over-the-cabinet 4-foot long fluorescent tubes were eliminated, since the 2-foot fluorescent "wall washers" provide very bright but diffused light. The total cost of $742 was acceptable, since the system is highly functional as well as attractive. The Pugh method was crucial for clarifying criteria, generating viable options and identifying the optimal solution. The homeowners are happy with the new lighting system.

An individual, not a team, conducted this application of the Pugh method for evaluating different options and developing a best solution. It illustrates that this evaluation technique can be used profitably by anyone, as long as the evaluator maintains an unbiased viewpoint when judging each concept and obtains information and ideas from experts as needed for developing good alternatives, as shown in this example.

> ## Points to Remember about the Pugh Method
>
> → In each round, look at the concepts with the largest numbers of positives—merely having no negatives with a few positives does not make for a best solution!
>
> → The overall aim must always be to try to eliminate all negatives (the weaknesses) in the highest-ranking concepts!
>
> → Always use the concept with the most positives from the last round as the new datum. Keep improving all concepts and the criteria for the next round (including the datum)!
>
> → If you are planning to start a business, you will have many opportunities to use the Pugh method, beginning with product ideas, as will be discussed in Parts 2 and 3 of this book.

APPLICATION EXERCISES

5.1 Application to a Current Problem or Project

a. Along the lines of the kitchen lighting example, select a project in your life—either alone or with a small team of friends, colleagues or family members—where you have (or need to develop) several options. Use the Pugh method to find and "engineer" an optimum solution; then summarize what you have learned about this creative idea evaluation tool.

b. Design a simple hourglass timer that makes a sound when time is up—a useful feature for avoiding arguments in the heat of a game or competition. Come up with at least three different concepts—then evaluate them with the Pugh "fast-track" approach.

5.2 Improve a Business Procedure

Think of a business process, paperwork, or way of doing something that could be simplified or made more efficient through creative thinking. Brainstorm a list of criteria and develop alternate solutions; then find the "best" using the Pugh evaluation in two or more rounds.

5.3 Teaching the Pugh Method

Teach the Pugh method to someone by going through an application at home or on the job. As a student, you might have a great opportunity in a student organization or as part of a team project in a concurrent or future class.

REFERENCE

5.1 Stuart Pugh, *Total Design: Integrated Methods for Successful Product Engineering*, Addison-Wesley, New York, 1991. This book provides the framework and many examples of a disciplined design and evaluation method for creating products that satisfy the needs of the customer.

Synergy happens in two ways in the Pugh evaluation process:

(a) at the team level through the team discussion process, and

(b) in the emergence of a superior solution from many different stepping stone ideas.

Part Two

Product Development

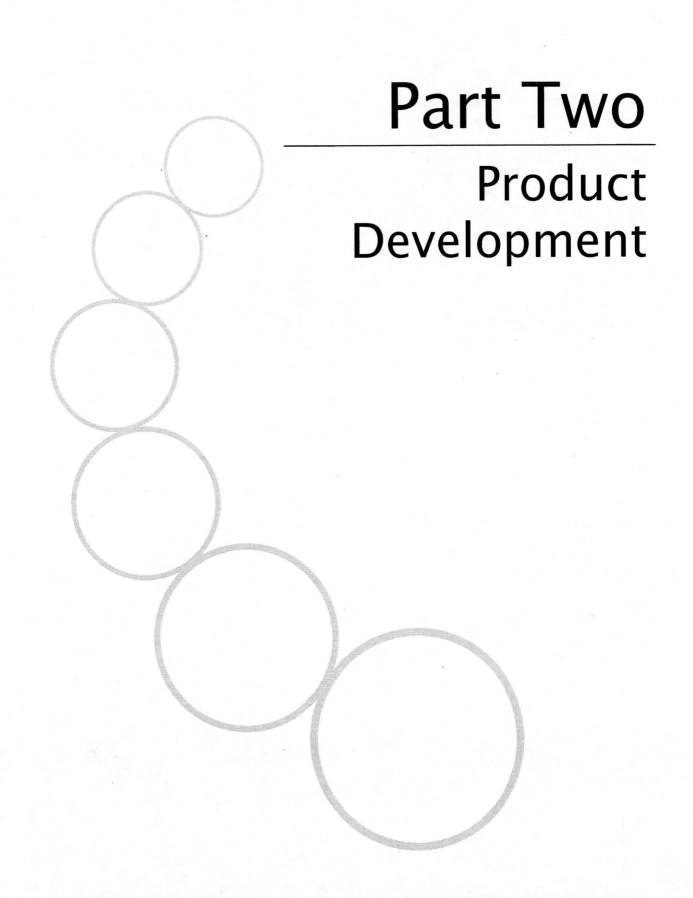

6   Finding a Problem to Solve

What you can learn from this chapter:
- How to find a problem to solve in the explorer's mindset.
- How to play the "Don't Sell Me" game.
- How to document an invention.
- How to narrow your search in the detective's mindset.
- How to do a customer survey and Pareto diagram.
- How to apply your learning in a team project.

Now that you have gained an understanding of entrepreneurial thinking tools in Part 1 of this book, are you ready to discover their application all the way from generating a creative idea to starting up a business and sustaining it through innovation? The three chapters in Part 2 will concentrate on product development. In Chapter 6, we will explore how to identify consumer needs, and in Chapter 7, we will focus on idea generation and how to protect an invention. Then in Chapter 8, we will look at the product development process in the context of the Pugh method evaluation, as initial ideas are sifted and synthesized to a best solution. A number of analyses are available that can assist in decision making which ultimately should result in a proto-type. Part 3 will show the application in business development, and Part 4 will discuss management and leadership for innovation and its importance to creating a sustainable and successful business.

INDIVIDUAL AND SOCIETAL PROBLEMS

Economic development at its best is often referred to as "Pareto optimal"—it increases economic welfare without causing a reduction in the welfare of any other individual or groups. This principle is central to the application of the creative problem solving process. Individual and societal problems often constrain economic development. Therefore, they represent potential areas for applying new ideas and enterprises and may range from the minor inconveniences associated with everyday life to the major challenges of our times confronting society.

It is often assumed that entrepreneurs act on the belief that they have a particularly appropriate and possibly unique solution to a prevailing problem for which people would be prepared to pay good money. This responsive alertness to opportunities is a characteristic of the Austrian school's view of entrepreneurs as described in Chapter 2. We believe that this interpretation can be taken a step further by encouraging the potential entrepreneur to actively seek out opportunities by adopting an explorer's mindset to discover new areas of activity that have not been addressed before.

USING THE EXPLORER'S MINDSET

In Chapter 4, we presented an overview of different tools that can be used to identify an opportunity or clarify a problem area. Here, we will give some additional tips and guidelines to help you toward finding a problem area with a good potential for generating a viable enterprise.

PERSONAL PROBLEM FINDING

Listing problems is a first step to help you decide which ones may be worth solving. It transforms a body of information into a set of components that can then be restructured, redefined, checked, and searched. Keep a journal of problems that you find personally interesting and that might be worth your while to resolve. You may chance upon a problem area with a large potential market for a good solution. The personal questions in Table 6.1 may help you get started; then let these questions incubate in your mind for a while.

Table 6.1   *Personal List of Questions*

1. What would you like to have or to accomplish?
2. What would you like to do better?
3. What do you wish would happen in your job or in your study area?
4. What do you wish you had more time to do?
5. What are your unfulfilled goals?
6. What more would you like to get out of your job?
7. What excites you in your work and in your hobbies?
8. What annoys you in your environment or angers you at work?
9. What have you (or others) recently complained about?
10. What would you like to get others to do?
11. What changes would you like to introduce?
12. What takes too long? What is too complicated?
13. In what ways are you inefficient? What is wasted?
14. Where are the bottlenecks? What wears you out?
15. What in your job turns you off?
16. In what ways could you make more money?
17. What misunderstandings have you encountered recently?

The following activity has a double purpose—it can warm up your right-brain thinking while at the same time give you insight into a technique that can help you identify customer needs and viewpoints. So let's take a break and have some fun in the explorer's mindset!

The game forces you to zero in on intangibles and use words to communicate different ideas. It asks you to think more about implications, less about the task itself. It moves your perspective away from things and more toward feelings, hopes, emotions, and benefits. "Don't Sell Me" is the scenic route to new awareness of the essence of your task.

Activity 6.1: The "Don't Sell Me" Game

Objectives

The game is based on what people want and respond to in order to have their basic needs and desires satisfied. For example:

Don't sell me clothes; sell me attractiveness and comfort.

Don't sell me books; sell me knowledge that makes me successful.

Don't sell me the Beatles; sell me a nostalgic mood and great memories.

This activity takes you right to your mission's core, but from a variety of emotional directions. An individual or team that is low in quadrant C thinking preference may find this very difficult to do at first, but don't give up too soon!

Instructions

Define your mission. What are you trying to accomplish or change? Who is your audience? In your notebook, complete the following statement:

Don't sell me .... (your task in concrete terms).

Sell me .... (your task in abstract terms).

Complete each statement as quickly as you can. Fill in the blank a dozen times or more. You're looking for "soft" stuff—the feelings, emotions, attitudes, results, consequences, secondary benefits, gut instincts, intuitions, and perceptions that drive your day-to-day life. Then set the list aside for ten minutes and do something else. Let it incubate; let your subconscious do some of the work.

When you return to your list, focus on each completed statement, one at a time. Concentrate on the pieces, not the aggregate, since you can quickly become overwhelmed when you attack a problem in its totality. Do some divergent thinking now. Use each one of your statements as a springboard to new ideas. What new thoughts does each statement prompt? Look at each statement as an opportunity to solve a part of the task. Consider each as an element of the challenge, or a new direction from which to approach the challenge. Let each represent a separate need. Address emotions, feelings, and perceptions. Look for weaknesses to fix and strengths to trumpet. Ask two or three people to join you to get additional insight and new ideas.

Practice problem

If you are having trouble playing the game in a selected problem area, practice first with "Don't sell me CREATIVITY BOOKS; sell me ......" You may use the answers below as thought starters.

Don't sell me CREATIVITY BOOKS ... Sell me "confidence in my brain."

Don't sell me CREATIVITY BOOKS ... Sell me "creative juice."

Don't sell me CREATIVITY BOOKS ... Sell me "a renewal of my childhood."

Don't sell me CREATIVITY BOOKS ... Sell me "success in the corporate world."

Don't sell me CREATIVITY BOOKS ... Sell me "a life I can be excited about."

Don't sell me CREATIVITY BOOKS ... Sell me "a blueprint for greatness."

Don't sell me CREATIVITY BOOKS ... Sell me "lasting enthusiasm and energy."

Don't sell me CREATIVITY BOOKS ... Sell me "a way to discover my real self."

Don't sell me CREATIVITY BOOKS ... Sell me "a leadership tool."

The ideas of "confidence in my brain" or "lasting enthusiasm and energy" help us think about the importance of courage and a positive outlook, along with inspiration and wherewithal to challenge conformity. The ideas of "success in the corporate world" and "a life I can be excited about" show that seeing creativity in action is important in the professional environment and in our personal life.

You can also search for a problem to solve and needs to meet in the business world and your professional environment. Table 6.2 lists some thought-starters especially suited to people already working in a company.

Table 6.2 *Typical Business Challenges*

1. What business idea would you like to work on?
2. What business relationship would you like to improve?
3. What new product is needed to satisfy a customer want?
4. How can you cut costs and increase production?
5. How can you better differentiate an existing product from all others?
6. What extension of a current product's market is needed?
7. How can you sell twenty percent more than you are at present?
8. How can you become indispensable to your company?
9. How can customer complaints be handled better?
10. How can you improve the role of service in the sale of your products?
11. How can you become more customer-oriented?
12. In what ways might you outperform the competition?
13. Which of your products could you potentially make into a true innovation and market leader?
14. What is an important issue or challenge in your present business?

TREND WATCHING

As we have seen earlier (refer to Table 4.3 for tips), one of the most important explorer tools is watching for trends. When you scan the messages bombarding you daily through news and advertisements in the media, be constantly on the lookout for developing trends. Use a variety of sources: TV, newspapers, radio talk shows, blogs, professional journals and magazines. Some trends can be expected to last a long time (for example, those involving demographics and census data). An example is that the population in the Western cultures is getting older. Thus we have the problem of the "sandwich" generation: middle-aged parents being squeezed by responsibilities in caring for elderly parents while assisting their own children with careers or helping to raise grandchildren. In other cultures, the majority of the population is young—under 25 years old (which creates very different problems and opportunities, for example in the area of basic and high-tech education).

The longevity of some trends is difficult to predict. How long will the demand for increased security, especially for the traveling public, persist when the threat of imminent terrorist attacks has abated? Ideas that will help airlines reduce the long lines and waiting times at security checkpoints while maintaining security would certainly be welcomed with open arms. Timing is important. In the mid-1970s, energy conservation became a key issue, with skyrocketing oil prices and periodic shortages. In early 2002, energy prices

Breakthrough ideas are most likely to occur when you are actively, confidently searching for new opportunities.

Denis Waitley and Robert Tucker

were at a low point and energy conservation had disappeared as a policy or personal priority. However, in 2006—when the cost per barrel of crude oil rose at an all-time high—energy conservation was back in the public's mind.

SEARCHING THE INTERNET

The World Wide Web is a wonderful explorer tool in several ways. It has many web sites on creative thinking. You can get business ideas and ideas for inventions from specific sites, or you can surf the web to get more information on problems and their context. Patent searching in patent depository libraries used to be very time-consuming and tedious—now you can do preliminary patent searches right from your desktop. Some relevant starting sites for all these tasks are listed in Table 6.3.

Table 6.3   *Useful Websites*

Preliminary Patent Search and Information for Inventors	
www.inventnet.com	Patent searching tutorial (click on "patent search")
Patent Offices	
www.uspto.gov	Official U.S. Patent and Trademark Office site.
www.patent.gov.uk	Information on British patents.
www.european-patent-office.org	Information on European patents in French, German, English.

This list is by no means exhaustive. Go to any search engine and look up invention, entrepreneurship, innovation, patent search, or creativity and take a journey—a good activity to practice the explorer's mindset. Also use the search engine to explore key words and concepts in the potential problem area or to collect information about an identified topic.

WHY DO PEOPLE INVENT?

A wide variety of needs and motivations have led to inventions and innovations. A few examples are given below (more items are listed in Table 12.1).

- As a response to threat—radar, weapons.
- To win a prize—human powered aircraft.
- To overcome flaws—magic tape.
- To leave a legacy (by a cancer patient)—*MindManager* software.
- To eliminate an annoyance—Post-it notes.
- As a response to need—low-cost solar rice cooker.
- To solve a safety concern—traffic light.

SPECIAL RECORDING REQUIREMENTS FOR INVENTORS

If you are thinking of starting an enterprise based on a new product idea that you want to invent, be aware that inventors are required to document the invention process in an inventor's log. This log has two purposes: (1) to help you think through and develop ideas and (2) to protect the completed invention. It thus covers both divergent and convergent thinking. Key features of the log are listed in Table 6.4. Note that the witness should be someone knowledgeable in the area of the invention, but not a relative or close friend.

Table 6.4 *Guidelines for the Inventor's Log*

✓ Use a bound notebook and make notes each day about the things you do and learn while working on your invention.

✓ Record your idea and how you got it.

✓ Write about the problems you have and how you solve them.

✓ Write in ink and do not erase.

✓ Add sketches and drawings to make things clear.

✓ List all parts, sources, and costs of materials.

✓ Sign and date all entries at the time they are made and have them witnessed.

FOCUSING THE PROBLEM TOPIC

Once you (or your team) have identified a potential problem area or topic, you need to analyze it for size. It will be difficult to generate a good business idea from a topic that is too general or too large. On the other hand, a very narrow topic usually limits the creative possibilities in the solutions that will be generated. If you have a good topic but need to expand the problem, you can ask a series of "what is this about" questions. This technique invites divergent, contextual thinking.

Example of a diverging chain of questions

"What is this problem about?"
    Answer: "Housing."
"What is housing about?"
    Answer: "Being warm and cozy."
"What is being warm and cozy about?"
    Answer: "Feeling loved, cared for, and safe."

Note how this chain has brought out aspects of the problem that involve not only a physical need but also emotional needs. It helps to get the bigger picture. We must encourage our customers and other people involved with the problem to express the needs or dreams that are important but often remain unrecognized or unspoken.

At other times, to obtain a solution, we have to break problems down into smaller parts through convergent thinking. If we want to '"squeeze" a problem, we can use a chain question process by asking "why?" Such questions can bring out the real reasons why people have a problem or what is important about the problem.

Example of a converging chain of questions

"Why do you want to improve your budgeting procedure?"
    Answer: "Because I'm always late in paying my bills."
"Why are you always late?"

Asking "why" is a key approach to access the real motivation behind the entire creative problem solving process—from your own to that of the customers and other stakeholders.

Answer: "Because I have a habit of procrastination."
"Why do you procrastinate?"
Answer: "Because I hate paperwork."
"Why do you hate paperwork?"
Answer: "It requires quadrant B thinking which I hate."

Chain questions let us eliminate rationalization; we can zero in on the real motivation underlying a problem. Here, the real problem is a mismatch between the task and the person's thinking preference, not the budgeting procedure or the habit of procrastination. Unless the root causes are identified and addressed, the solutions that might be developed likely will not solve the underlying problem.

Do not be too concerned about selecting just the right size. The problem can be expanded during the idea generation phase by encouraging diverging, wild ideas. If the topic is too broad, it can be broken down into narrower subtopics during idea evaluation.

USING THE DETECTIVE'S MINDSET

Once the "explorer" has identified a tentative problem area, it is time for the "detective" to collect specific information. As "detectives" we search for clues to identify the "real" problem. As seen in Chapter 4, "detectives" ask a lot of questions. In the context of entrepreneurship, a critical factor is the ability to identify your customers and then to ask them the right questions that will give you the information you need for analyzing the problem. This will then allow you to make a decision as to the potential of the topic for generating a viable business idea through creative problem solving.

Every problem, from major ones, such as education and national health care, to mundane ones, such as an overdrawn checking account, can be viewed from multiple conflicting perspectives. And what drives these differing perspectives? Biases and mindsets, those unseen killers of objective truth, determine our perspective on any problem. That perspective, in turn, drives our analysis, our conclusions and rationalizations, and ultimately our recommendations. It is essential that we identify and separate the real problem from the apparent problem. It is crucial that you ask: "How do my potential customers see the problem?"

ASKING QUESTIONS WITH A CUSTOMER SURVEY

You may be able to find published customer surveys that relate to your problem—as for example in census publications. However, it is more likely that no previous information exists, since you are seeking to identify a neglected market niche. Thus you need to develop your own customer survey form. The survey can focus on problems (negatives), or it can focus on desired features and preferences (positives). Tips on how to design a survey of user needs or customer wants are given in Table 6.5. Other tools for collecting user needs data suitable for your purpose may be focus groups, telephone interviews, or simple observation of buying preferences.

Table 6.5   *Survey of User Needs*

Address the respondent. Thank the respondent for taking the time to complete the survey. Explain how the survey results will be used and whether they will be anonymous.

Configure for easy scoring. If possible, place the answer blocks directly on the question sheet. Try to keep the survey to one page; at the most, use the front and back of the same page.

Obtain needed demographics. This data can alert you to a non-representative sample group or confirm that it is representative. You may ask for sex, postal code, age range, family income, owned or rented housing, level of education, etc. Be aware, however, that some questions, such as age or family income, may be very sensitive. Ask only what you really need to know to help you make decisions about your planned enterprise. Avoid a data swamp.

Obtain user opinions or preferences. Ask each question in a way that maximizes the information obtained and minimizes the chance of misunderstandings. Ask as few questions as possible to get the needed information.

EXAMPLE (not very helpful):
1. Do you usually buy electronic Christmas gifts?
2. Do you personally prefer clock radios with CD or with cassette?

Improved version:
1. Last Christmas, approximately how much did you spend (total) for electronic gifts? $_____
2. About how much would you be willing to pay for each of the following radios for your own use, if all have equal high-quality sound and tuning capability? Check only one in each row.

	<$20	$20-39	$40-79	$80-119	>$120
Simple AM/FM clock radio with alarm	____	____	____	____	____
Alarm-clock radio with CD player	____	____	____	____	____
Alarm-clock radio with cassette player	____	____	____	____	____
Alarm clock radio with CD + cassette player	____	____	____	____	____

The survey can collect different types of information, either purely quantitative data, or "weighted" data—where people (for each question) can indicate how severe the problem is by ranking it as 0 for no problem, 1 for a small problem, 2 for a moderate problem, and 3 for a severe problem. A similar ranking can be done for preferences. The replies can be tabulated as total points, or they can be stratified into the number of answers for each severity level or strength of preference. Stratified data collection can give better insight. If possible, use a team to design the survey form.

Producing and administering effective survey instruments is a complex task liable to error, both in design and interpretation of results. Piloting new surveys on small population samples can help avoid some of these errors. Even deciding on the appropriate population to be surveyed merits much thought, especially if stratification of the population, whether intended or not, may bias the conclusions derived from the sample. Sample size depends on the level of uncertainty that will satisfy you. For sampling errors of 5 percent, appropriate sample sizes would be 80, 278, 370, and 384 for populations of 100, 1000, 10,000 and essentially infinite, respectively. You should also be aware that a typical response rate to a survey may be less than 15 percent.

Even if you think you already know the needs of a typical user, some minimal survey can be useful. If you are inventing or designing a product that you would like to use, considering yourself as typical of other users in the market invites gross misjudgment. Remember the goal of a "positive" user survey is to produce a list of desired features ranked according to preference—these are *the users' definition of quality* for the product (or service)!

TIPS AND SOURCES OF HELP FOR CUSTOMER SURVEYS

A search for "customer surveys" using an Internet search engine will yield an immense number of responses. Among these are software tools for designing surveys, consultant firms, books, on-line newsletters, sample questions, and other advice. According to Ken Miller, as quoted in an article at www.adamssixsigma.com/Newsletters/design_redesign.htm, most surveys could be greatly improved if they focused on three key questions:

Answer three basic questions:

1. Who are your customers?

2. Where are they?

3. How can you reach them?

1. What is expected or wanted in the product or service?
2. What was experienced with similar (or your) products or services?
3. What is the level of satisfaction with the product/service?

The article also identified these common problems with customer surveys:

- The wrong people are surveyed.
- The wrong questions are asked.
- The questions are asked the wrong way.
- The questions are asked at the wrong time.
- Satisfaction and dissatisfaction are assumed to be equally important.
- Those who did not buy or use the product/service are not surveyed.
- Surveys are conducted for the wrong reasons.
- The results are generalized to groups not surveyed.
- Surveys are used as a substitute for better methods.

A reliance on this kind of wrong information on the "voice of the customer" in shaping your decisions for developing a certain product or service can leave you worse off than if you had no information at all. Thus make sure you expend the necessary care to obtain reliable data that you can actually use, based on a good understanding of statistics.

DATA ANALYSIS AND THE PARETO DIAGRAM

It is important to summarize the results of the collected data and record it in the problem briefing. The ranked frequency of identified problems or causes of problems can be effectively visualized in the form of a Pareto diagram. A Pareto diagram is a specialized bar graph used to separate the most important causes of trouble from the more trivial items in order to identify those that must be addressed with creative problem solving. The vertical axis can be expressed in numbers or percentage of cases or in terms of the money lost due to the identified defects. For example, as shown in Figure 6.1, it was found in a survey of problems with toasters that two out of 92 toasters started a house fire. Even though the number of incidences was low percentage-wise, the cost of the damages caused was significant and made this a prime target for problem solving.

94   ENTREPRENEURSHIP—FROM CREATIVITY TO INNOVATION

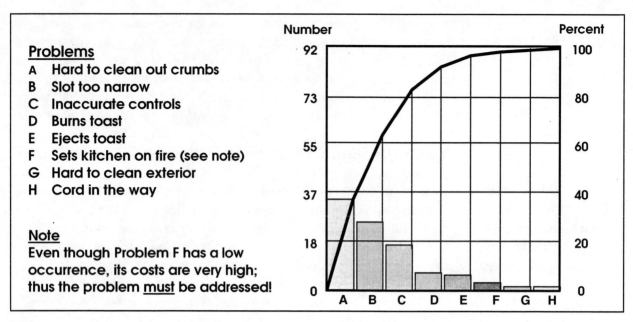

Problems
A   Hard to clean out crumbs
B   Slot too narrow
C   Inaccurate controls
D   Burns toast
E   Ejects toast
F   Sets kitchen on fire (see note)
G   Hard to clean exterior
H   Cord in the way

Note
Even though Problem F has a low occurrence, its costs are very high; thus the problem **must** be addressed!

Figure 6.1   Pareto diagram for problems with toasters

Vilfredo Pareto, an Italian economist, invented the diagram. He was struck by the fact that approximately 20 percent of the population in a country commonly controlled 80 percent of the wealth. In problem solving, this 80/20 principle makes it possible to concentrate resources on removing the top 20 percent of causes and thereby cure roughly 80 percent of the problems. The Pareto diagram is thus very useful for assigning priorities for continuous improvement. In the toaster example, addressing the top three complaints would take care of 76 percent of the problems.

IDENTIFYING THE "REAL" PROBLEM

Once a problem has been identified, it becomes important to discover the root causes that apply. Many apparent problems are simply symptoms of a deeper condition. Consider the problem of e-mail overload. At face value it might appear that too many people want to communicate with you through e-mail. However, a deeper inquiry into the root causes of e-mail overload would identify ease of access, convenience and the ability to pass on tasks and responsibilities with impunity as the real causes. Lazy people do not want to make a judgment on which trivial information could be useful to whom, so it is sent to all. Also, a substantial report or document that would have had limited circulation due to printing and shipping costs can now be circulated widely for comment. If problems arise later, the authors in defense can cite this wider circulation. Today, a major part of all e-mail is spam—firewalls have been unable to intercept much of this unwelcome solicitation.

When we are dealing with a very complex problem and have identified the most important root causes, we can then concentrate our efforts on one particular root cause. Then, as time and resources permit, new cycles of problem solving can address additional roots. For example, a student team should not select "how to reduce air pollution" as a suitable class project.

With automobiles being a major cause of air pollution in cities, focusing on cars would narrow the problem, but this would likely still be too complex since many factors contribute to the quantity of emissions, from size and efficiency of the car to fuel type, miles driven, traffic flow, and so on. But, "What can we as a family do to minimize our contribution to vehicular air pollution?" might constitute a more manageable project topic.

IDENTIFYING THE "REAL" CUSTOMERS

A survey of potential users of a silent signaling device for incoming telephone calls discovered, as expected, a high degree of interest among older people, since many suffer from some degree of hearing loss. But unexpectedly, the survey also found a high preference among office staff personnel who sought relief from the constant ringing of telephones.

The purchaser and the end user are frequently not the same person; thus the business concept must be geared to be attractive to both. Obvious examples are products for children that are purchased by adults. Services for the elderly (the primary users) are often paid for by social services, family members, or insurance companies, and thus the solution must appeal to a broad range of stakeholders which may not be apparent at first glance. Questionnaires can be designed to bring out these aspects. Also, will you primarily sell to other businesses, or do you need to attract walk-in or drive-by customers from the general public? The answer will influence your choice of business location. You may need to conduct a "traffic" survey and interviews with different local businesses to get a feel for the areas under consideration.

FINAL TIPS FOR PROBLEM DEFINITION

Someone that will not apply new remedies must expect new evils: for Time is the greatest innovator; and if Time of course alter things to the worse, and wisdom and counsel shall not alter them to the better, what shall be the end?

Francis Bacon

1. Before moving on to brainstorming, check that you used both mindsets—the "explorer" to discover the broader context and the "detective" to uncover the root causes involved in your problem. Opportunities for new ventures may be found in areas of weakness of existing products. A thorough investigation in this stage will avoid much wasted effort later.

2. If you have found several promising or challenging problem areas, you may want to do a brief Pugh evaluation to select the one you and your team want to concentrate on. However, successful entrepreneurs have found that it could be better to work with several ideas quickly and make the final decision later in the creative problem solving process, when more data on the potential products and markets are available.

3. Make sure you have included a preliminary patent search to avoid "reinventing the wheel." Although it is possible to work on developing improvements over an existing product, future profitability is usually much higher with a new product that meets an identified market need.

4. Once you have completed the "explorer" and "detective" tasks, it is a simple matter to summarize the collected information in a one-page briefing and to prepare a concise problem definition statement that will guide the direction of idea generation toward better potential solutions and marketable products as discussed in Chapter 4.

EXERCISES

6.1 Play the "Don't Sell Me" game

On the lines of Activity 6.1, practice the *Don't Sell Me* game with one of the following topics:

a. Don't sell me a financial plan; sell me ......

b. Don't sell me a knife sharpener; sell me ......

c. Don't sell me soft drinks; sell me ......

d. Or select a topic in an area where you have identified a market need.

6.2 What is the real problem at Algona?

Problem Briefing—The U.S. Environmental Protection Agency (EPA) has discovered volatile organic compounds in effluents from a processing plant of the Algona Fertilizer Company in Algona, Iowa. These toxic waste products bypass the city of Algona but are carried into the East Fork of the Des Moines River, a tributary that feeds into Saylorville Lake, the principal source of water for Des Moines, a city of more than 3 million people. The Des Moines city council, through news media and political channels, is putting enormous public pressure on state and federal environmental agencies to shut down the Algona plant. Environmental action groups, with full media coverage, demonstrated in front of the Iowa governor's mansion to demand immediate closure of the plant. Local TV news and talk shows are starting to focus on the issue. The company's executive board has convened an emergency working group to consider what the company should do.

a. Jot down what you think is the "real" problem at Algona.

b. Now carefully think about the different interest groups or stakeholders connected to this problem and jot down your ideas. Can you identify at least ten different groups?

c. What do you think is the "real" problem now? In what way has looking at the perspective of different groups given you insight into aspects of the problem you did not consider before? Write a revised problem definition statement that takes your new viewpoint into account.

Team Project Guidelines for Problem Definition

1. Form a mentally diverse team.

2. As a homework assignment, each member thinks about some problem topics that could potentially be used as a class project.

3. In a team meeting, use the Pugh method with a few criteria to select the "best" doable and interesting problem for the team to solve within the time constraints and resources of the class, unless the team comes to a quick agreement through simple discussion and voting.

4. Use the explorer and detective mindsets to define the "real" problem.

5. Who are your customers? Obtain data on how different customers see the problem.

6. If time allows, also do a preliminary patent search in the problem area. At the least, discuss the problem area from different points of view and thinking quadrants.

7. Write the briefing and a positive problem definition statement.

7

Generating Ideas and Protecting Inventions

What you can learn from this chapter:
- How to conduct a creative thinking warm-up.
- Using thought-starter tools to help generate creative ideas.
- What is intellectual property protection?
- When to protect an invention with a patent, and who can file.
- Steps in the patenting process and the costs.
- Useful links and tips for inventors and entrepreneurs.

USING THE ARTIST'S MINDSET

Characteristics of the artist's mindset were described in Chapter 4, followed by the procedure of how to conduct a classical brainstorming session. Here, we will illustrate three tools that can be used to enhance brainstorming. In addition, playing around with creative ideas is one way for us to exercise our brain in looking at things "differently"—an interesting database to explore and mine for all kinds of ideas are existing patents ranging from "wacky" to extremely useful and profitable.

EXAMPLE OF A CREATIVE THINKING WARM-UP

Brainstorming is not used just once in the process of becoming an entrepreneur and starting your own business. It is a tool to be used each time you are looking for more than one alternative, from identifying a customer need or market niche (as "explorers" and "detectives") to coming up with ideas for meeting the need, then finding the best approach to produce, develop, implement, and market the best idea, service or product.

Most people will dive right into brainstorming. The process can be made more effective when a creative thinking warm-up is used. This allows the participants to switch mentally away from other tasks they may have been involved in that day, especially if these were worrisome or heavily involved left-brain thinking modes. It also facilitates the transition away from the problem briefing and instructions toward the procedure to be used in the actual brainstorming process.

Use a flip chart or wall board to quickly jot down the warm-up ideas as they are called out. A small group may be warmed-up with twenty ideas—a larger, analytically minded group may take longer. Once unusual and funny ideas are brought forth and the group begins to laugh, the warm-up has succeeded and the regular brainstorming can begin immediately. Table 7.1 lists the ideas from a lengthy warm-up using a one-foot square of aluminum foil as the object. Note that an occasional "crazy" idea may appear early in the process, but it usually takes some time for the participants to purge their minds of the practical and mundane ideas before they become more daring, exploratory and humorous.

Table 7.1   Fifty Uses for a Square of Aluminum Foil

Wrap food for freezer	Cook (bake) food in it	Wrap for package/sandwich
Pie pan or candy mold	Emergency drinking cup	Use as lid
Holder for sticky object	Funnel	Table mat
Cake decorating tool	Grill cover	Drip pan liner
Scrub rust from metal tools	Shelf liner	Emergency gas cap for car
Protector for dripping candles	Gift wrap	Ball or toy animals
Airflow deflector	Window shade	Scarecrow
Vent cover	Bird cage liner	Picture frame
Sun reflector/signaling device	Shelf liner	Creative art material
Shade for transplanted seedlings	Make jewelry	Shower cap
Wrap for small flower bouquet	Make play money	Fold into artful bookmark
Stuffing for drafts/holes in walls	Make silver confetti	Make tinsel
Eye mask during carnival	Tin man costume for doll	Mouse suit
Catch water under flower pot	Garbage bag for "yucky" stuff	Emergency purse for small stuff
Christmas decoration or craft	Make relief print or "rubbing"	Punch holes to make sifter
Shoe insert for temporary repair	Shoe shield for walking in mud	Halo for Christmas pageant
Roll up to blow soap bubbles	Book cover for "silver" library	Boat for beetles or bugs or slugs

EXAMPLES OF FORCE FITTING

When we put two unrelated ideas together and try to make them fit, this mental exercise help us generate new and especially creative ideas. This activity can be used to energize a sluggish brainstorming session. It can also be applied to improve and hitchhike on ideas that have already been posed (for example during brainstorming or during the Pugh method evaluation in the engineer's mindset). For instance, the "best" cover design for this textbook resulted from force-fitting two good but very different concepts.

Example 1

Use the idea of caged white rats to improve business in a travel agency.

- Have a wild-animal decorating scheme (including live animals from a featured tour-of-the-month exotic location).
- Use a white rat escaping from a cage as the logo, as the agency features special trips to escape the "rat race."
- Special promotion of trips to the zoo (with low rates for kids).
- Have the staff dress up in white rat costumes and form a band.
- Feature special science tours to study some endangered species or ecological niche, or sponsor an environmental cleanup (locally or at an interesting travel location).

Can you see how different aspects of the two unrelated ideas lead to creative as well as practical ideas?

Example 2

Combine the two ideas of soap and paper.

- Paper soap; soap paper (noun-noun combination).
- Soapy paper; papery soap (adjective-noun combination).
- Soap wets paper; soap cleans paper, soap smoothes paper (verbs).

Then each of these concepts can be used as a trigger for creative ideas, depending on the original problem. In this example, this approach could lead to innovative ideas if you were looking to find a new way of packaging soap.

EXAMPLE OF A WACKY PATENT

For a good laugh, a creative thinking warm-up, and to learn what NOT to patent, see www.colitz.com/site/wacky.htm. A surprising "Wacky Patent of the Month" will appear, and you may also click on "Prior Wacky Patents." An example is given in Figure 7.1.

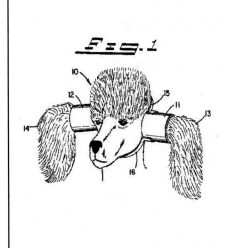

Animal Ear Protection
James Williams
Patented Nov. 18, 1980

ABSTRACT

This invention provides a device for protecting the ears of animals, especially long-haired dogs, from becoming soiled by the animal's food while the animal is eating. The device provides a generally tubular shaped member for containing and protecting each ear of the animal, and a member to position the tubular member and animal ears away from the mouth and food of the animal while it is eating.

FIELD OF THE INVENTION

The herein disclosed invention relates to devices for maintaining an animal's ears away from its mouth and food while it is eating.

Figure 7.1   Wacky Patent of the Month (Jan. 1998), U.S. Patent No. 4,2338,942)

EXAMPLE OF A THOUGHT-STARTER TOOL

Table 7.2 is an example of a thought-starter tool designed to help people generate creative ideas. The acronym SCAMPER will remind you of this list. A number of idea-generating tools have been developed based on this list and are available commercially as hand-held tools, wallet-size tables, decks of cards, large wall charts, or software packages. They are just different ways of asking *what if* and *what else*. Such a list is particularly useful for analytical thinkers who are not accustomed to switching easily to imaginative right-brain thinking modes.

Table 7.2   *Dr. Osborn's Nine Thought-Starter Questions*

1. **Substitute?** Who else? What else instead? Other place? Other time? Other tone of voice? Other ingredient? Other material? Other process? Other power source? Other approach?

2. **Combine?** How about a blend, assortment, alloy, ensemble? Combine purposes? Combine units? Combine ideas? Combine functions? Combine appeals?

3. **Adapt?** What else is like this? What other idea does this suggest? Any idea in the past that could be copied or adapted?

4. **Magnify?** What to add? Greater frequency? Stronger? Larger? Higher? Longer? Thicker? Extra value? "Plus" ingredient? Multiply? Exaggerate?

5. **Modify?** Change meaning, color, motion, sound, odor, taste, form, shape, or texture? Other changes? New twist?

6. **Put to other uses?** New ways to use object as is? Other uses or purpose if modified?

7. **Eliminate?** What to subtract? Smaller? Lighter? Slower? Split up? Less frequent? Condense? Miniaturize? Minify? Streamline? Understate? Simplify?

8. **Rearrange?** Other layout? Other sequence? Change pace? Other pattern? Change schedule? Transpose cause and effect?

9. **Reverse?** Opposites? Turn it backward? Transpose positive and negative? Mirror-reverse it? Turn it upside down or inside out?

Application

As an example, imagine that you are a manufacturer of nuts and bolts, and you were looking for new products. SCAMPER would give you:

- **Substitute:** Use of high tech materials for niche markets, such as high speed steel? Carbon fiber? Plastics? Glass? Non-reactive material?
- **Combine:** Integrate nut and bolt? Bolt and washer? Bolt and spanner?
- **Adapt:** Put Allen key or Star head on bolt? Countersink head?
- **Modify:** Produce bolts for watches or bridges? Produce different shaped bolts (e.g. screw in plugs)? Pre-painted green bolts?
- **Put to another use:** Bolts as hinge pins? As axles?
- **Eliminate:** Eliminate nuts, washers, heads, thread, etc.
- **Reverse:** Make dies as well as bolts, make bolts that cut threads for themselves in material, etc.

Source: www.mindtools.com → PRACTICAL CREATIVITY → SCAMPER. Many other tools for enhancing creative thinking are described on this site.

INTELLECTUAL PROPERTY PROTECTION

Let us say that your use of the creative problem solving process resulted in a very exciting and novel idea. So this is the time you may want to start thinking about what steps you should take to protect your idea. The form of protection depends on the type of intellectual property as listed in Table 7.3. The following information applies to U.S. laws and conditions—patent protection is different in different countries! But no matter where you want to apply for a patent, always check out the latest rules, terms, and costs on the nation's official patent office website.

Table 7.3 *Types of Intellectual Property*

Type of Asset	Type of Protection
Invention	Patent
Logo or mark	Trademark
Physical expression of information	Copyright (i.e., book)
Technology/marketing information	Trade secret

WHAT IS A PATENT?

A utility patent protects processes, machines, articles of manufacturing, and compositions of matter for twenty years. A design patent protects ornamental designs for manufactured articles for fourteen years. The idea must be novel and non-obvious. A patent protects the right of the inventor(s) to exclude others from making, using or selling the claimed invention or design during the term of the patent in exchange for public disclosure of the invention when the patent is granted. The patent can be licensed to another person or company. Patent rights are enforced by lawsuits in U.S. federal court to prevent infringement by unauthorized making, using, or selling.

WHAT IS A TRADEMARK?

A trademark can be words, names, symbols, and other devices to distinguish goods or services. The first user of the trademark can obtain protection. The mark is protected when it is registered by the U.S. Patent and Trademarks Office and used on goods and services. It is protected for an initial ten years and renewable for additional ten-year terms. The trademark protects the right to stop others from using similar trademarks that might cause confusion or deception regarding the protected item.

The entrepreneur's responsibilities:

1. Develop/provide:
- *new application*
- *new service*
- *new product*
- *new market.*

2. Make the public aware of it.

3. Convince the public that it works.

4. Make the public want or need it.

WHAT IS A COPYRIGHT?

Writings, music, and works of art that have been reduced to a tangible medium of expression (such as in books, audio tapes, video tapes, software) can be copyrighted. The subject matter must be an original creation—not copied—and the copyright notice must be applied when published. The originators of the work hold the copyright, but it can be assigned to others. The copyright holders need to apply to the Copyright Office for a registration certificate. Protection lasts for the life of the author plus 50 years for works created after 1977, and it grants the right to stop others from copying protected work unless granted permission by the copyright holder. Note that the materials can be used by anyone—only the unauthorized copying constitutes an infringement on the copyright.

WHAT IS A TRADE SECRET?

A trade secret can be a formula, pattern, customer list, device, program, or any other compilation of information. These items do not have to be patentable. A trade secret must be kept secret (through established internal and external security measures) and must be used in a business to give an advantage over others who do not know or use it. President Clinton signed the Economic Espionage Act of 1996 into law. Any person converting a trade secret to his or her own benefit commits an act of trade secret theft which is now a federal criminal offense. Civil courts can grant injunctions to prevent ex-employees from working for competitors when a strong likelihood of trade secret disclosure exists, even if unintentional or subconscious. The formula for *Coca-Cola* has been a fiercely guarded secret since its beginning.

INVENTION AND PATENTS

Entrepreneurs most likely want to seek intellectual property protection for inventions that they plan to sell (either through licensing or through manufacturing and marketing). Thus the next group of questions relate specifically to inventions, followed by questions about the patent filing process.

WHAT CAN YOU DO TO PROTECT YOUR INVENTION?

Patent rights enable patent owners to stop unauthorized use. Patent and design rights are destroyed by prior knowledge or use.

Eric Potter Clarkson, Nottingham, UK

- Make sure your invention is novel and practical or useful. It need not be entirely new but can be an improvement over an existing patent.
- Keep records that carefully document your discovery; be secretive at this point. If you do not have proof of the date of your invention, your patent may be invalidated.
- Carefully search and study existing literature and patents relating to your invention.
- If possible, make a prototype that works!
- Prepare and file a description of your invention.
- Be patient. It can take as long as two years to process a patent. It is also usual for the patent examiner to reject the initial application. You then must overcome the objections cited by the examiner before you can resubmit your application.

WHAT ARE SOME COMMON MISTAKES TO AVOID?

- Talking without protection (use signed non-disclosure forms).
- Poor prior art search.
- Leaving out claims that others can work around—a patent lawyer can be useful for carefully determining and expanding the areas of your claims.
- Selfishness—not rewarding or including co-inventors.
- Filing too many patents.
- Assuming a U.S. patent affords world-wide protection.
- Filing in too many countries.
- Assuming patent laws are the same around the world. For example, before telling anyone or using the invention in public anywhere in the world, the UK inventor must obtain confidentiality agreements from anyone to whom the invention is revealed in part or in full for development purposes. In the U.S., disclosure of an invention is OK if the patent application is filed within one year of invention.

- Assuming that all developed countries have the same degree of respect for intellectual property.
- Forgetting that the patent application will be published 18 months after filing under the Patent Cooperation Treaty.

WHAT IF YOU WANT TO KEEP YOUR IDEA A SECRET?

Not all inventions are patented. You may have some valid reasons for keeping your invention a secret and for wanting to save the costs of obtaining a patent. Trade secret protection might be the better choice, if you are sure you want to go into business by yourself, will only have a few people involved in the process, your idea would be difficult to copy, and you will be dealing with a rapidly changing product or market.

HOW DO YOU KNOW THE IDEA IS WORTH PATENTING?

Once you have completed evaluation and judgment in creative problem solving (including the Pugh method with some market analysis), you will have a fair idea about the merits of your invention. Chapter 8 will discuss several sources and processes that can help you evaluate your idea or product.

Important inventions are not always complicated, high-tech products invented by scientists and engineers. Sometimes, an invention has to wait for technological development (or another invention) before it becomes widely adopted—the can opener was invented 50 years after the first tin can was used to conserve food. Interesting information about different categories of inventors (including black, Canadian, Chinese, women, and young) can be found at www.inventors.about.com. This is just one example of a commercial website, and the viewer must be aware that such information may not be accurate or complete. Do not use such sites for patent searching; the example site given here is merely to show that anyone can invent something worth patenting. This site also has a "wacky patent" file with several funny subcategories. The odds of making it with your invention are increased substantially if you follow the creative problem solving process in this book.

Creativity and zest have become the prime creators of economic value.

Tom Peters

WHO CAN FILE FOR A PATENT?

In the U.S., it is the person who invents, keeps an inventor's log, and files a provisional patent—it is the inventor (or group of inventors) that can file for a patent. The inventors need not be U.S. citizens. The requirements may be different in other countries. For example in the UK, the first person to apply for the patent can receive the patent—this can be anyone: inventor, business partner, or sponsor. Patents can be filed by a single inventor or a group of co-inventors (see Table 7.4 on the following page for examples of a few famous co-inventors). Sometimes the organization licensing a product becomes more famous (and prosperous) than the original inventor. An example is Dr. Yoshiro Nakamatz, the original inventor of the floppy disk and virtually unknown in the U.S., although he holds over 2000 patents. Groups of technical people at IBM (including Alan Shugart and Dick Morley) worked on the development of the disk and are usually credited with being its inventors.

Table 7.4 Some Interesting Inventions and Inventors

Earmuffs were invented in 1873 by 13-year-old Chester Greenwood.

James Henry Atkinson, a British inventor, patented the "Little Nipper" mousetrap in 1897. It still has about 60% of the UK market today.

Charles F. Nelson received a patent for a mousetrap in the U.S. (Patent No. 661,068) in 1900.

Mary Anderson received a patent for windshield wipers in 1903.

Patent No. 821,393 for a "Flying Machine" was granted to Orville and Wilbur Wright in 1906.

Henry Ford patented a transmission mechanism in 1911 (Patent No. 1,005,186).

It took Guideon Sundback 30 years to perfect the slide fastener (zipper) patented in 1913.

Josephine Cochrane patented a dishwasher in 1914.

In 1921, Earle Dickson invented the Band-Aid to help his wife (who frequently cut her fingers while busy cooking); he was an employee of Johnson & Johnson and they soon marketed this product.

Garrett Morgan patented a traffic signal in 1923 in the U.S. and later also in Canada and England.

Two Hungarian chemists, Georg and László Biro, patented the ballpoint pen in 1938.

Marion Donovan received a patent for the first disposable diaper in 1951.

Bernard Silver and Joseph Woodland, two graduate students at Drexel, invented the barcode and received Patent No. 2,612,994 in 1952. Silver died in 1962 before seeing the invention commercialized. President Bush awarded Woodland the 1992 National Medal of Technology. Neither inventor made much money on the idea that started a billion dollar business.

Bette Nesmith Graham, a housewife and typist, invented "liquid paper" in the mid 50's; she obtained a patent and trademark, and her innovative company was sold in 1980 for over $47 million.

The Bobcat loader was invented in 1957 by Louis Keller, a North Dakota farmer with little education (with his brother Cyril, a blacksmith), to help a neighboring turkey farmer clean out the stalls.

Stephanie Kwolek, a chemist with DuPont, invented the miracle fiber Kevlar in 1971.

George De Mestral was granted a patent for an "Adhesive Element in Cloth Form" in 1973 (Patent No. 3,748,701)—we know it as Velcro.

Marcian Edward Hoff, Stanley Mazor and Frederico Faggin received Patent No. 3,821,715 in 1974 for a "Memory System for Multi-Chip Digital Computer."

THE PATENT FILING PROCESS

WHAT ARE THE STEPS FOR FILING FOR A U.S. PATENT?

The applicant must make sure to have the date of the conception of the invention protected by either having a witnessed, permanently bound, page-numbered notebook or other notarized records. Once the decision to seek patent protection has been made, the main steps in the patenting process for the U.S. are:

1.   A *disclosure* document in a standard format is completed and sent to the U.S. Patent and Trademark Office where it is held and preserved for two years (for a small fee).

2. The inventor needs to conduct a thorough search on patentability. It must be verified that neither the idea nor any of the possible claims are already protected by a patent.

3. If the invention has been shown to be original (or novel) and useful, the inventor can then file a *provisional application for a patent.* This establishes the filing date. The application should be as complete as possible but need not include all claims. This will allow the inventor to show "Patent Pending" on the product.

4. Within 12 months of the application, the inventor must file a *non-provisional application* including a declaration of inventorship. Upon receipt, the application is given a patent serial number and filing date and is then examined by a patent examiner. This application must be complete in all details and include all claims. For this reason, entrepreneurs and inventors with strong quadrant D thinking preferences are urged to seek the help of a patent attorney with quadrant B thinking skills to prepare the patent application. Although it is possible to complete the entire application alone, the risks of leaving out some claims on the patent drawing and application are great—anything left out leaves the product unprotected. Make sure you hire a reputable person—many scam artists fleece inventors by filing only a provisional patent (at high cost) and then letting the application expire.

5. If the patent application is rejected, it can be amended and resubmitted. Check with the U.S. Patent and Trademark Office as to the exact procedures that must be followed.

WHERE CAN YOU FIND MORE INFORMATION?

For more information on U.S. patent law and to obtain the required forms, go to www.uspto.gov.

As you can see from Table 7.5, www.inventnet.com has a slew of useful information, beginning with "Inventing and Patenting Help." Be sure to check "Invention Scams" and the separate warning at the head of the InventNET home page. Click on "International Patent Offices" and you will be provided with a list of links to patent offices in many different countries (in their own languages). Other sources of information are listed in Table 7.6.

To invent, you need a good imagination and a pile of junk.

Thomas Alva Edison

Table 7.5   Main Menu of Available Information from InventNET

• Inventing and Patenting Help	• Patent Attorney Directory
• Bookstore	• Inventor Trade Shows
• Patent Search	• InventNET Forum
• Invention for Sale	• Patent and Licensing Forms
• Get Your Free E-mail	• Classifieds
• Invention Scams	• Useful Links
• Prototype Work	• About InventNET
• Products and Services	• International Patent Offices
• Inventor Organizations	• Inventor Organizations

If you want to cut through the patent red tape and possibly save thousands of dollars, <u>Patent It Yourself</u> has all the forms and instructions needed to patent a product in the United States.

<u>The Washington Post</u>

Table 7.6 *Books with Patent Information*

David Pressman, *Patent It Yourself,* Nolo Press, Berkeley, California, 11th edition, April 2005, 608 pages. This book contains useful hints and forms for those who want to apply for their own patents.

U.S. Department of Commerce: *Patents and How to Get One: A Practical Handbook.* This paperback is listed at www.amazon.com as well as at www.barnesandnoble.com for $4.95 (less at some other sites) and represents a very good value.

Search www.amazon.com for books on "Patents" and then choose among a very long list of highly rated books for any that fit your particular circumstances and interests (and pocketbook).

COSTS

HOW MUCH DOES IT COST TO FILE FOR A U.S. PATENT?

Filing for a patent—the non-provisional application—can be very expensive. Check with the patent office for the latest pricing information. The costs are typically as follows, if the inventor asserts in writing that he or she is "a small entity" (otherwise the prices are double). The filing fee for a provisional application is $100 and for a utility patent $395 (higher for more than 3 claims). Maintaining a patent is expensive. At 3-1/2 years, the fee is $450, at 7-1/2 years, $1150, and at 11-1/2 years, $1900. These high maintenance fees again point out the importance of having an invention with marketability in the near- to medium-term.

WHAT HAPPENS WHEN A PATENT EXPIRES?

Many patents expire due to non-payment of the maintenance fee or because the protection limit has been reached. Others can then use the patent in their own inventions. Thus U.S. Patent No. 2,292,387 for a spread-spectrum communication system invented by H.K. Markey and George Antheil (an avant-garde composer) was recently used by another inventor in the Secure ID System (patent pending). H.K. Markey is better known as the Hollywood actress Hedy Lamarr, and the "secret communication system" was intended for launching torpedoes during WWII. Other current uses are in satellite and cellular telephone communication security. All later spread-spectrum patents acknowledge the original (which was kept classified by the U.S. government until 1985).

WHO PAYS FOR THE PATENT?

A critical issue in the protection of intellectual property concerns payment for patent protection. Often, those who file for patent protection then claim ownership of the intellectual property involved. It is crucially important to clarify and resolve this issue prior to disclosure and patent application. Consider the following four situations.

1. **University Staff and Students:** Increasingly, universities are being encouraged to develop and exploit their intellectual property. This affects both staff and students. When intellectual property with commercial potential is identified, it may be university policy to process and pay for patent applications centrally. In this case, the university staff member or student involved may lose ownership of the intellectual property. If you are a staff member or graduate student, you may have no choice but to turn over ownership to the university. Universities commonly have a person or an office responsible for intellectual property. If the university licenses your invention, you may be entitled to a certain percentage of the royalties. In any case, be very sure you check out your rights.

    TIP: The inventors may not have sufficient resources, time, interest, patience, or rights to pursue a patent application. However, they may be able to negotiate a percentage of future royalties. Such amounts are low, since the university is assuming the risk of paying for the patent up front without assurance that the invention will be commercially profitable. Typically, the royalty to the inventor is in the range of 5 to 15% at most.

2. **Employees of Companies:** As with universities, more companies are now actively encouraging the development of intellectual property and its commercialization within the business. Many large companies promote such activity by their employees by providing time and resources for this purpose. Again, it is vital that those who generate new ideas are fully aware of their company's policies regarding intellectual property.

    TIPS: Companies are more likely to pay a cash bonus for a successful invention than to assign a percentage of profits. If the invention was made as part of the regular employment and using the company's resources, little if any special recompense should be expected. However, if the employee has a creative idea and develops it in his or her own time at home (without any of the company's resources), the employee must carefully investigate if independent pursuit of the patent is feasible:

    - Is it allowed under company policy? Intellectual property developed by employees may be vulnerable to lawsuits even if generated on the their own time, particularly if the idea becomes very successful.
    - Is the market potential sufficient to warrant the time and costs of seeking a patent?
    - Can the employee afford the investment in time and costs?

3. **Government Employees:** Employees of national or local government departments may also develop intellectual property that has commercial potential. Again they should seek information and advice on the most appropriate strategy to adopt and the regulations that apply. Some government agencies (especially those working in the forefront of high technology development), may have some system of recognition or recompense available for their inventors. For example, NASA pays a bonus to employees who obtain patents (but only when the invention has a payback exceeding the cost for getting the patent).

There are many do's and don'ts in the invention game; learn the ropes—don't jump in head first.

www.inventNET.com

"He could have added fortune to fame, but caring for neither, he found happiness and honor in being helpful to the world."

Epitaph on the grave of George Washington Carver

4. **Intellectual Property Protection for Entrepreneurs:** The observations and warnings provided above should also be kept in mind by individual entrepreneurs. If you have checked out some of the information on the patenting process given on the recommended web sites, you will be aware that the decision about going forward with a patent application requires serious thought. Professional advice should be obtained to ascertain the most economical and appropriate way of proceeding before simply applying for patents as a matter of course or a matter of pride.

HOW DO YOU DEAL WITH PATENT INFRINGEMENT?

It only pays to carry on a lawsuit for patent infringement if you have a very successful product, because this is usually a lengthy and very expensive undertaking. A settlement recently in the news was for the hand-held *Black-Berry* e-mail device, where NTP, the patent-holding company, sued RIM, the Canadian developer and manufacturer of the *BlackBerry*. This lawsuit was in litigation for 5 years before RIM agreed to pay NTP $612.5 million for the patent rights (and damages).

INTERNATIONAL PATENT PROTECTION

FOREIGN PATENTS FOR AMERICAN INVENTIONS

Under U.S. law, it is necessary, in the case of inventions made in the U.S., to obtain a license from the Commissioner of Patents and Trademarks before applying for a patent in a foreign country, if the application is made prior to or within a period of six months after filing the U.S. application.

In most foreign countries, publication of the invention before the date of the application will bar the right to a patent. For this reason it is wise to file the U.S. application prior to public disclosure.

There is no such thing as an international patent that covers all countries. You must apply for a patent in each country where you wish to market your product, if you want to be protected in that country. Also, most foreign countries require that the patented invention be manufactured in that country after a certain period (usually three years). If there is no manufacture, the patent may be voided, or a compulsory license may be granted to someone else.

The right of priority under the Paris Convention allows public disclosure after the filing of a U.S. patent application but before any international applications are filed. This applies only to countries that are members of the Paris Convention (which includes most industrialized countries). Although each foreign country's laws are different, international treaties help when applying for international patent protection, including the Paris Convention Treaty and the Patent Cooperation Treaty.

PATENT COOPERATION TREATY (PCT)

This patent treaty facilitates filing patent applications on the same invention in member countries, because a single application filed at an official PCT site can constitute an application for a patent in one or more member countries.

A single application is less expensive than individual national filings. Although the applicant will eventually be required to pay the fees when the PCT application is filed with the requested national patent offices, the PCT procedure allows these costs to be delayed for up to 18 month. This time will allow the inventor to analyze the patentability and profitability of the invention and thus make a more informed decision on where it should be filed.

ADVICE FOR BRITISH INVENTORS

1. File a UK patent application (see Table 7.7). Under the relevant international agreement, you have 12 months during which you must file any foreign, European or world patent application you wish to pursue.
2. Alternatively, you can file a European or world patent application directly. However, there are clear advantages to filing your application in the United Kingdom first:
    - Early, cheap search report from the UK Patent Office. You can use the UK application as a basis for claiming priority for an application filed in most other countries.
    - You need to obtain security clearance from the UK Patent Office before you can apply for a patent abroad.
    - You can use the UK search report to assess your invention before starting the costly process of obtaining protection abroad.

Table 7.7 *Steps in the UK Patent Application Process*

1. The description
2. The patent drawings
3. The claims
4. Patent Application Form 1/77
5. Processing the application.

For more information, see www.patent.gov.uk

FILING FOR AN INTERNATIONAL PATENT

The PCT provides for the filing of an international patent application. It may be filed by nationals or residents of a PCT member country (say for example Singapore). After the international filing, the application subsequently passes into the national phase of designated countries. Going through the PCT process has several advantages:

1. This single application covers North America, Europe, and South-East Asia and gives at least 18 months of product development and market research time to decide which countries to actually go for.
2. The PCT patentability evaluation should lead to more uniform results regarding patentability of the invention in each country. A positive PCT decision can have a persuasive influence on national patent officials.
3. It allows advanced application and early results from the European Patent Office and makes delay into the U.S. Patent Office possible. Filing a patent in the U.S. is expensive. Discuss these advanced application options with a qualified patent attorney experienced in PCT applications.

Inventing is a combination of brain and materials. The more brain you use, the less material you need.

Charles F. Kettering

Much information is available on line, both from official government offices and private firms. For example, the www.epatents.gov.sg site of the Intellectual Property Office of Singapore has search links to the UK, U.S., European, China, Japan and Taiwan patent offices. The South African government website at www.cipro.co.za/products_services/patents_corptreaty.asp has a nice timeline and description for the process of applying for international patents by first going through the PCT process.

EXERCISES

7.1   Application of an Idea-Generator Tool

For fun, or when your team is "stuck" in a brainstorming session, use one of the idea generator tools discussed in your chapter or in the list below:

- **http://www.creativethink.com** Click on "Whack"—look at the picture and text to see what creative ideas you can discover. Repeat a few times.
- **http://www.ideachampions.com/idea_lottery.shtml** If you some time, you might find it productive to learn to play the "idea lottery" and then apply it to a problem your team is facing.
- **http://gocreate.com/tools/jobs.htm** This thought-starter tool asks you to think about, "How would someone in a different job solve the problem?" Try it!

7.2   Patent Search in Product Development

Depending on your interest, need and prior experience, choose one of the following areas for a patent search:

a.   Go through a patent searching tutorial to learn the process.

b.   Use it as a creative thinking warm-up.

c.   Do it as an exploratory search to get ideas about possible products.

d.   Do it as a check to see if a promising idea has already been protected.

e.   Do it as an exhaustive search to ensure your invention is not infringing on an existing patent.

f.   Or you can do research to identify funding sources that might be available to pay for patent searching and patent drawings for students.

Team Project Guidelines for Idea Generation

1.   In preparation for the upcoming brainstorming session, review the problem briefing and problem definition statement with your project team.

2.   Next, using the artist's mindset, conduct a 5-minute creative thinking warm-up.

3.   Immediately move on to brainstorming creative ideas for solving your defined problem. Be sure to write down all ideas on a board or flipchart.

4.   Finally, write down each idea on a separate note card or Post-it note for further processing in the engineer's mindset.

8 Developing a "Best" Product

What you can learn from this chapter
- You will gain a deeper understanding of Phase 1 of the Pugh method, as concepts are being developed. Concurrent activities are: patent searches, technical analysis, feasibility analysis, and initial assessment of market and profit potential.
- You will gain a deeper understanding of Phase 2 of the Pugh method, as products begin to converge to a "best" concept. Concurrent activities are: detailed market research and analysis; check of market value; risk and resources assessment; cost estimates, and naming your product.
- You will learn how product development is connected to business development and why it is important to have a prototype.
- You will be able to review your chances of success (as an inventor) and your motivation for starting an enterprise.

This chapter is focused on the development of a product as concepts pass through Phase 1 and Phase 2 of the Pugh method. Several analytical tools are employed to help improve, evaluate, and rank these concepts. This process culminates in a "best" concept which is then demonstrated in a prototype. The two chapters in Part 3 will focus on business development. Be aware that business development activities may coincide with product development, or they may occur in succession. Product development with the Pugh method combines right-brain thinking—when additional creative concepts are generated—with left-brain, analytical activities in the engineer's mindset. Some people with strong dominances in quadrant D thinking may find reading the "dry" material in this chapter not very interesting, but this knowledge is essential to future success. Many inventors have fallen prey to scams which could have been avoided had they done their analytical "homework."

PUGH PHASE 1: DEVELOP BETTER IDEAS

To make it easier to develop different but well thought-out concepts for the Pugh evaluation matrix, we recommend that you process the many ideas that come out of the first brainstorming session in a round of creative idea evaluation—essentially a second round of brainstorming which employs both the artist's and engineer's mindsets—as discussed in Chapter 4. Depending on the problem topic, the outcome of this activity will be either a smaller number of better, more practical ideas, or a list of design criteria or goals that the solution or new product must meet to satisfy the customer needs. This is the starting point for the Pugh evaluation.

EVALUATION CRITERIA

The first item needed for the Pugh evaluation matrix is a set of valid evaluation criteria. Alone or preferably with a diverse team brainstorm a list of criteria and then narrow the list down to about ten to twenty of the most important items. Make sure these criteria address all important customer needs and the concerns of all stakeholders—a problem rarely involves only one customer. For example, the end user is a child in the case of a juvenile car safety seat. Other customers would be the purchasers (likely a parent or grandparent), the retailer or store manager, the seat manufacturer and the carmakers, insurance companies, and perhaps repair or maintenance persons as well as law enforcement and emergency personnel, and finally society (for the recycling and other environmental aspects in addition to the general child welfare and safety concerns). As you develop your criteria (including cost factors), you may want to look ahead and think of what you will do with your developed product. Would you like to sell or license it to another company, or would you prefer to manufacture and market it yourself? Your answer to this question may influence some of your evaluation criteria.

The Pugh method of concept evaluation increases visibility.

"It helps everyone to find out what other people are doing and why."

Stuart Pugh

The result is more effective communication and synergy, ultimately yielding higher productivity.

DEVELOPING DIFFERENT CONCEPTS OR DESIGNS

Based on the problem briefing and an understanding of the problem-solving goal, work on the improved ideas to create several distinct solutions in the artist's and engineer's mindsets. The concepts need not be perfect at this point, but each concept should constitute a *very* creative approach for solving the problem—the natural process of critical evaluation later will tend to make these concepts more practical. Each concept should be worked out to about the same level of detail. For designs, prepare a large sketch that shows the major features of the product. For services, solutions and other intangible options, prepare a condensed description of the major features and post each concept on a flip chart page or poster. Have a minimum of three or four alternatives as a start—more will be generated as the process continues. In an engineering design team, it is often expedient to have each team member develop a separate idea or concept—but only after the entire team participated in brainstorming and improving the initial ideas. This approach can of course be used by any product development team.

PATENT SEARCHES

Phase 1 patent searches can be idea starters as you develop different concepts, as shown in Chapter 7. They can be applied to the entire concept or just to certain parts or features. Since roughly eighty percent of patents are not entirely original but are improvements of existing patents, this can be a source of good ideas for your concepts, either by adding practical aspects, or by prompting your mind to make a creative leap through force-fitting or overcoming some "ridiculous" idea. During Phase 2, patent searches should become more focused in the area of the emerging winning solutions.

EVALUATION MATRIX AND REVIEWS

Using the brainstormed criteria and the initial concepts, set up the matrix and conduct the evaluation as discussed in Chapter 5. Then review the results and continue to improve the concepts in two or more rounds, with the highest-scoring concept chosen as the datum for each subsequent matrix.

ANALYSIS TASKS DURING PHASE 1

The merit of the top-ranked options at the end of Phase 1 can be evaluated in terms of technical analysis, feasibility, and initial assessment of market and profit potential, as indicated in Figure 8.1.

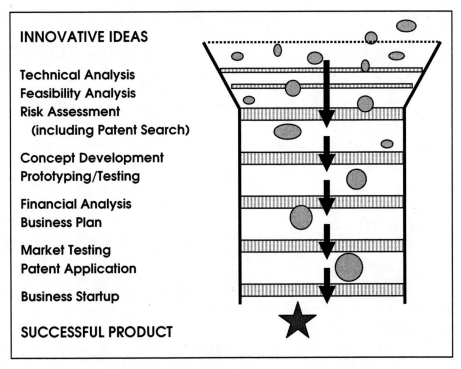

INNOVATIVE IDEAS

Technical Analysis
Feasibility Analysis
Risk Assessment
  (including Patent Search)

Concept Development
Prototyping/Testing

Financial Analysis
Business Plan

Market Testing
Patent Application

Business Startup

SUCCESSFUL PRODUCT

Figure 8.1 Innovative ideas pass through many assessment "filters" to distill out the best concept with the potential for development into a valuable and successful product.

TECHNICAL ANALYSIS

The proposed concepts should be analyzed as to their technical aspects. Does the concept use existing technology? Can it be used as is? Will it have to be modified? Will it have to be purchased? Is it protected by a patent? Does it need development? If yes, what is the time line? What would be the costs? What would be the competitive advantages? What are the trends—is rapid change expected, and how would this affect you?

This analysis may point out three options, where one definitely involves a long-term view:

1. Go with existing technology.
2. Go with existing technology, with adaptations.
3. Go with existing technology, while simultaneously working on developing an advanced concept to maintain or expand the future market for your product or business.

Thus this analysis can point out the most promising areas for R&D investments for your business.

FEASIBILITY ANALYSIS

This involves the whole context of what you want to do with the "best" idea once you have developed it, from business planning to obtaining financing and ethics. Some of these aspects will be discussed in Chapters 9 and 10. At this point, you merely need to have a rough yet realistic estimate of the scope of your potential enterprise and if it appears to be doable.

INITIAL ANALYSIS OF MARKET AND PROFIT POTENTIAL

All the work you have done in developing an invention or other business idea will come to naught if you give little thought to the market. Who will buy your product or pay for your idea? What will be your profits after you have paid for all your expenses? Later in this chapter you will find some questionnaires that will help you think through a market assessment.

After two or three rounds of the Pugh method, you and your team will begin to have a fair idea on the strengths (and weaknesses) of your ideas and concepts. You may want to check out the market potential with a typical sample of customers—information on survey forms was given in Chapter 7. If you have made an invention and your research has shown that nothing like this is being sold anywhere, could the reason be that you have come up with a breakthrough idea or that there is simply no market or interest in your idea? Critically evaluate these two possibilities, without personal bias or blind spots. An ideal situation would be a market where potential customers show interest and have no other loyalties or brand preferences.

You can begin your search for market information on the Internet and in public libraries (look for special reports on markets in your product area in business magazines, for example). A very structured, highly competitive market is difficult to enter, whereas a fragmented or emerging market may have many niches that can be filled with new products. Keep in mind that having a lot of published information available about a market's high potential also means shrinking opportunity because many competitors can be expected to enter such a market.

Many organizations and companies offer to assess the market potential or value of a new product or invention. Our first advice is to check out the advice given on www.inventNet.com on how to beware of scams. Table 8.1 lists examples of the types of resources available that can analyze the market potential (or marketability) of your idea or invention—of course for a price.

IMPORTANT TIP

Don't think invention.

Think business opportunity!

IMPORTANT RULE OF THUMB

The product's selling price should be three to five times its manufacturing cost, or you will be unlikely to make a profit.

Table 8.1　*Who Can Analyze the Market Potential of Your Ideas?*

Innovation Institute: www.innovation-institute.com/about.htm

　　This is the primary site in the U.S., with considerable experience and reasonable cost ($200 for U.S. residents, $220 if you live abroad). This organization at Southwest Missouri State University will assess inventions as well as existing products. Recommendations: Do **invention evaluation** during the early design stage (before extensive product development and prototyping). Do **market evaluation** before applying for a patent. A **product assessment** is especially valuable in times of changing market conditions.

Patent Café: http://evaluation.patentcafe.com/

　　This has a do-it-yourself program from PatentCafe to evaluate, score and chart your invention's success potential. It is easy to use, on-line, with no software to install, with immediate feedback, and includes a manufacturing assessment, a safety evaluation, an invention development financial analysis and a budget planning report (among other items), all for $199.

Canadian Innovation Center: www.innovationcentre.ca/innovator/iap.html

　　This center is equipped to do technology-centered as well as enterprise-centered assessments. Check out their website for the different services and resources offered. Its "Critical Factor Assessment" gathers information demonstrated over time to be the key for successful commercialization; they investigate 40 issues that have proven to be crucial in scoping risk and opportunity, for a fixed fee of just under $1000.

Neustel Law Offices: www.uspatentlaw.com/evaluation.htm

　　This site has a free 20-question evaluation form. It differentiates between market analysis and marketability evaluation and warns of promoters who charge high fees ($600-$1500) for worthless market analysis (which can be done for free at most local libraries or by using free Internet resources such as American Demographics, Biz-Lib.Com, Industry Research Desk, and the U.S. Census Bureau.

PUGH PHASE 2: DEVELOP A "BEST" SOLUTION

In the rounds of Phase 1, you and your team have most likely come up with several additional ideas or concepts. In Phase 2, you will begin dropping the weakest concepts and more fully develop the stronger solutions. Eventually, the process will converge to a single, best or optimal solution that is supported by the entire team. However, to be able to judge the merits of different concepts that remain in the running toward the end, it will be advantageous to conduct additional analyses.

REFINING THE EVALUATION CRITERIA

Not just the concepts, but also the criteria are being developed and refined during Phase 2, based on the discussion during the completion of the evaluation matrix as well as data obtained from the analyses being done. Key factors from marketability analysis and business development (if carried out concurrently) need to be incorporated into the list of criteria. For example, the product needs to fit into the planned business area. If you have your mind on adhesives, ideas involving hardware-type tacks may not meet your requirements. On the other hand, your conceptual product may drive business development, and this, too, should be expressed in the criteria.

DEVELOPING BETTER AND MORE DETAILED CONCEPTS

In each round, the concepts are worked out in more detail (with data from the technical and cost analyses, together with input from potential customers). In some projects, you may not have time to continue the process until you have convergence to a single, best solution. In this case, it will be especially important to supplement your evaluation of competing concepts with data from the Phase 2 analyses.

EVALUATION MATRIX AND DOCUMENTATION

It is important that a careful record be maintained of the results of each evaluation as well as of the descriptions or drawings of each concept being evaluated, together with notes on the evaluation process and discussions. Also record the rationale why particular concepts are being discarded.

ANALYSIS TASKS DURING PHASE 2

Three different types of analyses are very helpful to determine the merit of the final ideas: a detailed market analysis, a risk analysis (including an assessment of resources), and an analysis of costs (for development, for manufacturing, and for marketing).

Successful innovators were seen to have a much better understanding of user needs (from the Project SAPPHO Study of Innovation, University of Sussex, 1970-1972). They get this superiority in different ways:

1. Some may collaborate intimately with potential customers to acquire the necessary tacit knowledge of user requirements.
2. Others learn about these explicitly through market studies.

DETAILED MARKET RESEARCH AND ANALYSIS

If you have not explored these areas during the problem definition phase, start your market research by making a list of different categories that might be related to your concept or product (where the "product" can be a service). These are called research fields. Get ideas for fields by:

- Searching through different companies on the web
- Visiting stores
- Looking through catalogues of related products
- Talking to experts
- Attending trade shows—the offerings are vast.

We cannot overemphasize the importance of attending trade shows, especially if you can do so for two or three years in a row. You may have been playing around with a potential idea, and at the trade show you may find it developed into a superior product and ready for sale at an astonishing low price. Many of these technological innovations are now coming out of China.

Trade shows are designed to let entrepreneurs meet potential customers. Beyond that, you can check out the competition and prospective suppliers.

MARKET VALUE

For your idea to have market value, determine the following:

- Will your invention (product or process) work as intended?
- What is the competition? If there is no competition, BEWARE!
- Is there a need for this product?
- What future changes or paradigm shifts could affect demand?

For some inventions, there is no question of the value (such as a vaccine to eradicate a deadly disease). But for many products, you will have to create a market (as was the case, for example, for the Post-it notes). From the Pugh method, you will gain a clear idea of the customer benefits: Does your idea perform a task that has not been achieved before, or can it do the task faster, better, easier, or at substantially lower cost? Table 8.2 lists some initial questions that you need to answer to gain an understanding of the market conditions your product will face. If your answers are different from those indicated, evaluate why and investigate how the obstacle can be overcome with additional problem solving as you develop your concepts.

Table 8.2 *Self-Assessment Questions Related to the Market*

Competition

1.	Are similar products or ideas already on the market? *Conduct a product search.*	No
2.	Are there previous relevant patents or patent applications? *Conduct a patent search.*	No
3.	Is the market very competitive for these types of products?	No
4.	Could competitors quickly catch up and take a substantial market share?	No
5.	Can you effectively compete in price, quality, and service?	Yes
6.	Are your product's features unique?	Yes
7.	Are your product's benefits obvious?	Yes
8.	Does your product provide more customer choice and value?	Yes
9.	Will increased competition affect your profit level negatively?	No

Market

1.	Do you know who the customers will be and the size of the market (local, regional, global, private, industry, commerce, wholesale, retail, government, etc.)?	Yes
2.	Will the product or service be in constant demand?	Yes
3.	For something entirely new, can you create a demand for the service or product?	Yes
4.	Is the potential market likely to grow? How fast?	Yes
5.	Are there additional applications for your product?	Yes
6.	Is your idea filling a market gap (open door) by meeting a clear customer need?	Yes
7.	Will your market be immune to overall economic conditions?	Yes
8.	Are there legal, regulatory, environmental or other factors hindering market entry?	No
9.	Could an existing company introduce your idea with a better chance of success? *(If yes, consider licensing your idea to them.)*	Yes/No

RISK AND RESOURCE ANALYSIS

Table 8.3 gives some self-assessment questions regarding manufacturing risk and resource requirements. If you can answer all the resource questions in the affirmative, your risks will be relatively low. The majority of new businesses start with an initial investment of less than $10,000. Thus only a modest investment is at stake should the enterprise fail. And the value of what can be learned from the failure may far outweigh this initial loss if it forms the stepping stone to a successful business later.

Table 8.3   *Self-Assessment Questions Related to Risk and Resources*

Risk

1. Is innovative technology needed for producing the idea?
   The more innovative the technology, the bigger the risk to the manufacturer.
2. Is the idea a new application of an existing product or process?   *This may be less risky.*
3. Does your idea depend on at least one other innovation being operational before it can become successful?   *This dependency vastly increases the risk.*
4. Will the product be cheaper when produced in larger volumes?
   The higher initial costs increase the initial risk.
5. Is the technology involved relatively simple?   *The risks are lower.*
6. Are several complex systems integrated in your innovation?   *This will increase the risk.*
7. Do you have a working prototype?   *This decreases the risk and development costs.*

Resources

1. Can you develop and exploit your idea with little or no additional resources?
2. Can you start exploitation with small resources and expand later?
3. Can your idea be implemented quickly (in less than two years)?
4. Are external funds available for development?
5. Can you do the development yourself, preferably with little additional training?
6. Are you able to obtain assistance from people with know-how when needed?
7. Will you be able to cope with short-term ups and downs?
8. Will patent protection for your product outweigh the costs?
9. Will your product be easy to distribute (at low cost)?

COST ESTIMATES

It will be very helpful at this stage to prepare a realistic estimate of the development, manufacturing and marketing costs, especially if you are comparing two or three good but very different "better" concepts. Your final decision on which product to choose for your enterprise will have to weigh these costs against your available resources and the level of risk you can live with. Chapter 9 includes a discussion on how to assess the profit potential of your "best" product emerging at the end of the Phase 2 Pugh evaluation.

NAMING YOUR PRODUCT

The Pugh method evaluations may also give you good ideas for a creative name for your product and possibly a memorable logo for your business. In the early rounds, you can play around with several ideas, and you can come up with interesting, original, and descriptive names for each of the concepts being evaluated. This is your chance to have more fun with creative thinking.

Once you have identified or developed the best concept or product, use the creative problem solving process to brainstorm and develop a unique name for your product. Do not underestimate the importance of the product's name. Sometimes, the name as an asset can be more valuable than the product itself. You will have to verify that the name you have selected is not already owned by someone else and protected by a trademark. Then protect your product's name. Even if you are not planning to manufacture or market your own product, an interesting name may get the attention of a large company to where you will be invited to make a sales presentation.

BUILD A PROTOTYPE

So now you have a best concept or invention. Are you sufficiently motivated to move from idea to product development—to make a prototype of your product? Do you have the passion and discipline, as well as the ability to work with others if necessary for a successful invention (this requires both quadrant B and quadrant C thinking modes)? If your business idea is a service, not a product, your "prototype" may be in the form of a small-scale pilot project, to demonstrate the feasibility of your concept and provide you with valuable customer feedback and operational information. The prototype is the central achievement of the product development phase. After this, our attention will shift to business development (see Fig. 8.2), although the product may undergo further refinement and innovation to enhance its marketability within the context of sustaining a profitable business venture.

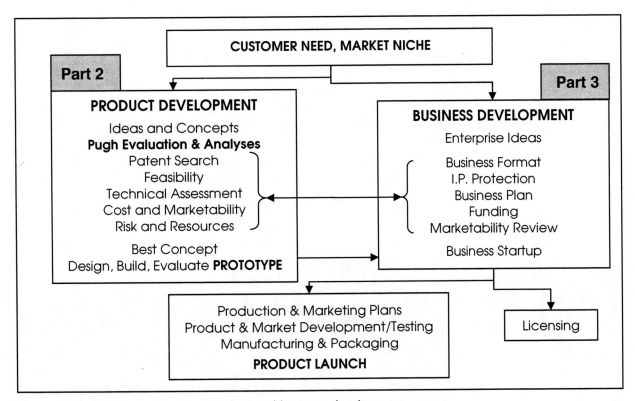

Figure 8.2 Connection between product and business development

THE PURPOSE OF A PROTOTYPE

The prototype made—based on the best solution coming out of a Pugh method evaluation—is strictly for the purpose of confirming the soundness of the concept and to demonstrate it to potential purchasers. It is nearly impossible to find a licensee unless you have a working prototype. The biggest deal killer in business is to have a prototype that is not exactly like your proposed product. Sometimes, prototypes are needed to test a number of options or alternate designs or to prove the robustness of your product. If your product involves new, unproven technology, testing may have to be quite extensive to create confidence in your product and confirm the estimated performance. The stages in prototype development are listed in Table 8.4.

Table 8.4   Stages in Prototype Development

1. Design stage (during the Pugh method evaluation).
2. Procurement stage (obtaining the materials and/or making the parts).
3. Assembly stage.
4. Testing stage.
5. Final industrial design stage (with full engineering drawings and specifications for production). Increasingly, this information may be in digital form to save time to market.
6. Other drawings as needed—artist's concept to sell your product and patent drawings in the specific format required by the Patent Office.

PROTOTYPE TESTING

Typically, all or parts of a technical design require testing to validate the decisions made. If the product will depend on new technology or application of existing technology in new ways, tests may be required to confirm the effectiveness of the technology in the design. Sometimes a test is needed to confirm estimated performance simply because the complex interplay of environmental and operating variables cannot be modeled with a computer. The construction of test models, prototypes and test apparatus can consume inordinate amounts of time and resources. And yet, all too frequently, the tests do not provide the validation needed by the designers because the test was not well planned. Table 8.5 provides guidelines for setting up a test plan.

Table 8.5   Elements of an Effective Test Plan

- Statement of the specific purpose of the tests. Which decisions will the test validate or illuminate? If the test does not bear on a design decision, it most likely will not be needed.
- Specific test objectives. What needs to be measured during the test, and what equipment and specifications are required?
- Outline the step-by-step procedure to be used for conducting the test. If possible, use a standard protocol. What variables need to be monitored or controlled?
- Outline the expected results, preferably in the form of a data sheet—if we do not know roughly what will happen, data collection and analysis are threatened. Also specify if the product is expected to be tested to destruction.

PROTOTYPE EVALUATION

After the tests have been run, prepare a summary of the results and conclusions drawn from the testing, together with the recommendations for design changes and plans to implement the changes (if any). Make sure that no further design changes after this stage are anticipated since changes after start of production are very expensive and can cost you market share.

In addition, confirm that your product meets customer expectations and marketability. Typical questions to obtain customer feedback would be:

- What do you like about the prototype?
- What do you dislike about the prototype?
- Any suggestions for improvement?
- How well do you think the product meets your needs?
- What do you see as the key advantages of this product over other similar products?
- How much would you be willing to spend for this product?

SPECIAL TIPS FOR ENTREPRENEURIAL INVENTORS

If your product is an invention, does it meet most of the criteria for success listed in Table 8.6? These tips for inventors were prepared by the National Endowment for Science, Technology and the Arts (NESTA) in the UK.

Table 8.6   When You Invent—Strategies for Success

- Don't expect anyone to beat a path to your door (if they do, they may intend to rip you off). Good things will happen only if you get out there and make them happen.

- Frequent complaints are that inventors aren't on the same wavelength as the companies. To you, your idea is your baby, precious and unique. To companies it's just another log on the fire. Swallow whatever it is you need to swallow and get on the other party's wavelength.

- Innovation brings rewards but it also brings risks, so ALWAYS control your costs and ALWAYS limit your risk.

- A typical development time scale is 2 to 3 years—often more and rarely less. So plan carefully and never rush into anything.

- Learn continuously, especially about the market and the companies you're aiming for. You'll get lots of conflicting advice along the way, so you need much knowledge to make sound judgments.

- Be as professional as you can in all your dealings. Claiming that because you're more of a creative type it's okay to be disorganized, unreliable and inflexible just won't wash.

- No matter how highly you rate your own abilities you won't be able to do everything on your own, so be prepared to be part of a team that shares the work and the spoils fairly.

- In the interest of self-preservation, regard being an inventor as a short-term job with a limited aim: to develop your idea only to the point where potential licensees, partners, investors or buyers can clearly judge its commercial worth.

- Beyond that point, either back off and leave the licensees to get on with it or—if it's your own business—forget being an inventor and go full tilt for entrepreneurial success.

Here is a final checklist if the invention is to become a reality:

_____ The product should be easy to distribute.

_____ The product's technology must be relatively simple.

_____ The product's features must be unique.

_____ The benefits of the product should be obvious.

_____ The product's selling price should be three to five times the costs it takes to manufacture it.

_____ The product concept must have some type of protection (patent, copyright, trademark, or license).

Team Project Guidelines for Idea Evaluation and Implementation

Creative Idea Evaluation

1. In the engineer's mindset, sort idea notes into categories.
2. Work with one category at a time and try to synthesize more complete concepts.
3. Next, force-fit the initial ideas from all categories to obtain comprehensive solutions.
4. Come up with a least three very different but potentially innovative concepts to take forward for judgment and optimization with the Pugh method.
5. Name (and sketch) each concept.

Evaluation Criteria

1. Brainstorm judgment criteria for the Pugh method. Think about different customer groups, acceptance and marketing.
2. Have one criterion as "high innovative or entrepreneurial potential."
3. In the judge's mindset, narrow the list down to ten or more of the most important criteria.

Pugh Evaluation Matrix

1. Mainly using the engineer's mindset, follow the process for three rounds as illustrated with the kitchen lighting example in the textbook, or if appropriate, use the "fast-track" approach illustrated with the moisture-barrier example.
2. In the criteria, also think about implementation in the producer's mindset. Keep adequate records of the Pugh evaluation process, as this information will be needed for your final project report.
3. If done on the same day, take a brief break before commencing a new round.

Solution Implementation

1. At the end of the project, the teams will be asked to make a 20-minute oral team project presentation on the best concept coming out of the Pugh evaluation.
2. Learning from the product and business development topics (Parts 2 and 3) should be incorporated into the presentation, including the 30-second message technique.
3. Also jot down notes on your entire creative problem solving and teamwork experience so you can later write a summary in an individual learning report (if required).

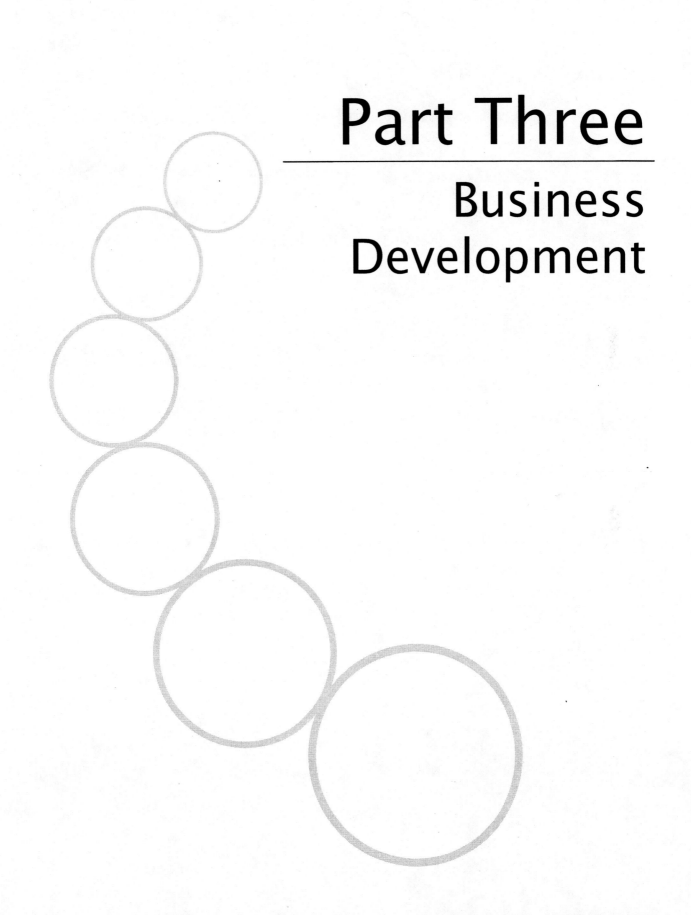

Part Three

Business Development

9 Developing Your Business

> **What you can learn from this chapter:**
> - Review of your motivation for starting a business (in quadrant C):
>   — Do you have the necessary passion and value added?
> - A chance to look at the big picture (with quadrant D thinking):
>   — Does your product make sense?
> - How to assess the profit potential of your product (in quadrant A).
> - Information about possible legal forms for businesses.
> - Details about other business decisions: name, timing, location, and knowing why thorough documentation is important (quadrant B).
> - Thinking about marketing: strategies, marketing plan, and pricing.

Through the Pugh method approach in product development, you will have obtained an in-depth understanding of the merits of your best solution or concept (be it a new product or an innovative service). Now you have to decide what to do with it. First, we recommend that you obtain an unbiased commercial assessment of your idea (as discussed in Chapter 7), if you have not done so already, because from here on, your investment costs will go up substantially. Then you must decide if you want to sell the patent rights, license the product, or start your own business. If you decide to start your own venture, you will need to select the most appropriate business form—individual proprietorship, partnership, LLC, corporation, or franchise.

RIGHT-BRAIN BUSINESS DECISIONS

The purest treasure mortal times can afford is a spotless reputation.

William Shakespeare

Judgment is commonly perceived to be a very critical, analytical, logical, rational activity—in other words, a strictly left-brain approach. However, to make the best business decisions, we must also consider right-brain input—the intuitive modes of quadrant C and quadrant D.

HOW STRONG IS YOUR PERSONAL MOTIVATION?

If the following five factors are present, you will know intuitively that your best idea is "it."

1. You really, really, really care → **PASSION**
2. The idea just won't go away → **OBSESSION**
3. Others care as much as you do → **CONTAGION**
4. Making it happen is fun for you → **FULFILLMENT**
5. The idea is *much* better than other alternatives → **SUPERIORITY**

ARE ALL CUSTOMER NEEDS MET?

You may have a personal stake and pride in your idea or invention, you may be in love with your idea, but you must not think invention—remember to THINK MARKET! Right now, go back to the original problem definition and make sure that all customer needs have been met. Sometimes, novel ideas can get the problem solving process sidetracked away from the original goal—thus it is important to make this final check. And if you have to decide between two or more top-ranked ideas, use the checklist in Table 9.1.

Table 9.1 *Checklist for Final Idea Selection*

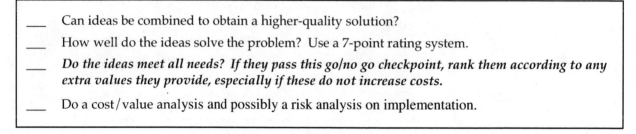

____ Can ideas be combined to obtain a higher-quality solution?

____ How well do the ideas solve the problem? Use a 7-point rating system.

____ *Do the ideas meet all needs? If they pass this go/no go checkpoint, rank them according to any extra values they provide, especially if these do not increase costs.*

____ Do a cost/value analysis and possibly a risk analysis on implementation.

WHAT VALUE CAN YOU ADD?

The concept of value added is very important if you want to have a competitive product or service. Customers often are willing to pay more if substantial added value is provided. The best scenario of course is if this can be included at no extra cost. Value can be tangible or intangible, real or perceived. For example, if your product happens to be at the forefront of a developing trend or fits in with the goal of a particular environmental movement, this could represent an intangible value. Aspects of being in the right place at the right time come into play here—and often this depends on luck. Remember the saying, "Luck comes to those who are prepared."

CAN YOU VERIFY THE INDUSTRY CONTEXT?

Frequently ask the paradigm question posed by Joel Barker (Ref. 1.5):

"What is impossible to do in my field or business today, but if it could be done, would fundamentally change what I do (or what people do)?"

This angle becomes important when you prepare your business plan. You must be up-to-date and well informed about what is going on in the industry that relates to your product. Motorola missed a big opportunity by waiting with the development of the digital phone. When AT&T was looking for a supplier, Nokia, a small company in Finland, was ready and thus quickly gained a large market share. Studying trends in your industry (and society) is not just a creative thinking exercise (though valuable in itself)—it has real economic implications in the timing and success of your planned enterprise.

WHAT CHANGES WILL YOUR PRODUCT CREATE?

We live in a rapidly changing world. Many changes are positive, others negative. Try to anticipate the changes involved that might be associated with your product, so you can emphasize the positives and minimize the negative effects. Be aware that most people are wary of change. If priorities and values must be changed in order to innovate, intense communication will be necessary (more information on coping with change is provided in Chapter 11).

LEFT-BRAIN BUSINESS DECISIONS

If everything so far looks GO, there is one important item to check: Will your product earn enough money so your business will make a profit? The task of assessing the profit potential of your idea or product mainly requires left-brain critical thinking and analytical decision making in the judge's mindset.

ASSESSMENT OF PROFIT POTENTIAL

To make an assessment of profit potential—which will be required for the business plan (Chapter10)—you will need the information and calculations listed in Table 9.2.

Table 9.2   Cost Items Needed for a Profit Potential Assessment

1. Determine the startup costs.
2. Determine the annual costs of running the business.
3. Do not forget to include a realistic value of your own time.
4. Determine the sales price of your product.
5. Determine the monthly sales (from market potential analysis).
6. Determine the monthly profits (for 2-3 years).
7. Calculate the return on your investment (ROI).

By the time you have the prototype (or pilot) of your concept, you will have a good idea of the direct production costs. As you make the business development decisions outlined in this chapter (and go through the start-up checklist in the next chapter), you will be able to ascertain the costs associated with each item, both for starting up and running your business. Your market research, marketing strategies and marketing plan will yield information about the projected scope of your enterprise.

As soon as the figures for these costs are on hand and the appropriate sales price has been decided (the first five items in Table 9.2), it is possible to calculate the stream of profits that will be generated by the planned enterprise. These monthly projections (for two or three years) will be vital when completing the financial sheets of the business plan. They are also central to the final decision of whether to proceed with the enterprise.

When estimating the various costs involved, it is important to ensure that these are as accurate and "complete" as possible. A common fault when calculating startup and operating costs is to omit or undervalue the entrepreneur's own time—often a very high number of hours per day or week. This value must be included to make the correct decision as to whether the enterprise is sensible or not. A simple way to value your input is to calculate what you could earn at an hourly rate if you spent the time working on another project or as an employee.

The market research and comparisons with competing alternatives analyzed during the Pugh Method evaluation will give a good indication of the price that will attract the levels of demand that have been assumed in the calculation of operating costs. Monthly revenues are simply calculated by multiplying this price by the expected level of sales. In many cases there is a considerable time lag—certainly weeks, and sometimes months—between selling (invoicing) and payment. Typical payment terms of key market customers should be ascertained and built into the monthly projection of revenues. This delay or "trade credit" may also be available to the entrepreneur, although it is often the case that new businesses with little or no track record will be required to pay suppliers in advance until their creditworthiness is proven through experience.

The pressure upon the cash flow of a business caused by delayed payment by customers and advance payment to suppliers can vary significantly. Many retailers can often benefit from immediate payment by customers and one month's trade credit from suppliers. These pressures may impact service providers less strongly than manufacturing firms. An example is the publishing business. Printers have to be paid upon delivery of the books. These are then shipped to bookstores which may take many months before selling and then paying for the books. These pressures (and the high costs of carrying large inventories) have led to the development of an innovative business model—known as print-on-demand publishing. Here, after the initial prepaid setup in digital format, books are printed from paid orders. It takes at mind-boggling speed of 90 seconds to produce a paperback—which includes doing a cover in color, binding, and cutting to size. The point is—do not forget to account for the cost of credit or prepayments in your calculations.

The decision to proceed can be viewed as a decision to invest in the enterprise. When making an investment, one of the main aims is to maximize the returns that will be generated. In short, the decision to proceed makes sense only if there are no alternative investment possibilities that would provide a higher return for the same level of commitment. At its simplest, this could be the earnings possible, if the funds were deposited in an interest-bearing bank account.

Once you have estimated the monthly profits (revenues minus costs) for the first two or three years, you can compare this profit stream with the investment income if the start-up investment earned interest in a savings account. This straightforward calculation refers to the net present value (NPV) of future profits generated by the business (also known as discounting).

A formula for this calculation is given in Table 9.3 (with an alternate step-by-step format given in Table 9.4 for the less mathematically minded). Since it is not unusual for an innovative company to run at a loss for a number of years before the idea "takes off," it may be necessary to run your profit projections beyond the near term. Also, during the start-up years, entrepreneurs cannot always expect to be paid a salary equivalent to what they might be paid as an employee in a comparable position elsewhere. Entrepreneurs are advised to keep their current jobs until their projections show the new enterprise can support them at least at a level of sixty percent of previous salary before they resign and work full time in their new business. This is a difficult call to make because of the risks and intangible benefits involved.

In the course of such complex operations, there is an abundance of obstacles to be surmounted, anxieties to be repressed, misfortunes to be repaired and expedients to be devised.

Jean Baptiste Say

Table 9.3 *Formula for Calculating the Future Value of Money*

A simple formula can be used to calculate the future value of money.

$$\$_{Future} = \$_{Present} (1 + i)^n$$

where n is the number of yeas and i is the interest rate.

For example $100 for two years at an interest rate of 10% is

$$\$_{Future} = 100 (1 + 0.1) (1 + 0.1) = \$121.$$

For discounting, you simply find the present value of future money, or

$$\$_{Present} = \$_{Future} / (1 + i)^n$$

Thus, $121 two years hence at 10% would have a present value of

$$\$_{Present} = 121 / [(1 + 0.1) (1 + 0.1)] = \$100$$

Table 9.4 *Calculation of Net Present Value*

Most people understand the process of discounting much more easily when it operates in the opposite direction. If asked the value of $100 in a year's time at 10% interest, most will crack straight back with the correct answer of $110. If you left it gaining interest for an additional year, it would grow to $121 ($110 + 10% of $110). Discounting is simply the same process in reverse. $110 in one year's time with an interest rate at 10% has a present value of $100. $121 in two year's time with a prevailing interest rate of 10% also has a present value of $100.

To calculate the present value of the profit stream expected from your business over future years, simply follow these steps:

The present value of the profits (or losses) made after one year is arrived at by dividing these by the rate of interest. For example, if the rate were 10%, you would divide by 1.1, if 5% by 1.05, if 20% by 1.2. In the example above, this would mean dividing $110 by 1.1, giving a present value of $100.

To find the present value of the second year's profits (or losses) simply divide in the same way, but apply the interest twice. If the interest rate were 10%, this would be 1.1 x 1.1 = 1.21, if it were 5%, it would be 1.05 x 1.05 = 1.1025, and if the interest rate is 20%, then this would be 1.2 x 1.2 = 1.44.

In the case of the third year, use exactly the same calculation but simply multiply the interest rate three times rather that twice to arrive at the figure by which you divide the profit (loss). Continue this process of multiplying for each additional year the interest rate for that year until you reach the end of your projected profit stream.

Finally, sum the numbers calculated for each year and subtract from this the start-up costs of the business.

If the resulting figure, the Net Present Value, is higher than your start-up costs, your business expects to generate a higher return than would result from investing the start-up costs in a savings account at a prevailing rate of interest. If it is lower, then proceed no further!!

The Say quote on the opposite page (from 200 years ago but still valid) emphasizes the importance of allowing for the unexpected in your calculations. Sales may not go as expected, and payment delays may be longer than your market research indicated. Similarly, certain costs may be higher than anticipated, or suppliers may let you down in terms of quality or promptness of delivery or both. It is sensible therefore to recalculate the net present value with more pessimistic assumptions about revenues and costs in order to ascertain how sensitive the business fortunes are to changing market conditions. To cheer yourself up, you might also wish to recalculate on the basis of more optimistic assumptions, so long as you treat these as "hoped for" rather than actual. They may turn out to be realistic, but don't bank on it!

You may be surprised to observe how much higher than the cost of production the price of your product or service has to be to ensure an acceptable return on your investment. As mentioned in Chapter 8, a rule of thumb for a manufactured product's selling price states that the price will need to be three to five times the production costs in order to realize a sufficient level of profit to justify the investment. In the case of services and retail trade, this ratio may be lower but should still be more than 2:1. The reason for this will be clear if you have properly calculated the full costs of taking your concept to market. In addition to the hidden labor costs that you and others may contribute, many other large commitments are involved with marketing and making the target consumers aware of your product or service and the related benefits. And even if you start out in modest quarters, you must not neglect overhead costs: rent, utilities, office supplies and equipment, telephone, computer services, and so on.

Authentic marketing is not the art of selling what you make but knowing what to make.

It is the art of identifying and understanding customer needs and creating solutions that deliver satisfaction to the customers, profits to the producers and benefits to the stakeholders.

Philip Kotler, U.S. marketing guru

TIPS: If the return from your business is only slightly higher than prevailing interest rates, you should explore the financial press to determine whether there is a consensus as to the future direction that interest rates might take. If they rise significantly, your investment could cost you dearly!

If you found the calculations of cost and profit potential difficult, we recommend that you either take a course in business accounting or at the least acquire a trustworthy partner with accounting skills.

Based on the results of the commercial evaluation and information given in Chapter 7 on the patenting process, make the decision about obtaining a patent for your invention or product. Unless you have the time and ability to conduct the final, exhaustive patent search yourself, hire a competent patent attorney and initiate the patenting process. In most cases, a product that is not protected with a patent has little commercial value, either for licensing or giving your business a longer-term market advantage. Then don't forget to add this cost to the calculation of your profit potential assessment.

FINAL DECISION ON DIRECTION

Now comes decision time. Let us assume you are convinced that anyone can be a potential entrepreneur by using appropriate thinking modes and tools, either alone or with a team. Also, you have completed the process of product and business development and have determined that you have a viable product, a good market niche, and acceptable profit potential. Now, before you decide what to do with your product, you need to answer one remaining question: Do you *want* to be an entrepreneur? So here, in Table 9.5, is the final decision matrix on the more intangible, personal factors.

Table 9.5 *Final Startup Decision-Making Walk-Around*   © 2006 The Ned Herrmann Group

A	D
How good are you at making decisions? *Your skills are enhanced by understanding the HBDI model and using the Pugh evaluation process as a decision making tool.*	**Are you willing to take calculated risks?** *You had a chance to learn quadrant D thinking skills from this book, and you can minimize risk by using all four quadrants in decision making.*
How well do you plan and organize? Are you a self starter? *If you have come to recognize that these are your weak points, you can get a partner with these skills or hire help.* **B**	**How well do you get along with people?** *Also, do you have the physical and emotional stamina to run a business? Are your motivation and drive strong enough to get you through rough spots? How will your business affect your family?* **C**

Of these, "How well do you get along with people?" is the key consideration. To run a successful business, you will have to deal with all kinds of people, from customers to suppliers, from employees to partners, from bankers to lawyers, and so on. If you find it hard to frequently interact with people, seriously consider a partner having these skills. Steve Jobs of Apple Computers is reputed to have trouble getting along with people. His company is a leader in technological innovation—but as we shall see in Chapter 12, it has had difficulties in the business portion of the enterprise which could in part be attributed to its founder's personality.

Now you are ready to decide what to do with your patented product. You can sell the patent outright or license someone to manufacture and market the product—in essence taking the easy way out—or you can go into business yourself.

LICENSING

History shows that many inventions and patents were sold to companies for relatively small fees, with the companies later making huge profits from a successful product. Today, the trend is more toward licensing products that have a good market potential and fit in with a company's business.

The advantages of licensing are that you keep ownership of your product, yet you have low overhead, no need to hire employees, few administrative responsibilities, no cash flow worries, and no buying, selling, and bill collecting. Your licensor will market your product, keep inventory, and take care of distribution. Depending on the product, the licensor may also be involved in manufacturing or assembly (or farm these tasks out). Since the licensor will have existing infrastructure, there is a substantial time saving in getting the product out.

The main disadvantage of licensing is loss of control of your product. You will be tied to the fortunes of the licensor, and the deal may not bring in large revenues. Charles Stanley, Vice President at Motorola, lists key items you need to watch if you want to sell an invention to a large company (see Table 9.6).

Table 9.6   Selling Your Idea or Invention to a Large Company

1. Your intellectual property must be protected. Companies are leery of accusations of cheating, especially if the company is working on a similar idea.
2. Don't consider companies as venture capitalists.
3. Your idea must be closely related to the company's core business.
4. Do your homework! Be sure your idea is not obsolete, wrong or economically nonviable.
5. Be realistic in your royalty expectations.
6. Have an "elevator" speech ready (see Chapter 10).
7. Use the web and go to conferences on topics related to your idea to discover company champions.

Before contacting a company, make sure your product is ready for the marketplace. Have a working prototype! Contact a person with a title such as New Product Development Manager, Director of Marketing, or Director of R&D. Establish your credibility and be businesslike, not an image of a far-out "wild-and-crazy" inventor. The good news is that most large companies buy more ideas and technology from outside than they develop internally.

DECISION TO HAVE YOUR OWN BUSINESS

If you decide you want to run your own business, you have several options for the legal form your business can take.

1. You can buy an existing business—either one that is thriving or one that is in bankruptcy. Depending on your business idea, this may be an ideal fit, and you may acquire the infrastructure, a good location, and a customer list, saving you much time and trouble. The key is to make sure that you have a good fit.
2. You can buy a franchise, as discussed later in this section.
3. You can buy someone else's business idea, patent or invention through a patent broker or from InventNet or a not-for-profit R&D institution or university, perhaps as part of further developing your concepts, but then you will still need to decide on the legal form of your business.

Sell yourself.

Sell your invention.

SELL THE BUSINESS OPPORTUNITY!

LEGAL FORMS OF BUSINESSES

If you must have complete control and be the person solely responsible, the sole proprietorship is for you. But make sure your own qualifications and competencies are sufficient to start and run your own business.

Or could you profit by including others with complementary skills? If you decide that you need partners, good judgment will be required to set up the best ownership structure, controls and incentives. These need to be established at the outset and will have a strong influence on the future success of the business. If you need expert help in running your business (including financing) and if you have already worked with a co-inventor or co-developer team (or a close friend or family member), then a partnership might be the ideal setup. A strong team can make the difference between success and a marginal or failed venture or between a so-so and a great company. Setting your business up as a corporation is another option. Corporations have distinct characteristics:

- A corporation is a legal entity ("person") chartered by government—(states in the U.S.)—separate from the owners (shareholders). Its purpose is described in its Articles of Incorporation.
- The corporation can sue, be sued, buy and sell property, produce products and services, commit crimes and receive punishments imposed by courts, and it pays taxes.
- The shareholders elect a Board of Directors who appoint the officers of the corporation (President, Vice President, Treasurer and Secretary as a minimum) to run the day-to-day affairs of the firm.
- The Board must meet at least annually and keep minutes of the meeting. There is also a substantial reporting requirement to the shareholders and various levels of government.

In the U.S., the Subchapter-S corporate structure with a small group of shareholders closely holding their shares and substantially participating in running the business may be an alternative with attractive tax advantages. We recommend that you research your options carefully and consult an attorney to set up the legal structure of your business. Make sure you obtain all necessary local and State licenses and registrations. Table 9.7 compares the advantages and disadvantages of the different legal forms.

Table 9.7 *Legal Forms for Businesses: Advantages and Disadvantages*

Sole Proprietorship	
Advantages - Easy to start, understand, and dissolve. - Generally owned and operated by one person. - The proprietor is in complete control of the business. - In the U.S., revenue and operating expenses are treated as part of the owner's personal finances for tax purposes. - Losses (common during startup years) can offset income the proprietor has from other sources and thus will lower taxes.	**Disadvantages** - The proprietor is liable for all of the business debts—a lawsuit by an injured customer or employee can claim many of the proprietor's personal possessions, including the family's home.
Partnership	
Advantages - Two or more partners combine their funds and talents to start and run the business. - It is like a sole proprietorship in terms of taxes.	**Disadvantages** - More complicated than a sole proprietorship. It is crucial to start with a written agreement to specify what happens when one of the partners leaves (through death, divorce, disagreement, etc.). Otherwise, the business may collapse. - It is like a sole proprietorship in having unlimited liability for business debts and lawsuits.

Corporation	
Advantages	**Disadvantages**
<ul><li>Ability to attract the resources of a large number of investors.</li><li>Shareholders have limited liability—they can only lose their investment in the corporation.</li><li>The investment is liquid—shares can be sold.</li></ul>	<ul><li>Complicated to set up, operate, and dissolve.</li><li>Because the shareholders are the owners, it is possible for the founder to lose control.</li><li>Double taxation: the corporation pays taxes on profits as well as dividends to shareholders (who in turn pay tax on the dividends).</li></ul>

Sub-S Corporation	
Advantages	**Disadvantages**
<ul><li>Limited liability for shareholders.</li><li>No problem with double taxation; profits are reported on Schedule K-1 and taxed as personal income.</li></ul>	<ul><li>It is important for the owners to keep personal and corporate assets separate and to always identify the corporation with its full name (including "Inc.") in all its contracts.</li></ul>

Franchise	
Advantages	**Disadvantages**
<ul><li>Significantly better success rate than a new business (more than 90% survive after five years, compared to one-third of independent businesses).</li><li>Reduced risk and less operating capital.</li><li>Marketing plan and promotional materials in place.</li><li>Quality control standards established.</li><li>Available technical and management assistance (including training).</li><li>Opportunity to gain experience in running a business.</li><li>Opportunities for growth through the right to sub-franchise.</li></ul>	<ul><li>Service cost.</li><li>Restrictions on freedom of ownership.</li><li>Limited expansion.</li><li>Termination of agreement.</li><li>Low performance of other franchisees can influence your business.</li><li>You will be selling someone else's product, not your own invention.</li></ul>

Limited Liability Company (LLC)
Advantages
In the U.S., an LLC combines the best aspects of partnerships (pass-through tax structure) and corporations (limited personal liability of members). The number of owners (called members) can range from one to unlimited. It is low-cost and simple to set up by filing the "articles of organization" with an appropriate state office. It is recommended that the members have a written operating agreement.

FRANCHISING

This provides easy access to an established product, thus reducing the many risks of a new business. However, franchising requires all the self-analysis of starting a small business. Best obtain legal help when you get to the step of examining the franchiser's contract, since franchisor and franchisee enter into a long-term interdependent strategic relationship for mutual benefit.

Three factors are especially important for building and maintaining a good relationship with customers:

✓ A brand recognized widely to attract initial customers.

✓ A tried operating or delivery system to keep customers.

✓ Ongoing support and training for expanding the business.

Franchisees receive help in building relationships with key resource people, such as suppliers, lenders, real estate developers and advertisers for startup and operation.

When checking out a potential franchisor, consider the following list of items. If you are thinking of starting an independent business, these are things your competition will be doing (and you might have to do better):

____ Proven location or chains of stores?

____ Strong management team as well as field support staff?

____ Sufficient capital to sustain the franchising program?

____ Distinctive and protected brand or trade identity?

____ Proven method of operation not easily duplicated by competitors?

____ Comprehensive training programs (initial and on-going)?

____ Strategic plan and legal assistance?

____ Demonstrated market demand for products or services?

____ Site selection and architectural standards?

____ Understanding of competition (and trends)?

____ Franchisee standards and screening system?

____ Effective reporting and record-keeping requirements?

____ Research and development activities for introducing new products?

____ Effective communication system?

____ National, regional, and local advertising, marketing, PR programs?

Simple Example: Taxi Driver as a Franchise

A major city in Canada has only one taxi company. A franchisee is assigned a taxi for which he or she is required to pay a fixed amount per month. The franchiser provides maintenance of the taxi, dispatcher services, and company name, the franchisee the gasoline and oil. Minimum contract agreement is for one year. In the agreement, franchisees are not allowed to start a competing company for at least one year after the termination of the franchise contract. Because of the increase in business, two new taxi companies are now starting to compete with the existing monopoly. This begins to seriously cut into the business of the existing taxi company. Some drivers signed the original contract with the knowledge that business would increase because of increasing population and industrial growth. Now they see decline rather than increase in their revenue and opportunities.

Moral of this example: Look carefully before you leap into a franchise!

NAME YOUR BUSINESS

To establish the legal form of your business, you must have a name. You can employ creative problem solving to develop a name and logo (and perhaps a slogan) for your business. A slogan example (for an insurance firm) is "You're in good hands with ALLSTATE." The goal is to have a name and slogan that are easy to remember while also giving a picture of what you are all about. Again, do your research to verify that the name and logo are not protected by other firms or enterprises. Then protect your name, logo and slogan with a trademark.

DECISION-MAKING DOCUMENTATION

Why is it important to keep good records of your entire problem-solving and decision making process? The rationales for making decisions are frequently omitted from many project reports and design documents. If you have done a good job in making decisions and have selected the best alternative after a thorough analysis of all the options against the objectives (or Pugh method criteria), the rationale is simply a summary of the results of this process. Omitting this information might invite needless questioning about the decision later and perhaps repetition of the selection evaluation process.

Cases of "re-inventing the wheel" can sometimes be traced to a lack of information on why a particular choice was made upstream in the process. When competing alternatives are closely matched, there may be a tendency to omit rationales for decisions to avoid undermining confidence in the decision. This would be a mistake, since the recipient of the design would lose valuable information that may allow or dissuade a design change later on. More often than not, the designer or inventor may gain confidence and favor by bending over backward to describe the competing alternatives at least as well as the one selected. All designs and inventions must be sold to someone; most must be sold many times. It is simply not enough to present a drawing or a prototype. A concise and easy to follow summary of the evolution of the product which includes the rationale for all decisions is essential.

Also, having a good record of your invention's development (in the prescribed format) is crucial to substantiate your claim as the original inventor. In addition, a complete case file on the development of your product, including all information on the context, will be invaluable when you compile your business plan (in Chapter 10).

And last but not least, a complete documentation of your business startup (including both the successes as well as those things that did not work out as predicted) will become a valuable database for continuing improvement or for starting another enterprise.

Any communication or marketing professional needs cross-cultural research and communication skills to be able to succeed in the future.

Marye Tharp,
Chair, Marketing and Communications,
Emerson University

WHERE SHOULD YOU LOCATE?

Location is critical both in terms of the market being targeted and the costs that will confront the business. Choice of location may be one of the first tests of the entrepreneur's quality of judgment and decision making. Take the time and effort necessary to select the location of your business. Who are your potential customers and where are they located? Who will be your suppliers and where are they located? If you are dealing with perishable raw materials, this is not a trivial consideration. Who are your competitors and where are they located? Will you be able to find qualified employees when you are ready to expand? For example, one automotive design supplier chose a location 500 miles from Detroit (the home of the "big three" automakers) because of the extremely tough competition for skilled designers there. The new location, which has a technical university nearby, is a ready source of skilled designers at reasonable cost.

If you do not want to or cannot change your location, you can use creative thinking to identify a market niche or consumer need in your present location. Many startups begin in the entrepreneur's home or garage. In the U.S., the SBA estimates that as many as twenty percent of new small businesses are operated from the owner's premises (home or garage). With many new computer-based businesses, this number is growing. Contact the local Chamber of Commerce for information about locating your business in a particular location or about the availability of incubator facilities—with special support services available for startup businesses.

WHEN SHOULD YOU START YOUR BUSINESS?

Market conditions are often volatile both in terms of demand for products or services and in terms of the technological changes that are occurring. The timing of the launch may be critical in sustaining the business through the early and often most vulnerable stage of its development. Rushing to bring a product to market before its technical bugs have been worked out or producing a 2006 product for the 2007 or 2008 market are equally detrimental for the success of your enterprise.

If you have done a thorough job in going through the effective problem solving steps, completed your business plan and worked out your cash flow for one to three years, you will almost be ready to launch your business. You may want to do a last check with a trusted friend or expert who has had experience with launching a business. Also keep your eyes wide-open to economic conditions and trends, as well as unexpected surprises. Learn as much as you can, based on current information—then make your decision.

DEVELOPING A MARKETING PLAN

The key to your enterprise's success is of course being able to sell your product. You can profitably use the creative problem solving process to develop your marketing approach. If you are marketing an innovative product or invention that has no previous track record for marketing and sales, you may want to conduct some marketing tests using prototypes or trial runs of your final product. As you have seen with the example of the Post-it notes in Chapter 4, you may have to come up with an innovative marketing approach if traditional market tests fail but you are still convinced that you have a great product. Also, if you have an innovative product, you may need to have an innovative business model—to produce and market it effectively. This is another opportunity to apply the creative problem solving process.

The problem with covering the marketing topic in this book is the sheer size, complexity, and the huge amount of information available. At the end of the chapter, three basic books are listed as recommended references. When

If you do build a great experience, customers tell each other about that. Word of mouth is very powerful.

Jeff Bezos

MISSION OF MARKETING

Create and occupy a unique space inside the mind of the target customer!

"marketing" is entered in a Google search, almost a million items pop up. So the question is—where are good places to start? The two websites in Table 9.8 are excellent starting points.

Table 9.8 *Comprehensive Websites for Marketing Information*

U.S. Small Business Administration: www.sba.gov/starting/indexbusplans.html

Guidelines for developing a marketing plan are available as part of their materials on business planning. There are many links to subtopics such as "Market Research" and Marketing Strategies for the Growing Business."

Leading resource and reference site on marketing: www.KnowThis.com

The chief goal is to offer a web resource for providing unbiased, objective information as the marketing specialty area within the World Wide Web Virtual Library. They have tutorials, such as "Principles of Marketing," "How to Write a Marketing Plan," "Finding Information for Marketing Research," and How to Do a Market Study." It is interesting to note that this company is an example of a limited liability company (LLC).

MARKETING BASICS

To succeed, entrepreneurs must attract and retain a growing base of satisfied customers. As business owners, they should carefully plan their marketing strategies and evaluate performance to keep their market presence strong. Two key principles are:

1. All business activities should be directed toward satisfying customer needs (determined through market research).
2. Profitable sales volume is more important than maximum sales volume (returns are maximized through target marketing).

Marketing involves several key components, as listed in Table 9.9 (based on information in Ref. 9.1). The thorough understanding about your idea that you have gained from several rounds of the Pugh method and associated analyses on the way to developing a best concept will be crucial as you develop your marketing plan.

Table 9.9 *Key Elements of Marketing*

---

1. Market research—for understanding your customers, competition, and trends.
2. Advertising—to get your message to potential customers.
3. Sales—the outcome of marketing, with a satisfied customer and a fair price for your product.
4. Public relations—telling the story of your successful enterprise to create a favorable image.
5. Strategies—database marketing (from a purchased database) or direct marketing.
6. Product promotion—here you can be especially creative to quickly (and memorably) get your product into the marketplace.
7. Pricing—a crucial, though often neglected part of marketing; make sure you focus on value, not on lowest price to be competitive.
8. Distribution—how will you get your product to the customer? You may want to use more than one approach to meet your customer's needs.

Whether your business will be based on offering a product or a service, you may have realized by now that it will likely involve both to some degree. If you will sell a product, its competitiveness will surely be tied to the service that you intend to provide; if you offer a service, its satisfactory execution will often depend on the products or tools you will use or furnish as part of your service, so think about both aspects as you develop your strategy.

MARKETING RESEARCH

Initial market research and analysis should already have been done during product development. An inexpensive research program, based on questionnaires given to prospective (or current) customers, can often uncover dissatisfaction or possible ideas for new products or services. Marketing research will identify trends that affect sales and profitability. Population shifts, developments, and the local economic situation should constantly be monitored to quickly identify problems and new opportunities. Also keep up with your competitors' market strategies through a competitive analysis.

Great devices are created by engineers.

Great products are created by marketing.

Peter Drucker

MARKETING STRATEGY AND MARKETING PLAN

A good strategy helps a business focus on target markets—unmet customer needs that offer adequate potential profitability. It tailors product offerings, prices, distribution, services and promotional effort toward those markets.

The marketing plan will become an important component of the overall business plan (described in Chapter 10). Thus it is worth your time to very carefully compile the required detailed information and do the research about the customers and market niche you are targeting. You will also need to thoroughly analyze your competition. Typical questions to be investigated are given in Table 9.10 for the market analysis and in Table 9.11 for product and service analysis. Table 9.12 contains sample questions for marketing strategies. The source of the information in all three tables is SBA, the U.S. Small Business Administration.

Table 9.10 Examples of Questions Related to Market Analysis

- Who are your customers—private sector, wholesalers, retailers, government, other? What is the percent distribution for each?
- What is the target industry? What is the target geographic area?
- What product lines and sales will you target?
- How much will the selected market spend on your type of product this year?
- Who are your competitors? List each main competitor by name, how long in business, the market share, the price and strategy, and the distinct product and service features.
- List your strengths and weaknesses compared to your competitors (consider location, size of resources, reputation, services, as well as personnel).
- Look at the listed economic factors and consider how they will affect your product or service: country growth, industry health, economic trends, taxes, rising energy prices.
- What legal and government factors could affect your market? What are other environmental factors that could affect you, but over which you have no control?

Table 9.11 *Product and Service Analysis Questions*

1. Describe your product and what it does.
2. What advantages does your product or service have over those of your competition (consider unique features, patents, expertise, special training, etc.)?
3. What disadvantages does it have?
4. Where and how will you get your materials and supplies?
5. Where and how will you get qualified employees?

Table 9.12 *Examples of Questions Related to Marketing Strategies*

- What kind of image do you want to have (such as cheap but good, or customer-oriented, or exclusiveness, or higher quality, or convenience, or speed, or extra value, or innovative, or…)?
- What features will you emphasize?
- What is your pricing strategy (markup on cost; suggested price; competitive; below competition; premium price; other)? Are your prices in line with your image? Do your prices cover costs (sales, warranty, training, product development) and a margin of profit?
- What customer services will you provide? What are terms for sales/credit? What services does the competition offer?
- What things do you wish to say about your business (write a 40-word paragraph)?
- What promotional sources will you use (television, radio, direct mail, personal contacts, trade associations, newspapers, magazines, yellow pages, billboard, website, product demos or giveaway, other)? Why do you think the media you have chosen are the most effective? Will you use an innovative approach?

TARGET MARKETING

Owners of small businesses usually have limited resources to spend on marketing. Concentrating efforts on one or a few key market segments (target marketing) gets the most return from small investments.

1. **Geographical segmentation:** specialize in serving the needs of customers in a particular location (local, regional, national, or global).
2. **Customer segmentation:** identify those people most likely to buy your product; then target those groups.

INITIAL MARKETS

New firms generally start with a small market and, if successful, grow into larger and more varied markets. The initial market is often a niche market not adequately served by larger firms. Entrepreneurs should make sure that the chosen target market can be entered with confidence. Existing seller may have erected protective barriers against competition. Also, customers in high-tech markets are not a homogeneous group, as shown in Table 9.13 (from Ref. 9.2), and each segment requires a different marketing approach.

Various ways for obtaining information about customers are listed in Table 9.14. You should rely on more than one way and on multiple sources to get useful and reliable data.

Table 9.13 *Understanding Customers in a High-Tech Market*

Innovators must have the latest in technology. Though they are few in numbers, their acceptance encourages other buyers.

Early adopters buy because they need the perceived benefits.

The early majority represents perhaps 1/3 of the entire market, and they buy because they need the "proven" benefits. They will put up with having to learn the new technology.

The late majority represents another 1/3 of the market—they are not comfortable with technology, and it has to be "dumbed" down to their level. The product is now an industry standard, with much support available to help them learn how to use it.

Laggards resist new technology. They only buy when it is integrated in something else they need and when it requires no change in behavior or new learning on their part.

Table 9.14 *Collecting Information about Customers*

Personal contacts: Attend trade shows—talk to people. Become a customer of a firm in an industry you plan to enter.

Published information: Trade associations/journals, small business development centers, community economic units, chambers of commerce, as well as state and federal government publications have much data, and powerful web search engines can help find what you need.

Various types of surveys you design: This may include focus groups. Make sure you have a representative sample to get unbiased information.

Survey experts: If your product/prototype involves a new technology that requires people to change, the potential customers may not be able to tell you how they would behave—this may require a sophisticated survey structure (from survey experts) to get reliable results.

BRANDING, PACKAGING AND POSITIONING

Once you have selected a market, you can position your product—having the right product at the right time in the right place, packaged and priced right. For example, high-quality luxury items should not be sold in discount stores. And "first to market" conveys being most technologically advanced, with customers willing to pay a premium price.

Branding, packaging and labeling follow from positioning:

- Will you use your company's name or create a separate brand for your product or product lines?
- How does the customer use and store the product? Is the package easy to open, yet tamper-proof? Does it protect the product during shipping and storage? How can you add value to this important sales tool?
- Does the label match the product image? Does it give adequate information and instructions?

KEY COMPONENTS OF A MARKETING PROGRAM

Products and Services — Concentrate on a narrow product line; develop a highly specialized product or service; provide a product-service package with unusual, high-quality service.

Promotion — Good (attentive) salesmanship is essential for small businesses on limited advertising budgets. Good telephone book advertising is important. Direct mail is an effective, low-cost medium.

Price — The right price is crucial to maximize total revenue. Personalized service can often command higher prices.

Distribution — Working through established distributors is easiest for small manufacturers. Small retailers should consider cost and traffic flow in site selection. A low-cost, low-traffic location means spending more on advertising to build traffic. For impulse buyers, visibility is important. Targeted mailing lists now allow businesses to operate from any location to serve national or international markets.

PRICING

Break-even analysis in pricing is an algebraic model to determine the quantity of a product that needs to be sold in order to recover all fixed and variable costs. Variable costs per unit are: production labor and material, shipping, and so on. Fixed costs are items such as rent, facilities, administrative salaries and office equipment. As shown in Figure 9.1, the break-even point is when revenue begins to exceed total cost.

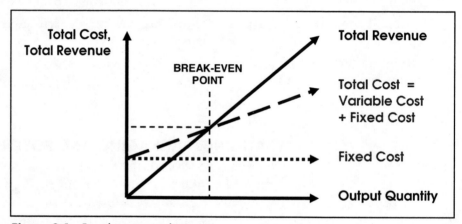

Figure 9.1   Break-even analysis

Other pricing policies that need to be considered are:

- **Product differentiation:** Estimate the likely share of the existing market with your product's unique features; then do break-even analysis.

- **Inelastic demand:** An increase in price does not lead to proportional drop in demand.

- **Intensity of competition:** This may dictate an upper limit on price, even if you have a superior product.

- **Business model:** With a long-term strategy of capturing a large market share, you want to charge a low price for a while to eliminate competitors. When the public cannot assess quality directly, it uses price as an indicator of quality—thus price yourself above the leading competitor. But if your product falls short of expectations, this strategy may backfire.

Also, keep pricing strategy in mind when making your branding and packaging decisions. When selling business-to-business, some products are sold to the end-user (consumer) at double of what you originally charged because of distributor and retailer markup, freight, taxes, promotion, storage, commissions, currency fluctuations and other fees.

PROMOTION

What promotional methods are you planning to use? What are your objectives? Do you want to communicate your message, create awareness of your product or service, motivate customers to buy, focus on increasing sales and market share? Objectives make it easier to design an effective campaign, choose the best method, and keep you on the right track. Also, what is your budget—what percentage of profits can you allocate to marketing? How will you measure results of your marketing campaign? Table 9.2 shows different approaches that can meet different objectives.

CONTACTS ➡ **PROSPECTS**

Build Awareness	Generate Interest	Educate Audience	Support Evaluation	Expedite Purchase
• *Advertising (paper, TV, radio, journals, flyers, etc.)* • *PR* • *Website*	• *Direct marketing (display, give-away)* • *Trade shows* • *Seminars* • *Website* • *PR* • *Customer profiles* • *Movie/video*	• *Brochures* • *Product briefs* • *Customer profiles* • *White papers* • *Websites* • *PR* • *Seminars*	• *Sales presentations* • *Concepts and facilities* • *Evaluation checklists* • *Product demos & trials* • *Websites*	• *RFP boilerplates* • *Trials and follow-up* • *Websites* • *Phone* • *Offer of customized products and service*

Figure 9.2   Approaches for different objectives when promoting a product

PLAN FOR PERFORMANCE EVALUATION

Plan to evaluate the performance of your marketing program after implementation. Set up performance standards so you can compare with quarterly performance. Research the norms in your industry as well as past performance to help set appropriate goals. You can use financial data (such as sales and return on investment (ROI), but don't neglect to get direct feedback from customers through interviews. Key audit questions to ask are:

- Is the company doing all it can to be customer-oriented?
- Do employees (and your web page) ensure that customers are satisfied and leave wanting to come back?
- Is it easy for your customers to find what they want at a competitive price, with timely delivery and superior quality?

An evaluation is meaningless if you do not plan to use what you learned to improve your product, service, and marketing approach.

It is easier to keep a customer than to attract new customers.

Don't ignore the effect of "word of mouth"—for good or bad.

CLOSING THOUGHTS ON MARKETING

All elements of your business must impress and satisfy the customer:

- Ads or promotional information.
- Ordering and payment process.
- Delivery, unpacking (and storage).
- Use (including access to technical support and easy to read manuals and accurate instructions—where the pictures match the actual product).
- Handling of complaints.

Final Marketing Tips

1. Customer expectations change. Be alert for quick response!
2. Learn from your competitors. Do not underestimate them!
3. Do not overestimate your product (or service). Be realistic!
4. Your employees project your company's image. Train them!
5. The customer is always right, at least almost always!

EXERCISES

9.1 Marketing: The Harry Potter Story

Research the influence of marketing behind the success of the Harry Potter books by British author J.K. Rowling.

9.2 Marketing Comparison

Compare the marketing approaches of Apple and Microsoft—in what way are they the same—in what way are they different?

REFERENCES AND RESOURCES

9.1 Jack Ferreri, *Successful Sales and Marketing: Smart Ways to Boost Your Bottom Line, Guide #1809*, Book 4 of Entrepreneur Magazine's Business Management Series, Entrepreneur Media, Inc., Irvine, California, 1999. For more information, see www.smallbizbooks.com.

9.2 G.A. Moore, *Crossing the Chasm: Marketing and Selling High-Tech Products to Mainstream Customers*, HarperCollins, New York, 1991.

Recommended marketing textbooks for in-depth learning

9.3 Philip Kotler and Kevin Land Keller, *Marketing Management: Analysis, Planning, Implementation, and Control,* twelfth edition, Prentice Hall, 2006.

9.4 J. Paul Peter and James H. Donnelly, Jr., *A Preface to Marketing Management,* tenth edition, McGraw-Hill, 2005.

9.5 Subhash C. Jain, *Marketing Planning & Strategy,* seventh edition, South-Western Publishing, 2004.

10   Starting Your Enterprise

What you can learn from this chapter:
- How to prepare a 30-second message for "selling" your idea (either to license or to get funding).
- How to give a formal team presentation.
- How to write a business plan—a requirement if you want to attract outside financing.
- Where to look for potential startup funding.
- Final preparations checklist for startup.
- Review of twenty ways to increase your chances for success.

In this chapter, we want to show you how to use the producer's mindset to do the tasks needed for actually starting a new business. Launching an enterprise (or implementing a solution) is in itself a new problem, which requires a new round of creative problem solving or whole-brain thinking, with emphasis on the producer's mindset. If you have decided that you want to license your idea, you need to "sell" the idea to an appropriate company—thus tips for making an effective 30-second sales presentation are given. If you have decided that you want to build a business on your idea, you need to know how to write a business plan. To obtain startup funds, the business plan and knowing how to "sell" your idea will both be very useful. Finally, we will review how to avoid common mistakes in launching your business.

IDEA "SELLING"—THE 30-SECOND MESSAGE

When contacting a company to sell your invention, you need to have four items ready: (1) be prepared to highlight the business opportunity, (2) have a working prototype, (3) have patent protection, and (4) give a short but effective opening presentation—a so-called "elevator speech."

WHY ONLY 30 SECONDS?

Milo O. Frank, a business communications consultant, has written a poignant book on *How to Get Your Point Across in 30 Seconds—or Less* (Simon and Schuster, 1986). This approach is especially helpful when you want a specific response from people—when you are asking them to do something for you. In our busy times, when our message has to compete with a bombardment of messages and information "noise" from many different directions and sources (just think of e-mail), how can we make sure that we are being heard? Some reasons for being brief are listed in Table 10.1. For optimum impact, short is definitely better than long in most instances.

Table 10.1   *Why Messages Should Be 30 Seconds or Less*

- Memos and letters of request are too long and thus frequently get tossed out unread.
- The attention span of the average person is 30 seconds.
- Doctors listen to their patients for an average of only 19 seconds before they start making a diagnosis and proceed with the physical exam (from research at Michigan State University).
- Time has become compressed; communication is often by e-mail or answering machine message.
- TV commercials do a good job of getting their message across in 30 seconds.
- In the U.S., TV news sound bites typically are 30 seconds long or they do not get air time.
- Most importantly, if you can't say it in 30 seconds, you probably are not thinking about your message clearly. You may need more time to present supplementary information (if asked), but the main thrust of your message should be very concise.
- President Abraham Lincoln's Gettysburg address is a brief but very powerful message. It is discussed at the end of this section.

PREPARATION

People often think that preparing such a brief message would be a breeze. However, it takes much thinking (using the creative problem solving process) and can easily take an hour or more, especially for beginners. The messages can be verbal or written: telephone requests and messages left with staff members; memos, letters, e-mail, thank-you notes, faxes; abstracts for proposals and scholarly papers, formal presentations at meetings, interviews, sales solicitations or complaints; social situations with superiors, chance meetings, and giving toasts. The 30 seconds in an elevator may be all the time you have to present your creative idea to a company's president.

As you prepare your message, you must determine your objective, your audience, and your strategy.

Objective: What do you want to achieve and why? You need a clear-cut, single, specific objective.

Audience: Who can get you what you want? Know what your audience is going to want from you. Make sure you go to the right person or group.

Approach: How can you get what you want? Brainstorm different ideas—then select the one that meets the objective and audience best; in form as well as content. Ask yourself: What is the basis of my game plan? What is the heart of my message? What is the single best statement that will lead to what I want? How will this statement relate to the needs and interests of the audience? What is my sales pitch?

MESSAGE

Next, you need to work on the three parts of the message: hook, subject and close (or if you prefer, hook, line and sinker).

Hook: To get attention, the hook is often in the form of a question. You may use humor (at your own expense only) or a visual aid. The hook should be a bridge connecting the audience to what you want. If you have a very brief message, the entire message can be the hook. You can use the "Walk-Around" from Figure 3.8 to make sure you communicate with your audience in all four thinking quadrants.

Subject: Answer who, what, where, when, why, and how as they relate directly to your explicit or hidden objective. Does the message correspond with your approach? Is it made relevant to your audience? What are the benefits to the audience?

Close: This is the bottom line. A message without a close is a wasted opportunity. Be forceful or subtle in asking for what you want, depending on your audience. Demand a specific action within a stated time frame, or ask for a reaction through the power of suggestion.

ORAL PRESENTATION

In an oral presentation, appearance, "acting," and mode of speaking are important since they help transmit the meaning of the message.

Style and appearance: Monitor your body language. Practice delivering your message in front of friends who can critique you in a supportive way. Or have your practice presentation videotaped—then critically evaluate your performance. Examine your facial expressions, eye contact, posture, gestures, and tone of voice. Do you know what types of clothes make you look your best? Are you aware that some features in your appearance (for example body piercing or dreadlocks) may give a negative impression? Consideration of others takes precedence over your own tastes. Be clean and well groomed. Learn about the do's and don'ts of communicating in other cultures.

Acting: Transmit a positive attitude. Smile. Focus on different people in the audience while you speak. Do not read off a script or memorize your speech. You may feel that you are being asked to pretend. On a way, that is what good communicators do—for example former U.S. President Ronald Reagan.

Mode of speaking: Do not use offensive words! Instead, show surprise, puzzlement, or concern in your facial expression and voice as you speak. Learn to modulate your voice (avoid a monotone); use strategic pauses. Practice breathing and relaxation techniques prior to the start to reduce your stress level and thus have your voice sound more natural.

PowerPoint: Keep it simple and go for a clean look. Use only one concept per slide with at most six points, in a size and font that are easy to read. Animation is cool but may go awry if you're nervous. The slides are best used as an organizational aid or prompt—the main focus should be on you.

WRITTEN MESSAGES

If done by hand, write legibly and neatly. If written on the computer, do not detract from your message by an overuse of fancy fonts, color and clip art—a little can go a long way and should always be in support your message. Use good grammar and correct spelling, then proof-read and double-check. Be positive and friendly (or polite and formal) depending on your audience.

Good leaders listen; they have personal humility, and they surround themselves with a few good critics.

Anne Mulcahy, CEO, Xerox

EXAMPLE: Abraham Lincoln's Gettysburg Address

Four score and seven years ago, our fathers brought forth upon this continent a new nation: conceived in liberty and dedicated to the proposition that "all men are created equal."

Now we are engaged in a great civil war, testing whether that nation, or any nation so conceived and so dedicated, can long endure. We are met on a great battlefield of that war. We have come to dedicate a portion of it as a final resting place for those who here gave their lives that the nation might live. It is altogether fitting and proper that we should do this. But, in a larger sense, we cannot dedicate—we cannot consecrate—we cannot hallow this ground. The brave men, living and dead, who struggled here, have consecrated it, far above our poor power to add or detract. The world will little note, nor long remember, what we say here, but it can never forget what they did here.

It is for us, the living, rather to be dedicated here to the unfinished work which they who fought here have, thus far, so nobly carried on. It is rather for us to be here dedicated to the great task remaining before us—that from these honored dead we take increased devotion to that cause for which they gave the last full measure of devotion—that we here highly resolve that these dead shall not have died in vain; that this nation, under God, shall have a new birth of freedom, and that government of the people, by the people, for the people, shall not perish from the earth.

The Setting

The battle of Gettysburg (in Pennsylvania) was fought on July 1-3, 1863. More than 7000 soldiers from the Union North and the Confederate South died there, and a national soldier's cemetery was created to properly inter more than 3500 Union casualties lying in hasty, inadequate graves all over the battlefield. (The Confederate remains were moved to cemeteries in the South after the end of the war.) The dedication of the national cemetery was held on November 19, 1863, less than halfway through the reburial process. Edward Everett (former governor of Massachusetts, President of Harvard University, U.S. Secretary of State, and noted orator) gave the opening speech. Next, it was the turn of Union President Abraham Lincoln. There was little reaction, and many of those present did not even realize he had been speaking.

The following day, Everett wrote to Lincoln (who had thought his speech a failure), "I should be glad if I could flatter myself that I came as near to the central idea of the occasion in two hours as you did in two minutes."

Importance

According to www.gettysburg.com/bog/ga.htm, the 272 words of the Gettysburg Address were formulated with great thought by Lincoln. He wrote the first draft in Washington shortly before November 18 and revised it at the home of David Wills in Gettysburg the night before the dedication. "The speech transformed Gettysburg from a scene of carnage into a symbol, giving meaning to the sacrifice of the dead and inspiration to the living."

According to http://usinfo.state.gov/usa/infousa/facts/democrac/25.htm, the short Gettysburg address came to be one of the most important documents in the growth of American democracy, because it asserted the true meaning of the Constitution, that all men *really* were created equal, slaves included. Also, before this speech, the United States were spoken of in the plural; after the speech, the United States truly became a union seen in the singular ("the United States is…").

Message Analysis

Object: To state the grand purpose of the war, "a union, with liberty and freedom for all," while giving meaning to the sacrifice made by the soldiers.

Audience: Attendees at the dedication of the battlefield cemetery, but with the press attending, the nation, and the world (posterity) were also included.

Approach: A concise statement in 10 sentences.

Hook: First three sentences, forming a bridge connecting the past vision to the present experience of the audience.

Message: Five sentences, dedicating the cemetery and honoring the sacrifice and bravery of the soldiers, living and dead.

Close: Two sentences, calling for the living to dedicate themselves to the work that the nation, under God, will be a government of the people, for the people, by the people.

Thinking Quadrants

A: Facts and time span in the "hook" (sentences 1, 2, 3).
B: "Proper" dedication (sentences 4, 5).
C: Personal commitment demanded and emotion expressed (close).
D: Grand view of "one nation, under God, with freedom for all."

SELLING YOUR IDEA—FORMAL TEAM PRESENTATION

Here are some tips on how to make an effective team project presentation (from 15-30 minutes in length). The credibility of your problem-solving project may hinge on how effectively you can present your solution. Even experienced teams can benefit from rehearsing their presentation—but it is essential for people who are not used to public speaking. Also, you must check out the audio-visual equipment and learn how to operate it.

Your main objective may be to inform your audience about your project and accomplishments. But keep a secondary objective in mind also—to give a presentation that will make it easy for your audience to remember your message. Some tips to accomplish this are listed in Table 10.2.

Table 10.2 Tips for Making an Effective Presentation

- Start and finish on time!
- Make sure each person on your team is introduced clearly.
- Speak the language of your audience and state the purpose of your presentation.
- Use visualization to aid in remembering your main ideas.
- Plan time for questions at the end; respond directly to the questions.
- Be yourself; project energy, enthusiasm, and competence. Don't exaggerate or criticize.
- Typical listeners can only remember up to five points, and if the points are reinforced!

    Thus you must: ... Preview the main points to have the listeners anticipate them.
    ... Continuously tie the points to the structure of the presentation.
    ... Provide summaries as handouts if you have many details.
    ... At the end, repeat the main points as you provide closure.

You can use these tips for making effective solo presentations. There are many opportunities for presentations when starting a business, but none is more critical than when asking for funding. Together with submitting a written business plan, you may well be required to make a presentation to the decision makers (bank, venture capitalists, or business angels).

WRITING A BUSINESS PLAN

Much of what you have learned in working through the previous chapters of product and business development in this book now comes together in the business plan. It is a written document that explains in quadrant B detail how you plan to implement your business idea. There are four main reasons or groups of people that will benefit from a good business plan:

1. **Yourself.** Especially if you are an enthusiastic, creative entrepreneur, writing the business plan will force you to realistically plan the implementation steps, identify potential problems and seek to overcome them in order to succeed in your venture.

2. **Potential lenders and investors.** These people need to understand what your business is about, that you have assessed your competition, and that they can have confidence in your ability to succeed—judging from the details and realistic financial information and forecasts included in the plan.

3. **Potential employees.** A new business needs multi-talented people, and they will take a risk committing to help grow a startup enterprise (since many startups fail, and employees could be left without a job and pay for months of their work). The vision of where you are planning to take your business can convince them to take a chance.

4. **Potential customers.** Especially if your business involves products and services sold to other businesses, these customers can have a key role in getting you started, by placing firm orders (and possibly even making advance payments). This in turn can help lenders and investors to make a commitment, and it can help you cover startup expenses.

The purpose of business is to create and keep a customer.

Peter F. Drucker

Although a business plan may serve to guide policies and strategies in your new business—and this is a very important point—a business plan is NOT the business. When conditions will change, you must have a flexible mindset to adjust quickly. Be prepared to look for opportunities in change, and do not follow the business plan blindly!

A simple plan may have a dozen or so pages; a more comprehensive plan may be forty or more pages long. Therefore, we will not include an example of a business plan here. However, we will indicate the main components of the plan and what information flows into it, and we will give you web sites where you can find examples and get useful advice for writing a business plan. As a guideline, keep in mind the key questions that must be answered by the business plan—not explicitly, but implicitly integrated into the different sections:

→ What is it that you expect to produce or provide, and why would anyone want to buy it?

→ Why would anyone want to buy it from you and not your competition, and why would they buy now?

→ How do you expect to make a profit?

Although the document is designed to project a positive picture, you must avoid the common errors people make when writing a business plan:

Do not exaggerate! You must be realistic and refrain from forecasting very rapid growth in sales (such as expecting sales to double every two years) unless you can substantiate your reasons for making this assumption. Just because one million people live in your trade area, you cannot *assume* that even a single person will buy your product, much less forecast that two or three percent would do so.

Do not ignore obstacles! Make a realistic assessment of what you might face and how you would address these. There may be global competition, patent infringement lawsuits, difficulties with obtaining permits and licenses, finding talented employees and dealers for your product, and developing effective marketing strategies, just to name a few.

Do not fail to prove your personal commitment! If you keep your present job as a hedge and do not invest your own money in the venture (i.e., by refinancing your home), lenders and investors will not want to risk their funds. They want to be sure that if you fail, you will suffer more loss than they would—as an incentive to try extra hard not to fail.

Do not fail to prove your competence! Ideally, you will have both business and technical experience, or you will have put a team together that will provide both. You need to have people (including employees) who can plan, organize, make decisions, budget, monitor performance and trends in the marketplace, and can manage to produce results. The special management skills needed for a new business will be discussed in Chapter 11.

THE ELEMENTS OF A BUSINESS PLAN

A typical business plan has four sections: (1) front matter, (2) description of the business, (3) financial information, and (4) supporting documentation. Make sure the information is as complete as you can make it, and take care to be neat and professional. Avoid using too much technical jargon and acronyms that are not defined.

FRONT MATTER

a. **Cover sheet**. Include your name as the contact person, the name of the business, a logo and/or slogan, addresses, phone numbers, and website.

b. **Statement of purpose**. Include names of all co-owners, amounts of financing desired (if applicable), and a confidentiality statement.

c. **Table of contents**. Include page numbers.

Entrepreneurs must relate customers (quadrant C) to profits (quadrant A) and creativity (quadrant D) to business processes (quadrant B) through management which encompasses planning, organizing, control, and communication.

But for real value to be created, these activities have to be governed by ethical standards.

DESCRIPTION OF THE BUSINESS

1. **Executive summary.** Include a brief discussion of the industry, your competitive advantage, the planned financing, key members of your business team, and any other important information. It is the most important section—if not well done, some readers will stop right there or at the least will be turned off to what else you have to say. Although this item appears first in the main body of the plan, write it last, after you have completed all sections. Do not exceed two pages!

2. **Context or background of your business.** Include a summary of the current state of the industry, market trends, and how you differ from your competitors, possible barriers to your entry, and the future trends and outlook of the industry. If you have completed a market analysis and the exploration of the industry context earlier, you should have the information needed to write this section. Make sure to present solid data and a realistic assessment of your competition.

3. **Description of your business.** Include the rationale for choosing its legal form. Describe the product(s) and/or services that you plan to offer. Indicate the location of the business, the targeted market or customers, and the competition you foresee facing. The key information on your product should come from your final round of the Pugh evaluation, the information on the customers from the original customer surveys as well as from the results of the marketing plan and market test (if any).

4. **Business strategy.** Highlight why customers will want your product. What will be your competitive advantage? How will you draw customers away from established businesses? Describe your market in terms of size and trends. Explain your pricing strategy and how it relates to "beating" the advantages of the competition, especially if they are much larger companies.

5. **Management.** Explain who will manage your enterprise. Include your own qualifications and the experiences of key personnel. List any consultants or services you are planning to hire (for example, accounting firms). Include an organizational chart if more than a few people will be involved. Investors and lenders will pay special attention to this information—since the manager can make or break a company.

6. **Operational plan and procedures.** Include—for a product—the production process, purchasing, and delivery and distribution, or—in the case of a service—the logistics of how you plan to deliver your services. Discuss how your approach compares with that of your major competitors. Also discuss the resources that are needed (and how these have been or will be acquired—including plant, offices, equipment, and all necessary permits). Explain where you will find the employees you need, and how you will train them. This information forms the implementation plan (in the producer's mindset, as described in Chapter 4). You can include a summary of your quality monitoring and continuous improvement plans here as well.

With this book, we have attempted to teach the fundamental thinking skills and models required for entrepreneurship.

High-tech business management also requires knowledge in specific areas such as accounting, law, science, engineering, technology, and marketing.

You can fill the gaps by educating yourself and by hiring people who can supply the knowledge you need in your business.

Plans are only good intentions unless they immediately degenerate into hard work.

Peter F. Drucker

7. **Marketing plan.** How will you generate the revenues you have forecast? Include your strategy (including pricing and packaging), methods of advertising, your advertising budget, and your advertising implementation and monitoring plan—how will you analyze and gauge the success of your promotional campaign? This information should be available if you have worked through the marketing topic in Chapter 9.

8. **Risk assessment.** Discuss how you see the risks in relation to your competition and its barriers to entry, trends, and anticipated future developments. Then outline the methods you plan to use to deal with the risks. Include a description of your insurance coverage. A risk assessment was recommended for the final solution(s) during the later stages of the Pugh evaluation. Include any late-breaking information here. Remember that any innovative enterprise carries with it a considerable degree of calculated risk—describe how you are prepared to deal with it.

FINANCIAL INFORMATION

You may need to enlist the help of an accountant to prepare these calculations and data sheets. The SBA web site on the next page gives detailed instructions on how to calculate and complete the financial data sheets. Make sure that all financial data is accurate or based on realistic projections.

a. **Overview of the financial plan.** This summary is especially important if a large amount of financial data is included here for starting up a substantial enterprise.

b. **Sources and uses of funding.** Include the loan applications if any (see the discussion in the following section for more information on different funding options).

c. **Capital equipment.** Also include a supplies list.

d. **Balance sheet.** Include a discussion of the assumptions that you are making for your projections.

e. **Estimate of your startup costs.**

f. **Break-even analysis.**

g. **Income projections** (profit and loss statements) in several formats:
   - 3-year summary,
   - first-year detail by month,
   - second and third-year detail by quarters.

h. **Cash-flow projections** in the same format as the income projections.

i. **Exit strategy.** Do you plan to sell the business someday, or will you be grooming a successor? When will the investors reap a payoff for their investment? If the business fails, how will the remaining assets be disposed of and the proceeds apportioned?

j. **Schedule of milestones and important events:** Although not always included, this information, possibly in the form of a Gantt chart, could be useful for the startup period, especially if you still have a long list of preparations to accomplish until the anticipated launch date.

SUPPORTING DOCUMENTATION

Here you can include tax returns of the principals for the last three years; personal financial statements (all banks have these forms); a copy of any relevant contracts (franchise, license, building leases or purchase agreements); a copy of the resumes of key personnel and principals, and copies of letters of intent from suppliers. Also include any other documents that can support your plan (i.e., a sample of your product brochure).

WEB-BASED RESOURCES

The U.S. Small Business Administration (SBA) has a wealth of free information available on business startup, including writing a business plan, at http://www.sba.gov. They also have a business planning course and a business planning workshop, as well as a link to http://www.bplan.com which has examples of 60 free business plans for many different types of businesses and many other resources—check them out! A step-by-step guide to business plan writing is found at www.inc.com/guides/write_biz_plan.

STARTUP FUNDING FOR ENTREPRENEURS

A study published in 1999 by University of Warwick economics professor Andrew Oswald found that seed money was the key factor in enabling people to run their own businesses. This was particularly true for people in their early twenties. Although a surprisingly large number of people in industrialized countries would like to be self-employed, the lack of capital is seen as the biggest hindrance, and funding is the area where entrepreneurs need help the most. Access to finance for entrepreneurial activity varies significantly according to the nature and scale of the enterprise. Figure 10.1 shows a diagram of the different funding paths.

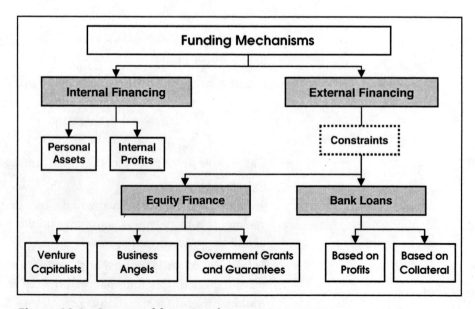

Figure 10.1 *Sources of financing for enterprise startup*

INTERNAL FINANCING

Many highly successful enterprises started trading at a modest activity level. The financial requirements for startup were similarly modest and within the capabilities of the entrepreneurs, their partners and their companies. *Organic growth* then provided sufficient profits for the enterprise to be self-financed. Short-term bank debt may be used to accommodate fluctuations in working capital (i.e., to compensate for seasonal cycles in the business or bridge predictable cash-flow problems), or customers may pay up front when ordering.

To help organic growth, startup entrepreneurs may take very little compensation from the business initially. Or they may support the business with income from a second job. A BostonBank study showed that the two most important funding sources by far for MIT-related startups (see Figure 10.2) were the founder's personal assets and company cash flow. Note that between 1990 and 2000, MIT graduates started over 2000 companies—of these, only about 100 were built on MIT licenses and patents.

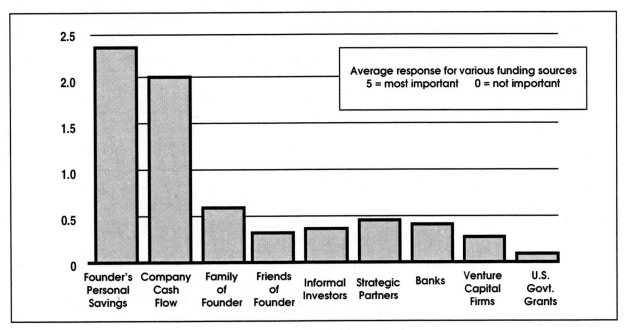

Figure 10.2 Funding sources for companies started by MIT alumni

FINANCING FROM EXTERNAL SOURCES

For many businesses, self-sufficient organic growth is not an option because:

- The lead-time from prototype to delivery is too long to be accommodated through internal sources.
- The minimum scale of operation for competitive startup is too large.
- The required growth rate for effective market penetration is too rapid.
- The entrepreneur has neither personal assets nor internal access to funds.

In all these cases, it will be necessary to access external financial support. When the only barrier is lack of personal resources, it might still be possible to pursue the organic growth option through a small injection of external funds to get started.

CONSTRAINTS INVOLVED IN EXTERNAL FINANCE

Access to external funding for entrepreneurial activity is constrained by the risk assessment made when an external provider is involved. Judgments about the use of internally generated funds are the responsibility of the entrepreneur and are made on the basis of the information available and the risk that is tolerated. The involvement of a third party introduces new elements to both the available information and the level of risk aversion. For the entrepreneur, the key issues are access to finance on agreeable terms. For the external provider, the key issues are risk and return. To assess these accurately may require significant amounts of information about the entrepreneur, the business and the market. Getting this information costs money.

The potential provider of external finance will have two key concerns when attempting to assess risk and return. The first is to avoid choosing badly and funding an enterprise that turns out to be far more risky than anticipated. The second is to ensure that the entrepreneur will stick to his or her side of the bargain and live up to the agreements made. To ensure that the business is run well may require significant monitoring activities. These natural constraints confronting entrepreneurs and potential providers of external finance are reflected in different ways according to the particular source of external support that is pursued.

EQUITY FINANCE

Potential providers of external equity are risking their money to buy a stake in your business. Their main motive is capital gain resulting from a rapid increase in the value of the business. They are risking their capital in the sense that if the business fails, they will lose part or all of their investment. Since they are investing in the prospects of your business, they must be prepared to invest in the evaluation and possibly, later, the monitoring processes required for effective risk and return assessment.

Venture capitalists — Institutional providers of external equity finance use their past and present experience of deal making as a guide to the potential costs of evaluation and monitoring. As a result they will tend to avoid smaller projects because the associated information costs prohibit further consideration. Although the threshold varies from one provider to another, it would be sensible not to take offence if rejected when your project is seeking external equity funding for amounts less than one-half to one million dollars. The difficulty of obtaining venture funding is illustrated with this story:

An entrepreneurship student getting ready to launch a company asked a business professor, "How do you get money to start a company?"

"There are two ways, the regular way and the miraculous way," the professor answered.

The budding entrepreneur begged, "Please explain this to me."

The professor replied, "The regular way is when the heavens part and angels come down to give you the money."

A look of surprise came over the student's face. "Well, Professor, what then is the miraculous way?"

"The miraculous way is when a venture capitalist lends you the money."

How you get things done is just as important as getting them done—there has to be honesty and integrity!

Rick Wagoner, Chairman and CEO, General Motors

Business angels — A more informal source of external equity funding may be available from business angels. These are high net-worth individuals who want to invest in new and exciting business prospects. The criteria a particular business angel applies to evaluate projects may differ from institutional venture capitalists and also from other angels. Although the risk/reward calculation is still critical in the decision-making process, there are other more personal factors that may drive the decision as to whether to consider a project and then get involved financially. Many business angels have their own experience of successful entrepreneurship they wish to apply to the benefit of new ventures. They may also wish to get closely involved in the operation of those ventures. Therefore, the business angel may be motivated to invest significant amounts of time and money to assess a potential prospect. The return sought may involve less tangible elements such as personal satisfaction in addition to financial returns.

Government grants — An additional source of effective external equity provision is in the form of government grants at a regional, state or national level. These are commonly designed to encourage particular kinds of business development in terms of the sectors or localities in which they operate. Such grants may not be conditional on the sharing of business ownership but represent external equity in the sense that they constitute risk capital with no recourse to repayment in the event of failure. Entrepreneurs should check the availability of such grants at an appropriate source such as regional economic development agencies or the Small Business Administration website at www.sba.gov (or www.nesta.uk in Great Britain) for further information.

Assistance or grants may also be available from regional government or private groups in the form of "enterprise zones" or business incubators, where no-cost or low-cost office space and staffing is provided to the entrepreneur for a limited startup period, possibly coupled with tax incentives.

But for the vast majority of startup businesses, external equity funding is not a realistic option. The amounts sought will either be too small for venture capitalists, not interesting enough for business angel participation, and non-qualifying for government grants. In this case, entrepreneurs who need external finance must consider going into debt.

FINANCING THROUGH LOANS

The evaluation and monitoring costs associated with external equity financing also influence an entrepreneur's access to borrowing. By far the most popular sources of debt finance for entrepreneurs and businesses are banks (and to a lesser degree credit unions and mortgage brokers). Although loans from family and friends are extremely important, they should be seen as external equity finance since those involved may not have a high expectation of repayment but may want to participate to some degree in the business.

To understand how banks approach the assessment of loan applications, it is helpful to consider two basic alternatives. The first refers to the "income gearing approach"; it focuses upon the profit prospects of the project for which the loan is required. The second is referred to as the "capital gearing approach"; it focuses upon the accumulated assets and credit history of entrepreneurs and their businesses.

The income gearing approach — Under this approach of assessing a loan application, bankers are primarily concerned about ensuring that the income generated by the proposed project will be sufficient to pay back the loan with interest and money to spare. In short, they will focus upon the prospects of the business and the extent to which it is likely to succeed. Thus evaluation and monitoring require very similar information, as was the case for external equity financing. It is rarely in the bank's interests to provide funding on this basis unless the amounts are relatively trivial (for example in the form of a line of credit not to exceed a few thousand dollars) or there is a long and close relationship between the bank and the entrepreneur.

The capital gearing approach — In order to avoid the information costs associated with an income-gearing or prospects-based approach, bankers will usually seek some form of security or collateral to set against the loan. For the entrepreneur with a startup enterprise this may present difficulties both with business and personal collateral.

With the exception of land and buildings, reliance upon business collateral in the form of plant and equipment may be problematic since the cost of their acquisition is not reflected in their value for collateral. The purchase price for the entrepreneur will typically be significantly higher than the collateral value to the banker because the entrepreneur will pay the market price for a productive machine whereas the banker will take a "carcass valuation" approach. For example, if a textile-based business buys a computerized knitting machine and there is a down-turn in the market which causes the business to fail, then the value of that machine, at auction, may be very low. For businesses intending to grow rapidly, this problem of business collateral valuation has particular significance since the costs of acquiring a new plant and equipment massively outstrip the extent to which these can be used for security and business collateral.

Because of the valuation problems with business collateral, banks will often seek personal collateral from the entrepreneur to secure a business loan, such as a home. This claim over personal assets may take a variety of forms but, effectively, removes the protection provided by limited liability. This means that the bank will have first call on these assets in the event of business failure and loan default. For potential entrepreneurs, there is a more serious consequence of this approach, because if they do not have sufficient personal assets, they may not have access to bank loans.

TIPS FOR GAINING ACCESS TO EXTERNAL FINANCIAL SUPPORT

1. **For venture capital**, entrepreneurs should:
- Prepare a very clear and persuasive business plan.
- Show in that plan an annual internal rate of return of at least 35%.
- Be prepared to share at least 30% of their business in terms of external equity participation.

By honesty I don't mean that you only tell what's true.

But you also make clear the entire situation.

You make clear all the information that is required for others who are intelligent to make up their mind.

Richard P. Feynman

2. **For business angels**, entrepreneurs should:
- Provide a clear business plan.
- Indicate the potential in that plan for significant annual internal rates of return often in excess of 20%.
- Be prepared to share a significant portion of the business in terms of external equity participation.
- Be prepared to involve the external investor in business operations.
- If the business angels are family members or friends, have a formal contract—deal with them professionally as outside investors.

3. **For government grants,** entrepreneurs should:
- Investigate what loan guarantees are available from local, regional or national government agencies, particularly if your business involves research and development in advanced technologies.
- Seek advice as to the evaluation criteria that will be applied to the grant application and the monitoring activity and performance levels that will be expected when a grant is awarded.
- Expect a large amount of paperwork—most likely more than the typical inventor-entrepreneur may want to live with.

4. **For bank loans**, entrepreneurs should:
- Ascertain the precise information requirements that the lending agency will impose and find out why this information is required.
- Be prepared to offer regular monitoring information about the business and the project's performance in advance or in excess of bank requirements. Research has shown that a more informed and closer relationship between banks and entrepreneurs results in improved terms for the loan and more effective bank support in the event of short-term and unexpected fluctuations in trading conditions.
- Be prepared to develop a clear business plan with explicit monitoring structures for obtaining business performance information.
- Be prepared to forewarn the lending agencies of changing future financial requirements.
- Be prepared to shop around at different banks to get the best deal.

5. **For encouragement**, all entrepreneurs should:
- Remember the adage "If at first you don't succeed, try, try again." Make sure your venture is skillfully presented as sound and exciting.
- Look at the situation from the viewpoint of the funding provider. Imagine that you are asked to finance a business—what information and assurances would you require? What criteria would you want met before investing in the enterprise?
- Consider operating on a shoestring. The need for "doing more with less" has been a powerful incentive for many entrepreneurs in starting their successful companies. Later, they felt that a large amount of available money would have been detrimental to their being lean and competitive. Too much startup funding has led to bad spending habits and the downfall of many a dot-com in the last few years.

To innovate successfully, you must hire, work with, and promote people who are unlike you.

Dorothy Leonard and Susaan Straus (Ref. 3.6)

BUSINESS STARTUP

Table 10.3 lists other questions you need to research before you start up your enterprise. A good place to begin is by entering the question into the FAQ link on the SBA website. We recommend that you review each topic to ensure you have not left out any important aspects or resources.

Table 10.3　Available SBA Web Information about Getting Started

1. How can I find qualified employees?
2. How do I set wage levels?
3. What other financial responsibilities do I have for employees?
4. What kind of security measures must I take?
5. Should I hire family members to work for me?
6. What kind of computer and telecommunications equipment do I need?
7. How do I set up the right record-keeping system?
8. Is it better to lease or buy the store, plant, and equipment?
9. Can I operate a business from my home?
10. How do I find out about suppliers, manufacturers, distributors?
11. Where can I go for help?
12. What do I do when I'm ready?

STARTUP CHECKLIST

This final list for "producers" getting ready to launch their enterprises includes many items that have been mentioned previously—check off all tasks that you have completed and cross out those that do not pertain to your particular planned venture. It is assumed that you are properly motivated, that you have determined your business to be feasible, and that you have a marketable product or service.

Financial info (from your business plan)

____ Assess your personal financial resources.
____ Calculate your startup and operating expenses (for two years).
____ Project your revenue (for at least two years).
____ Project your cash flow (for at least two years).
____ Assess the profit potential of your business (with timeline).
____ Investigate potential sources of funding, including family, friends, equity, and debt.

Research

____ Research your industry, your market niche/target, your customers, and your competition.
____ Research suitable locations and zoning laws; choose the "best" depending on your priority (lifestyle and profit expectations). Keep in mind that some localities and states (in the U.S.) are much more business-friendly than others. Also investigate if a location in a business incubator makes sense for you.

_____ Develop your business plan (including marketing).

_____ Create a company and product name; check for availability; file for trademark protection and domain name. If you have not yet done so, apply for patent and copyright protection.

_____ Research available free help or counseling from SBA Service Corps of Retired Executives at www.score.org or the small business development centers at www.sba.gov/SBDC/index.html.

_____ Research a suitable business model that matches your thinking style profile as well as the type of business you will manage. For the startup to be successful, you need to carefully plan how you will manage your employees, your business growth, your assets, as well as change and taking advantage of unexpected opportunities. The two chapters in Part 4 of this book will address some of these topics.

You need to formulate procedures to handle the paperwork of running a business efficiently.

Robert Gerrish, small business coach (London, Sidney)

External relationships

_____ Search out potential vendors and suppliers, as well as shipping and delivery providers if applicable.

_____ Select a suitable attorney, accountant, and insurance agent.

_____ Decide on legal business format; file with appropriate local, state, and federal agencies. In the U.S., apply for your FEIN number (from the IRS) and any other state and local franchise, property, and sales tax numbers as well as licenses and permits if applicable.

_____ Implement your funding plan; sign legal contracts as applicable.

_____ Establish a business bank account and credit card/line (if expedient).

_____ Join appropriate business organizations: Chamber of Commerce, Better Business Bureau, and trade organizations in your line of business.

_____ Create an advisory board (a source of valuable advice if chosen wisely).

_____ Arrange to have the business listed in local directories.

Infrastructure

_____ Establish record-keeping procedures.

_____ Decide on staffing and assign roles and responsibilities; hire and train employees as needed to meet the requirements (if not available from owners/partners). Have signed non-compete agreements to protect your trade secrets.

_____ Set up operational policies and procedures.

_____ Set up a monitoring system so all local codes and industry regulations will be met.

_____ Order raw materials or inventory.

_____ Set up a website.

_____ Set an official starting date; organize appropriate media notices.

_____ Put your sales/marketing plan into operation.

_____ Equip your premises (purchased facility, rented space, or home office or garage) including telephone, internet access/safeguards, and other utilities.

_____ Obtain insurance as appropriate: property, fire, flood, theft, auto, liability, employee group benefits (medical, life, disability), workers' compensation, and business interruption.

Twenty Ways to Increase Your Chances of Success

This quick review of the creative problem solving mindsets offers tips on how to avoid common mistakes inventors make when starting a venture. Inventions usually fail for one of two broad reasons: (a) development of the idea reveals serious technical problems, or (b) the inventor makes mistakes. In terms of sheer numbers, *inventor mistakes* win by a mile. The good news is that most of these failures are easily avoided by periodically going through the following checklist to make sure you have paid attention to these important items. They are grouped according to the steps in the creative problem solving process and were adapted from 2002 information at www.nesta.org.uk/topic/success.html.

Problem definition ("explorer and detective")

1. Do a proper patent and product search to ensure your idea is original. In most cases, unoriginal means unprotectable and therefore commercially worthless.

2. Research the market properly; interpret the findings realistically. Make sure that you are developing an idea that meets a demonstrated need. Do not skip the customer surveys and analysis.

3. Conduct a complete problem analysis. Are you addressing the real problem? Have you considered simplicity and reasonable costs? Have you minimized expected change in user behavior?

4. Are your knowledge and skills up-to-date? Do you know the latest trends and developments?

Idea generation, evaluation and optimization ("artist, engineer and judge")

5. Focus on progress and continuous improvement of your product or process. This is more important than merely having a good patent.

6. Make use of confidentiality agreements; this way, others can help in the developing process without affecting disclosure and patentability of your idea.

7. Use your available resources wisely. Going into debt can take your creative energy and focus away from developing your idea.

8. Iron out basic technical flaws before presenting your idea. Using such evaluation techniques as the Pugh method will help you identify and overcome flaws and bring out the strengths of your idea.

9. Consider working with experts for specialized knowledge to help you or views you may have overlooked. Or consider working with a mentally diverse team to gain different viewpoints.

10. Listen to good advice but beware of flatterers.

Solution implementation and "selling" your idea ("producer")

11. Carefully evaluate your associates and commercial firms you are hiring to assist you in the patenting or licensing process.

12. Investigate opportunities for a royalty deal in small companies, not just the market leaders.

13. Is business your true motive? Recognize that the ideas of others can make your idea work better (even if this may hurt your ego).

14. Make sure you have a complete idea or a working prototype before you make your presentation.

15. Use all your skills and careful preparation to make an effective presentation when "selling" your ideas to a company. Remember to interest your audience in the business opportunity aspects, not the invention!

16. Have realistic expectations about the worth of your idea when negotiating with a firm or investor.

17. Learn from good negotiating agreements; learn to recognize decent deals.

18. In a royalty deal, know that at some stage it is necessary to let go and give up control of your idea.

19. Have a Plan B (or even a Plan C) in case your Plan A for selling your idea fails. This prevents you from selling your idea for peanuts.

20. The actions of some inventors have created an adverse image of inventors. Thus make sure your idea or product is presented in a business-like, logical fashion, so you will be taken seriously.

EXERCISES

10.1   Role Reversal or "Devil's Advocate"

This exercise can be explored by an individual, but it is far more effective if done in a small team. The purpose is to anticipate as fully as possible any potential sources of resistance to the provision of external funds for a business project and then overcome these prior to actual submission. The process deliberately excludes many commonly accepted sources of potential resistance that have emerged from research over the years—in order to avoid "leading the witness." Explore and experience every aspect of this exercise.

Adopt in turn the different mindsets of the parties in the decision making process: the entrepreneur, the potential finance provider, and the business adviser. This will help you to understand more clearly the influences that shape their viewpoints. By the end of this exercise, you will be as well prepared as you can be for an initial discussion with potential providers of external finance. Further refinements will be required once you know the particular criteria and application processes they use.

STEP 1—The Provider Mindset

Scenario: This can be a venture capitalist, business angel, grant awarder, or banker. Imagine the following scenario:

- You have access to your own fortune of at least $10 million.
- You also have access to investments or deposits from friends you trust and who trust you.
- A stranger approaches you to request that you invest, support, or lend funds to carry out a particular business project.

Task: On lined paper, quickly list all the main areas where you require information and evidence in order to feel qualified to make a decision.

Possible outcomes from making the decision to invest:

a. If this action turns out to be correct, you will benefit significantly either through returns on your investment, welfare gains from grant provision, or interest on the supply of debt.

b. If this turns out to be an unwise decision, you will lose all or a significant part of the invested money.

STEP 2—The Entrepreneur Mindset

As the entrepreneur with a particular project in mind, describe the project and then try to calculate how much external funding you will need for the venture, both now and in the future. Make alternative estimates according to different assumptions as to the success of the project and its progress.

STEP 3—The Provider's Mindset

Review your list of questions in Step 1—then expand and modify these as appropriate to the project requiring external finance proposed in Step 2.

STEP 4—The Entrepreneur's Mindset

Provide answers to all of the questions resulting from Step 3.

There is no learning without some difficulty and fumbling.

If you want to keep on learning, you must keep on risking failure—all your life.

John W. Gardner

STEP 5—The Provider's Mindset

Decide what your decision would be and why, either for using your own $20 million or those of your trusted investors.

STEP 6—The Neutral Business Adviser Mindset

Critically evaluate every response of the entrepreneur to the questions from the Provider. Using the Pugh method with brainstorming, consider how each response could be improved and clarified.

GENERAL TIPS

In the areas of coverage, check that you have included those that would usually be considered when evaluating a new idea or innovation, such as:

1. **Impact on Society**
   - What is the effect on people's welfare?
   - Does it meet current laws and regulations?
   - What are the safety implications of using or abusing this innovation?
   - What will be the impact upon the environment of this innovation (in use or when obsolete?)

2. **Market Attractiveness**
   - What are the size and dynamics of the potential market?
   - How does it compare with the competition?

3. **Barriers to Acceptance**
   - What are the key barriers to acceptance and can they be overcome?

4. **Feasibility of Concept**
   - Can it be made?
   - Will it work?
   - Will it make money?

5. **Experience and Strategy**
   - What are the necessary marketing, financial, technical, management and production skills, and are they in place?
   - Is a new venture appropriate?
   - Is a partnership or licensing strategy appropriate?

Anyone who stops learning is old, whether twenty or eighty.
Anyone who keeps learning today is young.
The greatest thing in life is to keep your mind young.

Henry Ford

10.2   Pricing Concerns for an International Venture

A small publisher in the U.S. has found that a surprising market niche has developed overseas for one of the company's products. The decision was made to produce the next edition with an international print-on-demand company to reduce shipping time and costs to customers in South Africa, Europe, and the Far East. The product can be independently priced in U.S. dollars, British pounds, and Euros. Looking one, two, and three years ahead, what should the listed costs be for all three currencies, if the product sold for $20 in 2006 (keeping trends in currency conversion rates, trade agreements, and other possible factors impacting the publishing business in mind)?

Part Four

Managing
for Innovation

11 Management, Leadership and Change

What you can learn from this chapter:
- You will gain an understanding of the leadership requirements, as a business moves from startup to continuous innovation.
- You will gain insight into the role of manager.
- You will gain insight into the role of leadership.
- You will learn how to help people cope with change.
- You will understand the whole-brain management style and its implications for entrepreneurs.

If your actions inspire others to dream more, learn more, do more and become more, you are a leader.

John Quincy Adams

Leadership and management are often used interchangeably when talking about the top levels of organizations—yet they describe different concepts, with distinct characteristics. A good leader is not necessarily a good manager, and vice versa. Leadership can be an asset in a good manager, but it is not essential. In this chapter we will examine the qualities of management and leadership that would help an entrepreneur guide a company through several stages of development. In many self-evaluation checklists on entrepreneurial aptitude, the first question usually is, "Are you a good leader?" Assuming you fully understand what this means and answer yes, this is insufficient because one of the more important ingredients to be a successful entrepreneur is being a competent manager. As we shall see, the management (and leadership) roles change during the life cycle of a business.

THREE PHASES OF BUSINESS DEVELOPMENT

As seen in Figure 1.1, a product's life cycle is depicted from startup and growth to maturity and decline, unless a new cycle is initiated through continuous innovation. The same mechanism can also be said to hold for the development of a business, as it progresses through three phases: entrepreneurial, growth, and decline or renewal (Ref. 11.1).

THE ENTREPRENEURIAL PHASE

When starting up their new business, most entrepreneurs scramble to find a successful business model, develop a more competitive product, deliver exceptional service, and discover the most effective marketing strategy. As seen in Chapter 10, many companies, especially those started by young entrepreneurs, operate on a shoestring or bootstrap budget. The high energy and enthusiasm of the founders compensates for their lack of experience.

The key characteristics of the entrepreneurial phase are (from Ref. 11.1):

- Doing whatever it takes to survive
- Being adaptable and flexible to market needs
- Willing to take risks
- Having strong motivation and energy
- Practicing intense communication

According to U.S. government data, only one startup company out of ten makes it out of the entrepreneurial phase (with as many as two out of three not surviving past the seventh year). When the startup company finds its niche and becomes successful by having learned how to do most aspects of its business well, it moves on to the second phase.

THE GROWTH PHASE

This stage is characterized by rapid growth and expansion. An interesting thing begins to happen—instead of risk-taking, management now wants to control and safe-keep the process that has made the company successful. Bureaucratic policies and administrative procedures are being put into place.

The key characteristics of the early growth phase are (from Ref. 11.1):

- Market and financial success
- Focus on efficiency and effectiveness
- Development of systems, rules, and procedures
- Shift from entrepreneurial mindset to controlling management
- Excitement about growth

As we can see in Figure 3.7, this could be a business in the refining stage, where it is especially vulnerable to competitive pressures. The organizational climate has become rigid and averse to creativity. The original entrepreneurial founder may be forced out of the leadership during this phase (or may leave because the culture has turned "hostile" to creativity and innovation). The company may work hard at adaptive improvements in products and procedures to maintain success. Joel Barker explains (in Ref. 1.6), "When a paradigm changes, everyone goes back to zero." A company cannot rely on keeping a lead over its competitors by continuing doing business the same way. When the growth cycle peaks, there are two ways for the business to go: one is down to decline and demise, the other is up to renewal.

When the need to change is anticipated and the company culture is in the habit of looking out for new opportunities in the explorer's mindset, we create the conditions for continuous innovation.

> *I skate to where the puck is going to be, not where it has been.*
>
> *Wayne Gresky*

THE RENEWAL PHASE

This phase in business development is marked by the following characteristics (adapted from Ref. 11.1):

- Revitalization and rekindling of the entrepreneurial spirit
- Closeness to customers and market
- Willingness to take risks
- Change-friendly, open, flexible mindset
- Strong orientation to quality and innovation

Successful promising ventures require entrepreneurs with some special qualities and talents but not all-round super humans.

To grow into a large corporation requires entrepreneurs to develop new skills and to perform new roles. Only exceptional entrepreneurs have the capacity and the will to make such changes.

Amar Bidhé

This cycle also holds for individuals and explains why it is so valuable for everyone to develop an entrepreneurial spirit that will enable us to flexibly respond to changing conditions. If we have learned anything from the last few years, it is that the future is unpredictable. Such a climate demands new modes of thinking. It will also make us leaders of change who are able to motivate teams and support staff to continuously innovate.

Peter Drucker said, "Managers do things right, but leaders do the right things." We want to look in some detail at the two roles to discern what qualities are those that entrepreneurs must have or must develop to increase the likelihood that their enterprises will become successful and innovative.

THE ROLE OF THE MANAGER

How important is the manager to the success of a startup? The business plan has a section that deals with the qualifications of the management team, and the stakeholders who are participating in financing the business are indeed very interested in this item. The quality and abilities of management are important to the anticipated success, at least as important (and perhaps even more so) than the quality of the product line or the concepts around which the business is being built.

The purpose of management is...	*The primary thinking quadrants are:*
1. To make a profit	*A*
2. To do <u>tactical</u> planning	*B*
3. To organize and establish policies	*B*
4. To make decisions	*A*
5. To motivate and communicate	*C*
6. To control (and sometimes to rule)	*B (and A)*
7. To set goals and direct	*A*
8. To develop teams	*C*
9. To implement the business model	*A, B, C and some D*

The business model is central and must explain what your business is all about by answering the following questions (more will be discussed about the role of the business model for innovation in Chapter 12):

1. Who are your customers, and why should they buy from you?
2. What benefits are you offering—what is the value to the customer?
3. What is your competitive advantage and how will you maintain it?
4. What is the scope of your activities?
5. What profits are you planning on getting?
6. Why would anyone want to work for you?

Evaluate yourself as a manager, based on any previous experience and from what you have learned from this textbook. Even as a young person you have likely "managed" some project, either working with other students or doing something for your family.

Do a SWOT analysis—realistically.

- What are your **strengths**?
- What are your **weaknesses** (personally or in your business)?
- What **opportunities** are open to you that you might want to exploit?
- What do you see as a **threat**?

If you have great people skills but just never got the hang of math, you could really focus your attention on developing relationships with customers—but you might want to hire a trustworthy accountant to take care of the financial aspects of the business. You could take courses in finance instead, but you need to decide if this is where you want to put your energy.

Personal Example

One of the authors (Edward Lumsdaine) spent several years recruiting and managing a large group of professors and graduate students at Ford Motor Company. The following details some of his experiences.

The people being managed were mostly engineering professors and graduate students from major universities around the U.S. Also, a Ford manager worked closely with me. What was interesting is that both of us had similar thinking preferences. During the startup, our education program had many characteristics of an entrepreneurial enterprise—including some chaotic conditions due to rapid growth (and a lack of quadrant B thinking in the two of us).

As a manager, my functions included: recruiting and staffing, planning, organizing, budgeting, team-building, and resolving conflict. My job was to maximize output at a reasonable cost. Neither the Ford manager nor I were experts in the CAD/CAM/CAE/PIM software that the staff we were hiring was teaching—I merely directed the work (such as scheduling teaching assignments, developing the course catalogue and registration procedure, and passing the instructors through a certification process we had to devise). We simply hired people who were experts in the software, although we had the technical knowledge of the capabilities of these design programs. I was surprised how much time was taken up by having to deal with personal problems of employees.

Important **personal qualities** that managers should have include:

1. Integrity
2. Understanding the business (including the bottom line)
3. Team building skills
4. Decisiveness
5. Ability to listen, communicate effectively, and resolve conflicts
6. Ability to plan and organize
7. Ability and discipline to control costs
8. Ability to direct and monitor results
9. Continuous self-improvement and learning.

A manager must also know what is going on in the individuals that are being managed. For example, if someone is ill, the manager must have a plan for this type of contingency. Managers are more than just administrators—although they may need to do a fair amount of administrative work and wear many hats in the early days of a startup, perhaps even janitorial duties. But managers can be (and often have the opportunity) to grow into leaders.

THE ROLE OF THE LEADER

How important is leadership to the success of a startup? As we have noted, the leader's qualifications are important in the business plan. The entrepreneur's interest in starting and running the company must be supplemented with solid experience. One of the best ways to gain tacit and explicit knowledge is by working for the competition for a while. We have seen that managers chiefly need left-brain thinking skills, with the addition of quadrant C interpersonal abilities. Let us consider the requirements for leaders.

The purpose of leadership is...	The primary thinking quadrants are:
1. To develop and grow the business	D, A
2. To do strategic planning	D
3. To develop a vision	D
4. To write a mission statement	D, A, B, C
5. To assemble and motivate a team	C
6. To develop a suitable business model	D, A
7. To be focused, persistent, passionate	C, D
8. To be flexible, adaptable, competitive	D, A
9. To be a good communicator	C

It takes courage and intuition to be a leader. Entrepreneurs may be loners who "march to a different drum." For them, developing interpersonal skills and good communication will take much effort. Joining *Toastmasters* or taking a *Dale Carnegie course* are both good training grounds for developing these skills. A Hay Group study found that trust and confidence in top leadership was the single most reliable predictor of employee satisfaction in an organization—and effective communication was the key.

Personal Example (continued)

Edward Lumsdaine also spent many years as Dean of Engineering at three different universities. This position was mainly a leadership role, and he learned the following about leadership from his experiences:

As Dean, I frequently questioned and challenged certain policies and provided a vision for the college while examining ways to experiment with new methods and finding ways to innovate. My annual reports laid out the strategies, goals, and trends; they summarized past performance and otherwise attempted to convince the faculty that the new goals were in their best interest and in the interest of the university as a whole. A good leader takes blame when things go wrong and freely gives credit for the achievement of others—that was something I didn't do very well.

Leaders "must let vision, strategies, goals and values be the guidepost for action and behavior rather than attempt to control others" (Ref. 11.2). In my experience, it was a lot harder to be a leader than a manager. My experiences through many years of being a leader (as well as a follower) have convinced me that good leaders are made, not born. Unfortunately, most of what I learned came from on-the-job experience (the school of hard knocks)—I received no formal training in leadership.

Strategic planning was my strength, but I found it a challenge to "sell" my vision to a mostly quadrant B upper administration and a very change-resistant organizational culture.

Important personal qualities that leaders should have include:
1. Integrity
2. Understanding of the organization and its culture
3. Knowing how to motivate others
4. Decisiveness
5. Ability to listen, communicate effectively, and resolve conflicts
6. Ability to take calculated risks, make mistakes, and accept blame
7. Ability to make decisions on facts and intuition, not prejudice
8. Ability to persevere in the face of adversity
9. Continuous self-improvement and learning.

At the age of 22, I started a company. I had no knowledge about anything— I just threw myself into the water and learned how to swim.

Diane
Von Furstenberg

When comparing the ***personal qualities*** of leaders with those of managers, the only ones that are strikingly different are items 6, 7, and 8—for managers, they are truly quadrant B abilities, for leaders they are not so much skills that can be learned but character values needed to deal with the consequences of quadrant D thinking. There is a strong correlation between the qualities needed for an entrepreneur and the qualities exhibited by leaders. Why is this important for an entrepreneur? It was found that the major factor for small business startup failure is the lack of entrepreneurial qualities in the founder or founding team (Ref. 11.3). Starting a business may not be difficult, according to Amar Bhidé (Ref. 2.1), but the aptitude (and attitude) of the entrepreneur will largely determine if it will be successful.

According to Bhidé, most successful entrepreneurs start with a mundane idea rather than a unique one, without a lot of training. They simply get started, hustle for customers, get into a market niche and just work hard. However, if the enterprise is to be successful in the long run, entrepreneurs have to be part leader and part manager. They need the skills of both—by learning those they are lacking or by getting a partner or team with the missing capabilities.

Typical questions to assess your entrepreneurial aptitude would be:

Can you lead?
a. Can you motivate others?
b. Are you competitive?
c. Are you able to take calculated risks and learn from mistakes?
d. Can you communicate effectively and learn continuously?

Can you manage?
a. Are you organized?
b. Do you have self-confidence?
c. Do you have the ability to ride the ups and downs of a startup?
d. How are your conflict resolution skills?
e. Is your knowledge adequate of the product and service you provide?
f. How will you finance and budget for your enterprise?

And some personal questions you must answer are:
a. Are you in good health?
b. Are you willing to work long hours?
c. If married with children, is your family on board with the idea? They will be affected—instant success is almost unheard of in a startup.

COPING WITH CHANGE

Whether as manager or as leader in a startup company, you will have to deal with change. As an entrepreneur, you likely have a mindset that is flexible and thrives on change. But if you were careful to assemble a whole-brain staff team, you will have some people who may find change uncomfortable. You will certainly have potential customers whom you will have to convince that the changes your new product or service will bring will be beneficial for them. So here are some tips on how to deal with change.

First, let's think about some important changes of the last ten years:

- Personal computers
- Instant communication
- The Internet
- Digital data/records
- Distance learning
- Global commerce/competition
- Move from total quality to innovation
- Rise in medical costs
- Rise in energy costs and concerns about global warming
- Rise in terrorism

Change requires new thinking which is hard work.

Change seems to happen at an increasing rate, driven by changes in technology and global competition. Some changes are disconcerting and perhaps frightening, such as natural disasters or the terrorism threat and the probability that even long-established large companies have to downsize or go into bankruptcy or merge—all of which threaten job loss. Let's now look at the opportunities, not the danger aspects of change—remember *wei ji*?

WHAT IS GOOD ABOUT CHANGE?

1. Change helps us grow; it makes life interesting. "Continuity gives us roots; change gives us branches, letting us stretch and grow and reach new heights" *(Pauline R. Kezer, former Connecticut secretary of state).*

2. Personal and organizational changes help us survive and succeed in a rapidly changing world. "It is not necessary to change. Survival is not mandatory" *(W. Edwards Deming, quality expert).*

3. Change is not the problem—how we respond to change can be a problem. "When you can't change the direction of the wind, adjust your sails" *(Max DePree, former CEO of Herman Miller, Inc.).*

4. We can anticipate change. "Neither the wise nor the brave lie down on the tracks of history to wait for the train of the future to run over them" *(Dwight D. Eisenhower).*

5. If nothing ever changed, there would be no growth. "Change always comes bearing unexpected gifts" *(Katie McCain, President, American Water Works Association).*

6. Change can bring relief; it can be a second chance, and it certainly offers the chance of a new beginning.

Our response to change is our choice. We can react positively, with a flexible, can-do attitude, or negatively, with stubborn resistance. Our attitude is independent of our thinking preferences, or as Jim Henion of Cooperative Resources International said, "Misery is optional."

Change is a process. Change means the end of the old. This realization can be very painful for many people. Change involves a process of transition, and people need to be given a vision, goals, and direction, as well as time to navigate through this transition period. The two graphs in Figure 11.1 (by Jim Henion) illustrate two time frames for recovery from a painful change.

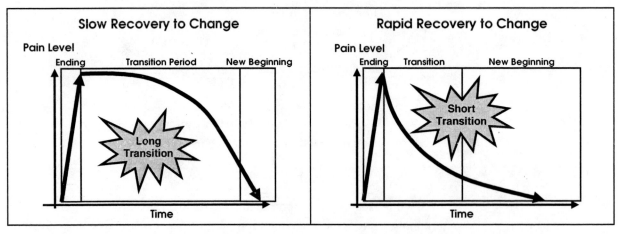

Figure 11.1   *People vary in how quickly they are able to recover from a painful change*

The time response is different for each person. Not everyone is at the same place at the same time and growing at the same rate. The rate of recovery can be shortened depending on how change is handled—personally and organizationally. Managers can encourage change by helping their people get through the transition period. To take ownership of change, people need practical ways to complete the learning cycle:

Step 1   Manager: Think about how to encourage each person's commitment to change.
Staff: Make a personal commitment (quadrant C).

Step 2   Manager: Create and then explain an understandable vision of a better future.
Staff: Join in supporting a mutual vision (quadrant D).

Step 3   Manager: Develop buy-in to an organizational goal for innovation.
Staff: Help in working out a common purpose (quadrant A).

Step 4   Manager: Develop specific step-by-step plans to implement the agreed-on changes and alleviate the fear of the unknown.
Staff: Follow detailed directions to implement change (quadrant B).

HELPING DIFFERENT THINKERS COPE WITH CHANGE

People with different thinking preferences respond to change in different ways. Managers must understand these differences, so they can tailor their approaches for best effect.

God grant me the serenity to accept the people I cannot change, the courage to change the one I can, and the wisdom to know it's me.

Author unknown

Quadrant A: To help these thinkers deal with change, management needs to explain the reasons and logic for the change—if they do not understand the need for change, they will not be motivated.

- They need information to reduce the uncertainty associated with change.
- They need time to do analysis and "think through" the issues involved.
- They need concrete, practical goals.
- To "win" they need to know the expectations as they strive for continuous improvement.
- They may prefer to work alone; they enjoy analytical problem solving, and they thrive on the challenge.

Quadrant B: These thinkers may find it the most difficult to change. Management needs to provide clearly defined rules to achieve a stated outcome, as well as sufficient time to adjust to the changes. Entrepreneurs who have a strong quadrant D mindset must be especially cognizant of how difficult and painful change can be for quadrant B thinkers:

- They have a need for protection, security, stability and structure because they are comfortable with the status quo and fear the risks and unknowns of change.
- They need direction and schedules, and the change process may have to be divided into small steps if possible.
- They want details on the effects of change and their role in the process.
- They have a strong need for specific procedures to manage innovation in their organization.
- They need to know that training will be provided, so they will have the skills needed to do well in the changed environment. They need acknowledgment of their struggles and reassurance that this state will end when the new will have become familiar.

Quadrant C: Since these thinkers deal emotionally with change, managers must emphasize the values that remain stable and provide an anchor.

- Quadrant C people need to understand the benefits to themselves.
- They need to know the available support.
- They need to be motivated to change.

Their strengths are that they intuitively know how others feel about change; as team members, they are supportive of each other. They like to work together; thus they can use the creative problem solving process as a team to deal with change. Good communication is especially important in times of change, and quadrant C people can be a valuable asset in this effort.

Quadrant D: Since these thinkers get the most out of change, managers can empower them to use their creativity and flexibility to initiate and encourage innovation and help others to cope with change, because

- They see the big picture in a changing world; they have vision and understand the context.
- They prepare for and create change; they live in an imagined future.
- They like change, understand the change process and want to participate—but they need patience to let the others catch up.
- They are able to focus on "what else" in life (beyond the change issues).

As leader or manager, expect many bumps as your organization goes through a change process. Deal with obstacles by using the creative problem solving approach. Accept that the results of change may come more slowly than anticipated. Especially be aware that the new may be perceived as criticism of the old (and as a loss of status for the experts in the old paradigm).

Also be aware that during times of change,

- **Quadrant A thinkers** feel more vulnerable to feelings and emotions. In addition, they may fear that the planned change will not make sense for the organization.

- **Quadrant B thinkers** perceive and fear a loss of security and control—they have a very low tolerance for change and will go to great lengths to try and maintain the status quo.

- **Quadrant C thinkers** are overwhelmed by the need for analysis; they fear losing something of value, such as familiar relationships.

- **Quadrant D thinkers** fear being boxed in, closure, and loss of "known" opportunity, and they may not understand the implications of change on the people who are not quadrant D.

The only person who likes change is a wet baby.

Since most people are double- or even triple-dominant, do not merely address a single quadrant's concerns. Most individuals and staff groups will need responses that will simultaneously address quadrants A, B, and C. Table 11.1 lists additional basic tips on how to help people cope with change.

Table 11.1 *How to Help People through the Change Process*

- Carefully listen to people's concerns.
- Share their concerns and apprehension with empathy; then talk about the benefits of change.
- Get people engaged; ask for ideas; develop a mutual plan of action.
- Change is stressful; thus offer concrete support for coping with stress.
- The quick course for the space age, www.angelfire.com/psy/change is an entertaining slide show with some interesting quotes, and does it ever give the "big picture"—it might provide a positive outlook and encouragement to someone struggling with a negative attitude. Caution: It contains New Age philosophy and some commercials.
- The Old Testament story in Exodus 3 and 4 gives a fascinating glimpse of how God is encouraging Moses to change out of quadrant B.

WHOLE-BRAIN MANAGEMENT

Entrepreneurial leaders—whatever their dominant thinking patterns—need to adopt what Ned Herrmann calls situational management. He identified nine different management styles, as summarized in Table 11.2. The whole-brain approach is the most flexible for matching the organization's operation to the leader's vision and meeting various needs and conditions (Ref. 3.3).

Table 11.2 Management Styles by Dominant Thinking Preference   ©1996 The Ned Herrmann Group

	Cerebral Management	
Quadrant A Logical, authoritative, analytical, technical and bottom-line tough. Decisions are made on facts for the "here and now."	**Quadrants A + D** Preference for technical and experimental thinking. A primary style for scientists, inventors and R&D organizations.	**Quadrant D** Holistic, global, visionary, risk taking and adventurous. Decisions are experimental, integrative, entrepreneurial, intuitive, and future-oriented.
Left-Brain Management	**Multi-Dominant Management**	**Right-Brain Management**
Quadrants A + B Practical and realistic. This combination makes this style appear strongly left brain and "hard" (i.e., engineer with MBA).	**The Whole-Brain Approach** **Ability to flexibly respond to diverse business conditions, issues, needs and situations for best results.**	**Quadrants C + D** Flexible, idealistic, intuitive, open-minded, prevalent in service-oriented businesses. This style appears "soft," very right brain, and informal.
Quadrant B Very detailed, structured, down-to-earth, and unambiguous. Decisions are timely and follow established policy, plans and procedure.	**Limbic Management** **Quadrants B + C** Combination of stable tradition with caring responsiveness. Employees, customers, community are seen as high-priority stakeholders.	**Quadrant C** Very participative, intuitive, personable, interactive and team-oriented. Human values and feelings rank high in management and decision making.

According to Ned Herrmann, the world is a composite whole brain—as confirmed by HBDI data from around the world. CEOs usually assume that their organizations as a whole are tilted toward left-brain thinking. But in any group of employees over 100 (and often for much smaller groups), all quadrants are represented with considerable diversity. Even for a class of senior engineering students in capstone design (Fig. 11.2) who have a typically left-brain dominance map (graph on the left), the composite (graph on the right) emphasizes the wide diversity for each thinking quadrant.

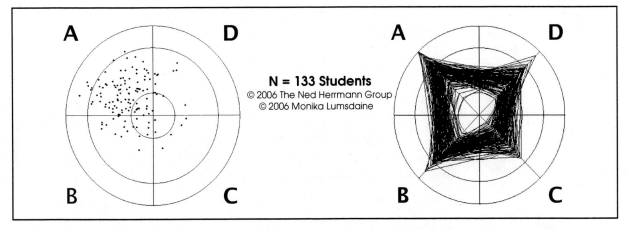

Figure 11.2 Brain dominance map and HBDI composite for capstone engineering design class

This has implications for communication (especially for teachers, managers, and leaders)—they need to go beyond their own much narrower thinking preferences and align their actions with the thinking and learning styles of their employees, customers, or students. Managing mental diversity is a major challenge for managers. Beyond communication, it impacts job design and placement, team formation, and organizational design. Flexibility in style (as outlined in Table 11.2) contributes to managerial effectiveness.

Ned Herrmann found that HBDI profiles for particular occupations have the same typical pattern independent of country, culture or ethnic background—"the more rigorous the professional requirements, the more likely it is that the profiles of occupational colleagues would be similar" all over the world. This suggests that each ethnic group has an equal potential for any particular occupational aspiration such as medical doctors, nurses, teachers, bankers, scientists, engineers, entrepreneurs, psychologists, and managers.

The Hay Group's study of international CEO leadership (of March 1995) has identified that the best CEO's shared some universal competencies:
1. Quadrant A: analytical thinking; strong drive to achieve.
2. Quadrant B: organizational know-how.
3. Quadrant C: good judge of people; social responsibility.
4. Quadrant D: conceptual thinking; broad view of business.

However, the CEO's were able to adapt these competencies to the local culture. For example, American executives learned that to conduct business in Asia, they had to take time to build a relationship of mutual respect (in quadrant C) before negotiating a contract. In contrast, in America, business contracts based on finance and quality (quadrant A) are paramount.

The implications for entrepreneurs are:
- Know your own thinking preferences—both strengths and weaknesses.
- Build your management team so you will have competencies in all four quadrants, while also considering the special requirements for the different phases: startup, growth, or continuous innovation.
- Develop your ability for whole-brain communication and using whole-brain, situational management.

Of 13,000 executives studied, 80 percent credited their success to intuition, although they relied on left- and right-brain skills equally.

Jagdish Parikh, Harvard University

REFERENCES

11.1 Ed Oakley and Dough Krug, *Enlightened Leadership,* StoneTree Publishing, Denver, Colorado, 1992.

11.2 Daniel F. Predpall, "Developing Quality Improvement Processes in Consulting Engineering Firms," *Journal of Management in Engineering,* pp. 30-31, May-June 1994.

11.3 James M. Louzes and Barry Z. Posner, *An Instructor's Guide to the Leadership Challenge,* Jossey-Bass, 1995.

11.4 Robert Sullivan, *The Small Business Start-Up Guide,* 1996, from www.isquare.com

11.5 Don Clark, "Concepts of Leadership," donclark@nwlink.com.

12   Innovation at Work

What you can learn from this chapter:
- A broader understanding of innovation from an expanded definition which includes the business viewpoint.
  - Why do people innovate?
  - Why do innovators occur at random?
  - Why is technological innovation not enough?
- The importance of business innovation to economic value.
  - Why is innovation in the business model the key ingredient?
  - How does the knowledge-creation model operate?
- The four pillars that encourage innovation in an organization: education, application, organizational climate and communication.
- Conclusion: What have you learned from this book?

Innovative ideas can be destructive, because they affect the value of investments in capital and equipment, as well as people's careers vested in an old paradigm.

On the other hand, they also represent opportunities for entirely new careers and investments, if we are flexible and see these changes coming.

Throughout this book we have discussed innovation and innovators. Nowadays, innovation is becoming increasingly important, especially as it relates to entrepreneurship, to the extent that we feel it necessary to devote the closing chapter of our book to this significant topic. However, this chapter does not give a recipe for building a creative company. Nor does it provide an algorithm for innovation, because none exists. Altshuller's book *Algorithm for Innovation* (Ref. 2.5) is a method for inventive problem solving—for these solutions to become innovation requires additional steps, as we shall see. Instead, this chapter will provide guidelines that will improve the chance for innovation to take place—and you will be able to recognize an innovative organization. With everything that you have learned, you should be empowered to work for change in any environment.

WHAT IS INNOVATION?

In Chapter 2, we gave a working definition of creativity, and we looked at innovation in its relationship to creativity, mostly in the context of product (and process) development and as they relate to different types of entrepreneurs and radical or incremental change. Creativity is a necessary but not sufficient condition for innovation. Although not always explicitly stated, the goal of innovation is to solve a problem, and the process requires many rounds of creative problem solving. Innovation is more than invention—it involves change, and it ultimately results in a useful product or process that is commercialized and widely disseminated. In this chapter, we will focus on the business and organizational angles and how an entrepreneurial mindset can help make business innovation happen.

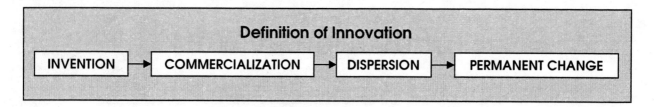

In this definition of innovation, just inventing is not enough. Commercializing the product is not enough. The invention must not only be commercialized, it must be widely dispersed to where its acceptance leads to a permanent change. Examples of inventions that demonstrate innovation with wide adoption and subsequent permanent change are the bicycle, radio, telephone, television, computer, quartz watch, and the Internet. Innovations need not be highly technical—the list of innovative products is almost endless but certainly includes mundane items like teabags, correcting fluid, Post-it notes, wheeled luggage, Teflon cookware, and the "spinning" toothbrush.

In contrast, the Segway scooter, a great invention introduced in December of 2001, is still waiting to turn into an innovation in human transportation. Several new modifications made in 2006 could improve its sales, but to become an innovation, sales must take off to where the scooter becomes a widely used option to get from here to there. PLATO, a software system for personalized instruction and standards-driven assessment and accountability, was invented over forty years ago to improve kindergarten to adult learning. This great invention has yet to make a basic change in education.

Understanding innovation is important to economics, business, engineering and technology, as well as sociology and government policy. The definition of innovation which includes going beyond invention and sales to a paradigm shift and permanent change in the way something is done is in line with Joseph Schumpeter's idea of creative destruction (described in his 1942 book, *The Process of Creative Destruction*):

> *The opening up of new markets and the organizational development from the craft shop and factory to such concerns as U.S. Steel illustrate the process of industrial mutation that incessantly revolutionizes the economic structure from within, incessantly destroying the old one, incessantly creating a new one ... [The process] must be seen in its role in the perennial gale of creative destruction; it cannot be understood on the hypothesis that there is a perennial lull.*

While innovation is usually seen as adding value, it can have a negative effect when those organizations that fail to innovate are left behind or when the innovators disregard the ethical boundaries in the management process of innovation as was the case at Enron.

WHY DO PEOPLE INNOVATE?

Research turns money into knowledge. Innovation turns knowledge into money.

Bayer Corporation, Germany

The question of why people innovate is linked to the question of what motivates innovators. The Bayer quote on the left may seem at first a bit humorous, but money is a key ingredient driving innovation—both making money and saving money. When Dr. Paul MacCready, one of the major innovators

of this century, was asked why he took on the challenge of m̶
human-powered flight across the English channel (in the *Gossame̶*
he replied, "For the money." He went on to explain that someone wa̶
to repay him a large sum of money. When he heard on the radio tha̶
Kramer Prize for crossing the English Channel had remained unclaimed ̶
decades despite numerous efforts by famous aerodynamicists, the sum mentioned was exactly what he needed. So he took on the challenge and won the
prize. It is easier to see why people invent rather than innovate. Table 12.1
lists common reasons and motivations for inventing new products.

Table 12.1 *Reasons and Motivations for Inventions*

1. As a response to existing need → can opener (invented 50 years after cans)
2. As a response to an imagined future need → high-temperature ceramics
3. To prevent accidents → cat's eye road reflector
4. To increase the chance of survival → pacemaker, smoke alarms, life-saving drugs
5. To make life easier → dishwasher and many other labor-saving devices
6. To increase comfort → waterbed
7. Through better problem solving → hydraulic propulsion system
8. As a deliberate synthesis → carbon brakes for aircraft
9. Through turning a failure into a success → Post-it notes, toilet paper (third try)
10. Accidentally, while working on something else → polyethylene, microwave oven, Slinky
11. Through cost reduction and quality improvement efforts → float glass
12. Through finding new uses for waste products → aluminum flakes in roofing
13. Through improvement of work done by others → piano, light bulb, ballpoint pen
14. By having research funds available to solve a specific problem → Kevlar
15. Through having new process technology → proteins from hydrocarbons
16. To meet tougher legal and legislated requirements → catalytic converter
17. From having been a dissatisfied user of a product → typewriter correction fluid
18. By finding new applications for existing technology → refrigerator
19. Through having new technology available → cell phone
20. Responding to a challenge by disgruntled customer → potato chip
21. To get around someone else's patent → changes to Microsoft Explorer browser
22. To pay a debt → safety pin
23. To satisfy intellectual curiosity → Velcro
24. For the fun of it → K'Nex (toy), the game of basketball
25. As expression of creativity → all inventions!

Some of the items mentioned in Table 12.1 were strong personal incentives for the inventors. Some of the items depend on the supportive environment provided by an employer—the invention of the transistor is a typical example. But even there, inventions frequently come from people outside
the area of expertise and from technological change originating outside an
industry. Although we usually think of inventions and innovation as products, processes are less frequently cited and sometimes more difficult to recognize as important innovations. Henry Ford combined the product idea of
Carl Benz (who designed and built the world's first practical automobile

...wered by an internal combustion engine) with the invention of Eli Whit-... (who mass-produced firearms using interchangeable parts) to come up ...h the assembly line way of manufacturing cars for the mass market.

HY DO INNOVATORS OCCUR AT RANDOM?

...illustrate this universal phenomenon—that innovation can come from ...one, anywhere, at any time—here is a story from Japan (see Ref. 2.3 for ...re details). It involves a project by Japan Railways East. While boring through Mount Tanigawa during construction of a new line north of Tokyo, engineers had a troublesome problem with water leaking into the tunnel. They drew up elaborate plans on how this water could be drained away. In the meantime, work crews inside the tunnel used some of this water for drinking. One worker noticed that this water had an exceptionally fine taste; he suggested that the company should bottle and market it as premier mineral water instead of pumping it into run-off channels. The brand name for this water is Oshimizu, and annual sales now top $67 million.

Another example (also from Ref. 2.3) happened at Hewlett-Packard. Two of their employees discovered that they could create small "explosions" when heating ink—which allowed the ink to shoot out in controlled bursts. No one understood how this process worked, and the company resisted developing this idea. Only when they looked at the economic potential of the inkjet did they begin to invest in its development. Today, with $5 billion in annual sales, the inkjet division of HP is larger and more profitable than many Fortune 500 companies.

Sometimes the biggest hurdle to acceptance is not technological difficulty but the reluctance of skilled workers to change their paradigm. Someone might say, "Oh, it was just a lucky accident." Yes, in many inventions we can see the vital role often played by chance. However, it takes a prepared mind—the mind of an "explorer"—to recognize when something is unusual and unexpected and to make use of the discovery. With the right organizational climate, it is possible to increase the probability of invention appearing at random and subsequent innovation succeeding in an organization.

WHY IS TECHNOLOGICAL INNOVATION NOT ENOUGH?

Innovation is one key to company success. But financial success depends on more than a company's ability to come up with new products. Consider Apple and Microsoft. In 2006, Apple was once again listed as the world leader in innovation in *Business Week* (Ref. 12.1). Microsoft ranked in fifth place, behind Toyota; it has never made it to the top of the list.

It is revealing to compare the worldwide market share and earnings between the two rivals over twenty-five years of growth and innovation. Apple presently commands two percent of the $180 billion worldwide market in personal computers, despite being the leader in innovation with products that are technological trailblazers. Apple in the past ten years was issued roughly 1,300 patents, which is about half of the 2700 for Microsoft. Yet the earnings of Apple are only 0.7 of one percent of Microsoft's!

(margin sidebar)

181

Creative acts are not planned for and come from where they are least expected.

Nobody can predict who will be involved in them, what they will be, when they will occur, or how they will happen.

Alan Robinson and
Sam Stern (Ref. 2.3)

The example I set is important, so it is critical that I encourage ideas.

Bill Gates

Many articles are written and many reasons given for the difference in performance between Microsoft and Apple (see for example Ref. 12.2). The first reason is always the fact that Steve Jobs kept his operating system proprietary whereas Microsoft had an open architecture where numerous software developers were able to participate. Other reasons include the serendipitous relationship Bill Gates had with IBM. However, James Andrews of the Boston Consulting Group maintains that "to be a truly innovative company is not just coming up with new ideas or products or services, it is coming up with the ones that generate enough cash to cover your costs and reward the shareholders." This involves inventing new business processes and developing new markets that meet previously unrecognized customer needs in new ways, fast!

It is quite interesting to examine Apple's approach in launching the iPod. According to Larry Keeley of Doblin Inc. (Ref. 12.1),

> *Apple used no fewer than seven types of innovation. They included networking (a novel agreement among music companies to sell their songs online), business model (songs sold for a buck each online) and branding. Consumers love the looks, ease and feel of the iPod, but it is the simplicity of the iTunes software platform that turned a great MP3 player into a revenue-gushing phenomenon.*

Thus, technological innovation alone is not sufficient for top earnings and increased market share. The Apple/Microsoft example should make you pause and think hard and fast about marketing and business innovation, not just about technological innovation, as will be discussed in the next section. One of the authors recently listened to a long presentation of a doctoral thesis about innovation. Not a word was mentioned about market development or cost to benefit ratio. We need to examine the critical elements of business success which go beyond mere technological innovation.

After ten years of research while at Harvard University, Amar V. Bhidé challenged the conventional wisdom about entrepreneurial success (Ref. 2.1). His conclusions about successful entrepreneurs are:

> *Most successful entrepreneurs start without a proprietary idea, without exceptional training and qualifications, and without significant amounts of capital. And they start their businesses in uncertain market niches. These entrepreneurs don't have anything that differentiates their business from other businesses in terms of technology or in terms of a concept. They just work harder, hustle for customers, and know that the opportunity may not last for more than six or eight months.*

This goes against the popular belief that a company is built around a unique proprietary idea. If we accept Bhidé's findings, entrepreneurs can start a business with a mundane idea. The author goes on to show that implementation of the idea—particularly overcoming the constraints of lack of money or track record—involves much creativity. To have a sustainable enterprise, innovation is essential, even for a small business, as indicated in Figure 1.1 of Chapter 1. However, in mid-1990, a survey of major U.S. companies found that eighty percent of firms said innovation was important but only four percent thought they did it well. A similar finding applies to the UK (Ref. 12.3). Thus for the remainder of this chapter, we want to take a closer look at business innovation.

BUSINESS INNOVATION

To produce true innovation that leads to permanent change—as defined in this book as a whole-brain process involving right-brain creativity and customer acceptance as well as left-brain implementation—we need to consider business models that enable the implementation portion of innovation. In Chapter 1, this is illustrated in the simple graph of Figure 1.2 and involves the bottom half of the cycle (which we have learned primarily utilizes quadrant B and C thinking, whereas much technological invention starts in quadrant D but stops at quadrant A). Figure 12.1 is an expansion of Figure 1.2 to highlight the central role of the business model in business innovation.

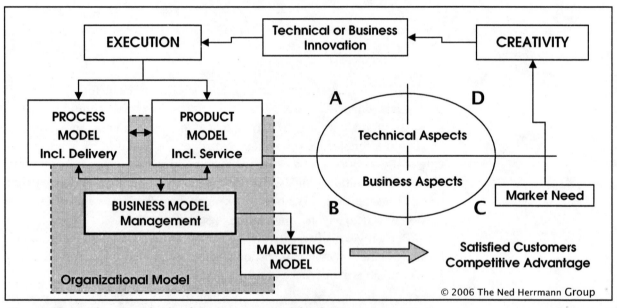

Figure 12.1   *The central role of the business model in business innovation*

THE BUSINESS MODEL

The business model is a key in the innovation process because it directs the way business is carried out. Examples are Dell (selling computers directly to the customers versus other companies who sell to retailers), Enterprise car rental (bringing the car to the customer versus other companies who mostly rent at airports), Southwest Airlines (providing low-cost, no-frills service), and Jeff Bezos (selling books online at Amazon.com). Basically, a business model is the *who, what, when, where, why, how and how much* of providing goods and services. "Innovation is any successful change in any element of the model that substantially enhances performance" and provides added value (Ref. 12.4). Business model innovation is a process that must be ongoing or repeated every two to four years to maintain competitive advantage.

Environmental concerns about over-packaging may lead to packaging innovations.

Established companies as well as startups commercialize technology with an approach determined by their business model. Sometimes, a new product can be innovated using a business model already in use. But often, there is a mismatch between the model, the new technology and the market opportunity. Technology managers must find and use a business model that will enable the venture to "capture value from that technology" (Ref. 12.5).

A subset of the business model is the *marketing model* where innovation involves development of new marketing methods to go hand in hand with improvement in product design or packaging, product promotion or pricing. Two packaging innovations are described in the following box.

Innovations in Packaging for Tea

Thomas Sullivan, a New York merchant, invented the tea bag in 1904. He packaged loose tea leaves in small hand-sown silk bags to hand out as samples to his customers. He was surprised when they brewed the tea in the bags—thus this also illustrates a serendipitous invention.

Later, bags were made of porous paper but retained a square shape. In 1989, Lyons Tetley began using round tea bags in the UK. The company had been slowly losing market share to cheaper generic teas. Eighteen months after introducing round bags, Lyons Tetley regained brand leadership and has since maintained a market share lead in the UK and significantly increasing world-wide sales.

Another packaging innovation was added by The Republic of Tea, who began selling round bags of specialty teas in cylindrical tins. The convenience and aesthetic appeal of a variety of handsome, airtight tins displayed on a pantry shelf soon became apparent to tea lovers.

When organizations innovate, they actually create new knowledge and information—from the inside out—to redefine both problems and solutions and, in the process, to re-create their environment.

Ikujiro Nonaka and Hirotaka Takeuchi (Ref. 4.2)

Product and service (and to some degree also process) innovations are discussed in Part 2, where the Pugh method can most appropriately be used to develop these innovative concepts, whether they involve technological innovation or not. But as we can see here, these potentially innovative solutions—to result in optimum benefit to the company's bottom line—give an impetus for business model innovation if this opportunity is recognized!

THE KNOWLEDGE-CREATION MODEL

To understand how technological and product innovation must be connected to the business model, we need to consider innovation from the point of view of knowledge creation. Ikujiro Nonaka and Hirotaka Takeuchi, in their book *The Knowledge-Creating Company: How Japanese Companies Create the Dynamics of Innovation* (Ref. 4.2) explain their detailed theory of the knowledge creation process as practiced in Japan. We were struck by the close correspondence between the four-quadrant knowledge creation model and the Herrmann model. These connections—for *goals* and actions—are shown in Figure 12.2. We believe this model can help us understand how teams learn to develop a mindset prepared to participate in innovation.

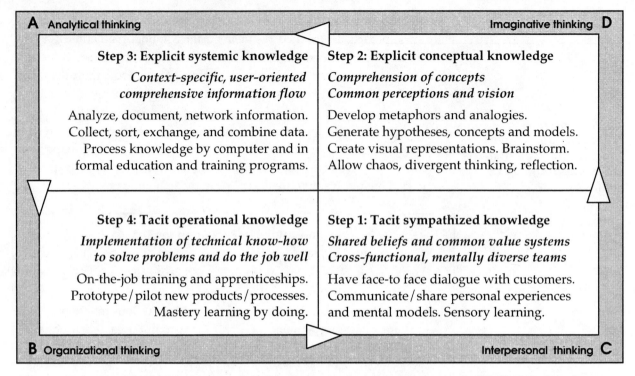

Figure 12.2 *The knowledge creation model superimposed on the Herrmann model (from Ref. 3.4)*

Learning in this model happens most effectively at the team level. It occurs in four steps, and knowledge is created in the course of moving from one quadrant to the next in an interactive social process:

- **Step 1** (in quadrant C): A collective commitment is made to learning and to sharing experiences and information, as well as developing a "feel" for new knowledge and cooperation.

- **Step 2** (in quadrant D): An intuitive understanding of concepts, change, and innovation is developed, with an increased ability to think flexibly, use metaphors, and explore new ideas.

- **Step 3** (in quadrant A): A synthesis of new knowledge occurs through combination and team synergy, together with continuous improvement through feedback from within and outside the team, going far beyond previously used approaches in information processing.

- **Step 4** (in quadrant B): The practical experiences from applying the new learning result in new tacit knowledge which can then trigger a new learning cycle at a higher level—involving new teams and new areas of learning, ultimately spiraling up to involve management and upper levels in the organization while yielding continuous innovation and competitive advantage at each level.

The term *learning* as used here is a whole-brain process; it is much more than passive acquisition of facts and information. Generally in Western culture, knowledge is seen as synonymous with data and information. Nonaka and Takeuchi call this *explicit knowledge* that can be expressed in words and

Effective teamwork embodies tacit knowledge as the members interact with each other and experience very different thinking styles in action.

numbers and shared for example in scientific formulas, principles, and procedures. They define *tacit knowledge* as highly personal and hard to formalize and thus communicate to others. It is deeply rooted in personal experiences, "know-how," perceptions, values and beliefs, as well as hunches, subjective intuition, and a vision for the future.

Knowledge creation is a new model that offers exciting possibilities for organizations to achieve continuous innovation. The case studies in Nonaka and Takeuchi's book give a wealth of practical applications. We want to include one example (in Table 12.2) that illustrates how the innovation process embodied in the automatic bread-making machine changed the entire company (based on information given in Ref. 4.2).

Table 12.2 *Knowledge Creation Cycles at Matsushita Home Bakery*

Cycle 1—Design Team Level

1. Identification of consumer dream—a home bread-making machine.
2. Vision of product as "easy and rich."
3. Prototype product; the evaluation discovers that bread is not "rich."
4. Software developer becomes apprenticed to famous baker to learn the art of kneading dough (the tacit knowledge needed to make excellent bread—a process that took many months).

Cycle 2—Design Team Level

1. When interacting with the design team, developer is eventually able to convey this new tacit knowledge as a mental image of "twisting-stretch" motion.
2. The improved design and prototype incorporates this motion—but it still takes a year through trial and error to produce tasty bread.
3. The project is transferred to the commercialization division but includes the original design team because of their valuable tacit knowledge of the product.

Cycle 3—Commercialization Team Level

1. Knowledge is shared to reduce cost and identify opportunities for innovation.
2. New concept: add yeast later in the mixing process—as it had always been done traditionally.
3. Design changes meet quality goals and reduce cost. The market delay is justified because the product now meets "easy and rich."
4. The success of this product shifts the focus of the entire company toward creating products that meet customer needs as well as "dreams."

Cycle 4—Organizational Level

- Engineers' attitude toward new projects and customers changes.
- Company now has a vision of "human electronics."
- New products (integrated coffee mill/automatic coffee brewer, large-screen TV, and induction-heating rice cooker) become bestsellers within the quality concept of "easy and rich."
- The process spirals up to higher levels and eventually changes the entire company through collaborative concurrent engineering. "Human electronics" extends to the company's employees—a 150-hour work month to give them more time with their families. This policy was first implemented as a pilot in one division to yield tacit knowledge of what a 150-hour work month would require to maintain the same productivity. One of the chief resulting strategies was to eliminate time wasted in meetings.

The knowledge creation model can help us understand how to foster the seemingly random creativity that is a prerequisite for innovation. As we shall see, it is possible to increase their frequency by optimizing the four conditions or *pillars* that can sustain creativity and innovation in an organization.

FOUR PILLARS FOR SUSTAINING INNOVATION IN AN ORGANIZATION

There are four main conditions—we are calling them foundational pillars—that will increase the likelihood of innovation in a company: (1) education, (2) application in teams, (3) organizational climate supported by management, and (4) open communication between all levels in an organization. They are not a prescription that will guarantee that innovation will happen—they are recommendations that will increase the probability of success. As we can visualize from Figure 12.3, if any one of the pillars is weak or missing, the potential for sustained innovation to occur will be diminished.

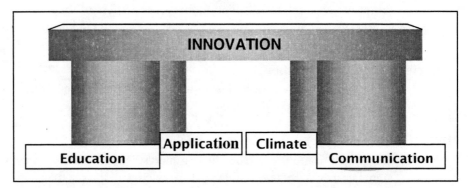

Figure 12.3   Innovation in an organization is supported by four pillars

The learning requirements for major innovation are high for everyone affected by the innovation. This is one factor why change is difficult.

Teamwork and communication are key in the organizational learning.

This is the crucial link (direct connection) between knowledge creation and innovation in the context of problem solving.

PILLAR 1—EDUCATION AT THE INDIVIDUAL LEVEL

Since invention and innovation originate with creative thinkers, it seems that training people in creative thinking and creative problem solving would be an obvious first step. Although many companies require their technical staff to periodically take education and training courses, creativity and innovation are rarely on the list. Creativity is in the same position as the quality movement was in the 1970s. Now TQM pervades the business world. Quality today is not the finish line but just the starting gate. This quality of "exceeding customer expectations" is essential if a product is to survive. Today, continuous improvement demands that businesses use a whole-brain approach and foster the creative and innovative potential of their employees. Systematically adopting the whole-brain knowledge creation cycle (Ref. 4.2) and a creative vision will prove more difficult but is necessary. As described by a former General Electric executive, companies must "innovate or evaporate."

What kind of education are we talking about? Universities (with rare exceptions) don't provide it; most industries don't have it, and only employees in a few organizations receive special training (mostly through consultants).

But with little accountability, the training seems to be largely hit-or-miss. Perhaps this is one reason why innovation is so random. Education in creativity and innovation must be of the same magnitude as that in the quality movement. If we are to increase the probability of success, it must become part of the organization's culture. This education is much more than a matter of taking creativity courses. Ideally, instructors working with teams must go to their work sites to understand the working environment and provide for just-in-time training and on-the-job tacit learning.

As a first step, those that have not taken college courses on creative problem solving should have at least one workshop on the subject, *followed by an implementation or case study assignment.* This is crucial because a group or team must have a common understanding and shared values about creativity and innovation. Another way to acquire tacit knowledge would be through a mentoring relationship with an innovator. Sustainable change does not happen when individuals work alone, are ridiculed for being different, are afraid of change, or cannot communicate the excitement of discovery. In the quality movement, industry was the driver and universities and colleges responded by offering courses focusing on quality issues. Will there be a similar development for creativity and innovation? The box below lists some encouraging global efforts we have personally encountered. Although many universities in the U.S. talk innovation, only a few "walk the talk."

Education— learning and then applying what has been learned— is above all the responsibility of each individual.

■ Nanyang Technological University and the University of Singapore (both ranked among the top five universities in Asia) are now required by their government to teach courses in creativity starting in the freshman year. The Innovation Centre at Nanyang Technological University is truly impressive and rivals many U.S. college campuses in size. ■ All engineering freshmen at the University of Pretoria in South Africa must take a course in innovation (which includes a team project) as a result of the university's focus on innovation. ■ The Nottingham University Business School is one of the first business schools in the UK to require all incoming students to undertake a module "Entrepreneurship and Business" to learn about invention and creative problem solving. This effort is beginning to spiral to other units at the University of Nottingham, including engineering departments.

PILLAR 2—APPLICATION AT THE TEAM LEVEL

Innovation is fostered when teams are trained and are routinely using the creative problem solving process. Teams are cross-functional and mentally diverse, and innovation is a shared goal. Teams understand that its members have different thinking preferences; they have learned to work together and value the contributions each person brings to the team. They do not segregate the process—for example, the brainstorming step is not assigned *only* to the quadrant D thinkers. Instead, everyone participates in the entire innovation process. This shared understanding enables the team to define problems properly, develop out-of-the-box solutions, and optimize. They also make an effort to build relationships with customers to gain tacit insight into needs, problems, and unspoken "dreams." In addition, it enables the team to develop effective "selling" strategies to get their idea accepted and implemented—thus possibly initiating a business innovation cycle.

The first principle of empowerment is the promotion of entrepreneurship— an insistence upon freedom in the workplace to pursue innovative ideas.

3M Company

Continuous improvement in the third step of knowledge creation occurs with two different feedback loops. The quadrant B loop leads to enhanced problem solutions and knowledge as people apply new information. The quadrant D loop achieves better solutions through additional creative thinking, brainstorming, and synthesis to eliminate flaws as part of creative problem solving. As we have seen, the Pugh method is such a feedback loop.

Patience is an important virtue for innovators and teams when selling innovative ideas. A book by Michael Geshman entitled *Getting It Right the Second Time* (Ref. 12.6) discusses forty-nine products that are now established household items but had serious trouble from day one in the market. It took a Herculean effort to bring them to being fully accepted by consumers. An example is Kimberly-Clark, the maker of such products as Kleenex and Kotex. Both of these products were unsuccessful initially—both were invented to use an enormous surplus of *Cellucotton* at the end of World War II. Kleenex was first marketed as a new way for ladies to remove cold cream from their faces. Kotex could not be advertised for its intended use at all, as the subject was unmentionable at that time. When Kleenex was creatively marketed for blowing one's nose and Kotex came in a white, plain package in vending machines (where women could anonymously buy the product) sales took off—the brand name now is synonymous with the product.

Just because an innovative idea, product or process does not succeed immediately (and it frequently won't), it does not mean it will continue to fail. Hundreds of products that are successful today can attest to this, including the Post-it notes, the Xerox machine, bar coding, and Jell-O. An organization can have training in creative thinking and a supportive climate, but if the problem-solving tools used routinely are strictly analytical, the likelihood of innovation will be significantly reduced. Creative problem solving must become the paradigm in the organization, not just in targeted projects, such as product development, but in solving many different business problems.

The essence of innovation is to re-create the world according to a particular ideal or vision.

Creating new knowledge is also not simply a matter of learning from others or acquiring knowledge from the outside.

Knowledge has to be built on its own, frequently requiring intensive and laborious interaction among members of the organization.

I. Nonaka and H. Takeuchi (Ref. 4.2)

When the chaos and messiness of creativity are feared instead of understood and appreciated, an organization can pilot a small scale implementation on the model of a "skunk works" where a creative team can operate outside the regular bureaucratic channels and control. Since nothing is more powerful than success when selling an idea, this may be an approach that can make the innovation process more acceptable in a very conservative, cautious organization.

The discussion so far has taken the view of supporting creativity through managerial leadership and providing the right kind of training in creative thinking and problem solving. But organizations can also grow creative—at least in the initial two stages—from the bottom up. Many organizations are at the first stage, where a few creative individuals work quietly in isolation so they will not be noticed and get into trouble. In the second stage, two or more of these people discover each other; they begin to collaborate and mutually enhance each other's creativity. This process may start a chain reaction and grow to involve teams—creativity has become contagious and acceptable. Finally, in the third stage, management will come to actively support these efforts with creative challenges and assignments. Good solutions will be evaluated, appreciated, and implemented, with the results that the organization will grow into a creative community because creative individuals have started the process. Several knowledge creation cycles are needed to spiral creativity up to the management and organizational level.

PILLAR 3—CLIMATE AT THE MANAGEMENT LEVEL

An important factor that influences the acceptance of new ideas is the current paradigm of the business. If someone came to 3M (which is a paragon of an innovative company) with an idea for a new zipper, that would be a much more difficult "selling" job than finding acceptance for a brand-new class of sand paper. Chester Carlson's invention was rejected by twenty companies over eight years—the photography business environment was not ready for this new idea of "electrostatic photography," now known as the Xerox process. Thus the environment includes not only a nurturing atmosphere within a particular company, but also an openness to new ideas coming from the outside, especially when the ideas might differ from the established business paradigm (as humorously illustrated in Figure 12.4).

Figure 12.4 *What response do new ideas receive in your organization?*   © *1999 Don Kilpela, Jr.*

To illustrate the influence of environment, consider the story of the bar code (from Ref. 2.3). In 1948, Sam Friedland, the president of Food Fair, the largest supermarket chain in Philadelphia, made a visit to the dean of engineering at Drexel University, a well-known private university that prides itself on innovative and cooperative programs with industry. Mr. Friedland wanted the dean to start a research project to automatically add up the prices of groceries at the checkout counter. His stores suffered huge money losses through clerical errors and inefficiency. The dean was not interested; he said it was not Drexel's mission to be involved in this type of applied research.

Bob Silver, an electrical engineering instructor at Drexel, was outside the dean's door waiting for his appointment and overheard the conversation. Later that day, Silver talked to Joseph Woodland, a colleague in mechanical engineering, and they decided to work on this problem. Through a chain of interesting circumstances, Woodland found himself on a Florida beach when the idea of the vertical bars for the code came to him as he happened to notice the pattern of streaks his fingers had formed in the sand. Friedland worked on developing a code reader, and by October 1949 they filed for the patent which they received in 1952. But it took more than twenty frustrating years before the bar code would be commercialized.

It is easy to blame the dean for being short-sighted. Most likely, he was only reflecting the view of the general university environment which valued fundamental research and disdained practical, application-oriented projects. Fortunately, these attitudes are now changing.

A good organizational environment is one that encourages employees to explore, network, experiment, question and think of more than one solution to a problem. A creative organization is a learning organization that is prepared to take calculated risks, because the initial application of new technology involves high risk and high failure. This is why these projects are frequently undertaken by quadrant D individuals (in their garages and a chaotic environment). When technologies are modified in a process of continuous improvement by a team in an organization, the risk is moderate. When the technology is developed and has matured for mass production and wide marketing to customers, the risk and failure rate are low, and the environment has become a quadrant B culture: ordered, disciplined, scheduled, and tightly managed. Unfortunately, this risk-averse behavior not only discourages the discovery of new paradigms and further invention, it leads to morale problems, as we have seen in Chapter 3, Figure 3.7.

Only the top leadership of an organization can quickly change a business culture by articulating a clear vision of where the organization needs to go and then supporting middle management in implementing the vision. When Procter and Gamble came up with their new innovation strategy—where fifty percent of new product ideas were to come from outside its own labs—each business unit added a manager for driving cultural change around the new model (Ref. 12.1). It is management that can counteract most of the barriers to innovation: bureaucracy, excessive control and segmentation, short-term thinking and lack of vision, as well as risk aversion, even if they cannot do much outside the company when the political climate is overly restrictive and has no understanding of how to encourage entrepreneurial activities.

Empowerment is much talked about these days, especially by upper management. Yet we often see a mismatch between the organization's vision (which may be expressed in quadrant C and D terms and values) and the controlling behavior (quadrant B) as day-to-day activities are carried out. At the level of middle managers whose main objective is to cut costs and do more with less, the only empowerment of employees is the right to quit—a typical response of a left-brain culture.

Charles Prather and Lisa Guntry (Ref. 12.7.) came up with nine dimensions or questions for a manager who wants to examine the organizational climate for innovation, as summarized in Table 12.3.

It is the dynamic process of interaction between individual and organizational learning spirals that fuels innovation and adds value, not information or knowledge per se.

Table 12.3 *Nine Dimensions of an Innovative Organizational Climate*

1. **Challenge and involvement.** Is the climate dynamic and inspiring? Are people engaged and motivated? As an example, one of 3M's "stretch" goals (not quotas)—publicized throughout the company—is to have thirty percent of its sales from products that are less than four years old, and ten percent from products less than one year old!

2. **Freedom.** Do the people have independence? Are individual employees and teams given autonomy to define and do their work?

3. **Idea time.** Do people have time to elaborate on new ideas or consider alternate solutions to a problem? The famous "15% of your time to pursue new ideas" policy at 3M is a good example.

4. **Idea support.** Are new ideas greeted with silence or an attitude of "We have done this before"? Or are they received in a supportive and attentive way?

5. **Conflict.** Do people behave in a mature way or are gossip, slander, plots, and traps part of the daily routine? It is important in creative organizations that people control their negative impulses because one negative person can pollute the entire environment.

6. **Debate.** Are diverse opinions in a group allowed and accepted?

7. **Playfulness and humor.** Are good-natured jokes and a degree of playfulness valued as part of a relaxed environment?

8. **Trust and openness.** With a few exceptions, are the doors to the managers' offices open? Do people have a sincere respect for each other? Or are things discussed behind people's backs?

9. **Risk taking.** Do people feel that whenever they are dealing with things with an unknown outcome, they are "going out on a limb"? Or are they encouraged to take a calculated risk? Do they feel protected when they are working on a new initiative on behalf of the company?

PILLAR 4—COMMUNICATION

Communication is central to innovation. There has to be communication between individuals, teams, and management. As a leader, you need to develop a plan to network and get information through to other people in your organization. Individuals or groups simply going about their business and doing their own thing will rarely innovate. Communication is the vital link between the pillars of education, application, and organizational climate and to make the knowledge-creation cycles operate effectively.

The 3M Company probably would never have developed *Scotchgard*, one of its most successful products, if it had not been for communication between a few key people. A young research chemist, JoAn Mullin, happened to spill three drops of a chemical onto her deck shoes. When she washed her shoes, she noticed that those spots simply refused to get wet. She knew that work was going on elsewhere in the company on oil- and water-repellent treatments, so she was excited about her discovery. However, no one paid attention to her, except her supervisor who eventually handed swatches of treated fabric for testing to the research group. However, nothing was done because of the failure of earlier tests. JoAn became so discouraged that she switched to another job. But her supervisor followed up. Fortunately, the timing was better this time around, as a young researcher had just finished a project and was ready to do something else. The results completely changed the direction of the research program. As it turned out, the spilled substance did not work out, but it was a stepping stone to the ultimate product. But JoAn Mullin never received credit for her original discovery (Ref. 2.3).

Open communication still goes against the grain for many people who are used to keeping good ideas to themselves. Some have learned through hard experiences that ideas get "stolen" by unethical colleagues. But in any organization, whether small or large, both formal and informal communication is necessary to discuss and grow innovative ideas. It is precisely the informal, unanticipated exchange between employees who do not normally communicate on a regular basis that often moves a project forward. Thus informal networking channels should be developed. For example, at 3M this happens through "creativity clubs." Companies should have a formal channel for employees to communicate ideas—possibly through committees, technical groups and management groups that regularly evaluate ideas. Indifference can squash ideas just as effectively as ridicule. Also, it should be part of the organizational culture that people are expected to respond to requests for help and information from others in the company and should be given the time to do so.

Activity 12.1: Identifying a Creative Organization

Table 12.4 is a checklist for identifying traits of a creative organization—for different users. No organization will have a perfect score on this checkup, but collecting this information and evaluating the answers objectively can give you a feel for the climate for creativity and subsequent innovation in the organization.

- If you are a student soon to enter the job market, the list may give you some hints—especially if you can talk candidly with some of the employees to collect the data.
- If you are part of an innovation team and want to work for change, the list helps identify areas that may need improvement.
- If you are a manager, the list can gauge the "state of your organization" and your own alignment; it will help you set priorities if you want to pioneer a paradigm shift.

Go/no go checkpoint for evaluating a job opportunity:

Evaluate the potential employer against the Table 12.4 checklist. Then look at the following cases:

1. If both you and the organization are creative, go for it—take the job.
2. If the organization is creative and you are not, you might get your creativity unleashed—if you get the job and are able to keep it. The assessment should give you confidence to take some risks.
3. If you are creative and the organization is not, you will have to use your judgment. If you need the job to survive, take it but be on the lookout for opportunities (within and outside the company)—you might be able to make a difference, but realize that it will not be easy. How good are your communication skills and your persistence? If these two characteristics are not your strong points, try to find a more favorable work environment.
4. If neither you nor the organization is creative, this may not be a problem in the short run, but in a globally competitive world and rapidly changing technological environment, this could hinder your future job opportunities and advancement. Learn to be creative and consider Option 3.

Table 12.4   Checklist for Identifying a Creative Organization

_____ Do all employees know the company's vision in the area of creativity and innovation?
_____ Do they support the vision wholeheartedly?
_____ Is everyone being encouraged to always look for improvement?

_____ Are managers aware that creative ideas can come from anyone, anywhere, at any time?
_____ Is technology recognized as a competitive tool that can make difficult products achievable?
_____ Is calculated risk acceptable and bureaucracy at a minimum?

_____ Are creative thinkers and innovators rewarded? How?
_____ Are employees encouraged to maintain a portfolio of creative accomplishments?
_____ Are people from different departments involved in creative problem-solving teams and in the evaluation and implementation process?

_____ Does the organization have policies and procedures that encourage a process of never-ending innovation and improvement?
_____ Are innovators allowed to learn and work by playing?
_____ Is management "walking the talk" about empowerment for creativity and innovation?

_____ Is management for creativity more than paying lip service by providing a "suggestion box"?
_____ Do definite mechanisms exist for developing and funding creative ideas?
_____ Does this system respond in a timely and fair manner, and are successes publicized?

_____ Is everybody in the organization able to recognize a potentially useful idea?
_____ Is it easy for an employee in one section to find out about ideas in a different section?
_____ What types of formal and informal networking opportunities and communication channels exist in the organization?

_____ How would the organization respond to an employee working "unofficially" on a project?
_____ Is there a process of appeal for independent review of an idea that has been rejected?
_____ Are people encouraged to look for the unusual and unexpected as a potential opportunity for creative ideas? Do they have permission to be creative and take independent action?

_____ Is there a policy of job rotation and developing new skills?
_____ Is the organization making full use of the skills and thinking preferences of their employees?
_____ How can you find out what skills and expertise are available?

_____ If contacted for help, how readily are people responding?
_____ Do employees have an opportunity for mini-sabbaticals to gain new stimuli?
_____ How easy (or difficult) is it in the organization to interact directly with the customers?

_____ What training programs in creativity, whole-brain thinking, and team development have been or are being used in the organization?
_____ Are people excited about their workplace, or are there morale problems?
_____ Besides your analytical evaluation, what is your "hunch" about this organization? Can you support its values, and will your job "turn you on"—will it stretch and grow you?

Failures in innovation have been widely researched. Some are caused by factors outside the control of the organization. Among the internal causes of failure, poor communication ranks at the top, followed by poor management and poor participation by teams, together with poor empowerment. If we consider the last item to mean a lack in encouraging and training employees in creative thinking, we can see that all four pillars are involved in some fashion. Poor monitoring of results was also mentioned and refers to monitoring all goals, actions and teams involved in the innovation process.

Here are some tips for doing innovation well in your own enterprise (from Ref. 12.2):

For innovation to flourish, both society and the organization must have a certain tolerance for failure for those who try something new.

Alan Robinson and Sam Stern (Ref. 2.3)

1. **Not all innovation is equal.** Technical innovation will earn you lots of fans (think Apple), but business model innovation will earn you lots of money (think Dell).

2. **Innovate for cash, not cachet.** If the cool new thing doesn't generate enough money to cover costs and make a profit, it's art, not innovation.

3. **Don't hoard your goodies.** Getting to market on time and at the right price is vital. If that means licensing your idea or invention to an outside manufacturer or marketer, do it.

4. **Innovation doesn't generate growth.** Management does. If you covet awards for your creativity, go to Hollywood. Managers get rewarded for results, which come from customers.

5. **Attention deficit has no place here.** Every innovation worth doing deserves your commitment. Don't leap from one new thing to another. If your creation doesn't appear important to you, it won't be important to anyone else.

WHAT HAVE YOU LEARNED FROM THIS BOOK?

We trust that what you learned here in this book will encourage you to start a creative enterprise. We strongly recommend that you keep notes about your process and periodically evaluate the results. As we have mentioned before, we cannot guarantee that you will succeed in your business if you follow all the steps for effective problem solving—there are too many intangibles involved. You can, however, increase the odds. According to Jeffry Timmons (Ref. 1.2),

> *Having relevant experience, know-how, attitudes, behaviors, and skills appropriate for a particular venture opportunity can dramatically improve the odds for success. The other side of the coin is that if an entrepreneur does not have these, then he or she will have to learn them while launching and growing the business. The tuition for such an approach is often greater than most entrepreneurs can afford.*

In the end, an entrepreneur learns by doing—like an apprentice. Many entrepreneurs experience false starts or even failures at various stages in product and business development. Yet what they learn through this process will help them to succeed in their next venture. Patience is required as a successful venture can take seven or more years before showing any capital gains. Also, we can learn from the failures of others—we can see them as opportunities for improvement. For encouragement, we recommend that you take the time to complete the following activity.

> **Activity 12.2 Creative Problem Solving and Success**
>
> Select a well-known product, company, or entrepreneur. Research their history from the very beginning. Were there any failures or detours on the way to success? This could be at any point: choice of product or name, timing, unwise use of startup funding, etc. Again, go through each problem solving step and mindset and analyze how well each step was followed. For ideas, see Reference 12.6 or Table 12.5. Assemble your findings in your notebook and then type up a two-page summary. What have you learned from this example?

Technology is neither good nor bad, nor is it neutral.

It has short-range and long-range impacts.

Impact may differ according to the scale at which a technology is applied.

Technology always entails trade-offs.

In short, technology has different results in different contexts.

Melvin Kranzberg, Founding editor of *Technology and Culture*

Table 12.5 *Examples of Failures that Became a Success*

Success after false starts and bankruptcy: Henry Ford
Failed experiments and product prototypes: Thomas Edison
Difficulty of finding a "concept" buyer: Chester Carlson
No sale of invention; became the product's manufacturer: James Dyson
Changed the product's name from SMP to *Mathematica*: Steve Wolfram
Changed marketing approach: Kimberly-Clark (Kleenex, Kotex)
Idea had to wait for supporting technology: Ralph Gillette
Change in product from pigs to fish: Kenny Yap
Change in "customer" (from arthritic to wealthy people): Jacuzzi Brothers
Old technology, no job—new partner, new technology: Jim Clark
High risk ad campaign; failures yield publicity: Richard Branson

ENDNOTE

In this book we attempted to meet the ambitious challenges of inspiring creativity and its innovation with a practical and relevant set of approaches and processes. Although we often focus attention on micro-level behavior and exercises, this still has clear and important implications for the more global picture. As decision making by individuals and groups is informed more effectively by creative insights and responses, the scope for improvement can grow in all areas of activity. The wider application of creative problem solving can make a significant contribution towards the generation of new solutions to the problems of an increasingly complex and precarious world.

EXERCISES

2.1 Interview with an Inventor or Innovator

If you have the opportunity to meet an inventor, prepare a list of questions ahead of time that you want to ask, so you can find out how the invention was made. What was learned? What were the motives, process, effort, and final outcome, as well as the rewards? Alternately, research an invention or innovator and try to find the answers to the same questions. For example, check out Dan Bricklin at www.bricklin.com.

12.2 Personal Application

How will you use what you have learned from this book? Describe how you will practice new thinking skills. Outline your short-term and long-term plans for entrepreneurship or entrepreneurial thinking.

12.3 Evaluating Your Teamwork

Write down a summary of your team accomplishments and interactions from your experience with your project team. What have you learned about communicating with people who have thinking preferences different from your own?

12.4 Organizational Application

How can you (with the help of a team) help your organization improve the climate for creativity, change, and innovation?
TIP: This could be a smaller group that is having to cope with a radical change—how would you help them overcome the fear of change?

12.5 Culture, Creativity and Technology

With a team, brainstorm and then discuss the values in your culture that support creativity and inventiveness. How can these values be strengthened? How do they support the integration of technology with the culture? Focus your discussion on one or more of the following: your family culture and heritage (and role models), your organizational culture, the culture of your local community (political unit, educational system, etc.) or the culture of your ethnic community.

12.6 Review of Your Journal or Notebook

Go back over the notes you took as you studied this book. Are there items you jotted down for follow-up or implementation? Make a schedule to do something about the best of these ideas—don't let them go to waste. Also, plan to keep your textbook; you will find it to be a valuable resource over time, worth many times the price you could get if you sold it.

12.7 Mini Case Study

a. Do a mini case study of the creative problem solving process, from finding a problem to implementing the solution and evaluating the results, similar to Example 3 in Chapter 5. You may invite family members, co-workers or a group of friends to participate. Use at least two rounds of the Pugh method. Write a report documenting all the steps. In some classes, you may have to submit it as part of your course assessment.

b. Since we are now publishing the book through a print-on-demand publisher in a digital format, we will be able to frequently upgrade the textbook to keep the material up-to-date. Thus we are on the lookout for good case studies (or other interesting and challenging exercise ideas) that can be added as we revise the book periodically. Please submit your contribution to the contact address at www.InnovationToday.biz.

Innovation—the successful exploitation of new ideas—is the key business process that enables UK businesses to compete effectively in the global environment.

Department of Trade and Industry, www.innovation.gov.uk

REFERENCES AND RESOURCES

12.1 "The World's Most Innovative Companies," cover story, *BusinessWeek* (online), April 24, 2006.

12.2 Carleen Hawn, "If He's so Smart… Steve Jobs, Apple, and the Limits of Innovation," *Fast Company Magazine,* Issue 78, January 2004, Page 68, as published on www.fastcompany.com.

12.3 Brian Clegg, *Creativity and Innovation for Managers,* Butterworth and Heinemann, 1999.

12.4 Donald Mitchell and Carol Coles, "Establishing a Continuing Business Model Innovation Process," article published by *The CEO Refresher* at www.refresher.com, 2006.

12.5 Henry Chesbrough and Richard S. Rosenbloom, "The role of the business model in capturing value from innovation: evidence from Xerox Corporation's technology spin-off companies," *Industrial and Corporate Change,* Vol. 11, Number 3, pp. 529-555.

12.6 Michael Geshman, *Getting It Right the Second Time,* Addison-Wesley, 1990. Although written for business people, it is fun for anyone interested in the history of consumer products.

12.7 Charles W. Prather and Lisa K. Gundry, *Blueprints for Innovation: How Creative Processes Can Make You and Your Company More Competitive,* American Management Association, New York, 1995. Concise, useful!

12.8 James Dyson, *Against All Odds (An Autobiography),* Orion Business, London, 1997. Written by the inventor of the dual cyclone vacuum cleaner, it illustrates a 15-year long process of innovation.

Movie/DVD: Tucker: The Man and His Dream (1988)

This film is based on the true story of Preston Tucker, a maverick car designer and his ill-fated challenge to the auto industry with his revolutionary concept. Directed by Francis Ford Coppola.

Website: www.bricklin.com

This is a fascinating website for seeing innovation "in action" by Dan Bricklin, the co-inventor of the first electronic spreadsheet, VisiCalc. It is constantly being updated. An article recently added is: "When the Long Tail Wags the Dog"—very inspiring for beginning entrepreneurs to read!

Michael Polanyi: Learning More about Tacit Knowledge

Michael Polanyi (1891-1976) was a renowned physical chemist and philosopher of sciences. If you are interested in reconciling the analytical approach of the scientific method with whole-brain "knowing," read Polanyi's book, *Personal Knowledge: Towards a Post Critical Philosophy* (1966) or Mark T. Mitchell, *Michael Polanyi,* ISI Books (2006).

Answers to Exercise Problems

CHAPTER 1

1.2 Diagnostic Question

This is the type of question used to identify people who can think creatively. Anyone giving more than one answer is able to go beyond the left-brain scheme taught in school that every problem has only one answer.

From college students, one of the most common answers is "ball rolling down a hill." Other categories of answers are: sun/moon rising/setting next to hill or building; various string toys; fasteners; nets; flying things, etc. One memorable idea was "bald man reading a newspaper (seen from above).

CHAPTER 2

2.1 Warm-Ups

a. Draw the track of the needle. Can you see the answer? One groove!

b. There are 25 boxes in all—one plus six plus eighteen. Did you draw a sketch? If not, draw one now and see how easy the question becomes.

c. You do not need to do any math—in fact, that mental language is a hindrance in this case. No matter how fast the two people travel or in which direction, at the moment they meet, they will be (by definition) in the same place and thus the same distance from City A.

d. Cook it when you catch it; freeze it; wrap it in paper; leave it in the water; switch to eating chicken; keep a cat around; burn incense; cut off its nose. Does this give you some additional ideas?

e. She bought three house numbers to make up the numeral 100.

f. They are two of a set of triplets, or two of a set of quadruplets, or …

g. Here it helps to have a consistent viewpoint: *Guests:* They paid £27; then *subtract* the boy's tip to get a room price of £25. *Proprietor:* He took in £30 and returned £5 (for a room price of £25) of which three pounds went to the guests and two to the boy.

2.2 Geese and Lambs

1. Use algebra: make up two equations with two unknowns:

    x = number of lambs, y = number of geese.

    $x + y = 8$ (animals) and $4x + 2y = 22$ (legs).

    Multiply the first equation by 2 and subtract from the second:

    $4x - 2x + 2y - 2y = 22 - 2 \times 8 = 6.$

    Therefore, $x = 3$ and $y = 5$. Check: $4 \times 3 + 2 \times 5 = 22.$

2. Use trial and error.

3. Use tabulation. Keep the total number of animals constant. Start with a maximum number of lamb legs (32) and corresponding geese legs (0); then 28 lamb legs and 2 geese legs, then 24 lamb legs and 4 geese legs, and so on, to 12 lamb legs and 10 geese legs (which gives the desired total of 22 legs). The tabulation could have been done in the other direction, or by keeping the number of legs constant and varying the number of animals.

4. Use a graph, with the total number of legs on one axis and the number of geese on the other axis. Then plot the number of legs of 0 geese (and 8 lambs) = 32, 1 goose (and 7 lambs) = 32, and so on until 5 geese (and 3 lambs) = the desired 22 legs.

5. The easiest visualization is this (invented by an elementary school child): Draw 8 circles representing the animals. Draw two legs on each circle, since the animals have at least two legs each. This makes a total of 16 legs. Then add two legs to one circle at a time, until 22 legs have been drawn. You will then have three circles with four legs (or three lambs), with five circles remaining that have only two legs (or five geese).

6. Other answers are possible, including using real animals or toys, for a hands-on learning experience.

Conclusion: Many ways of thinking are useful and valid for solving problems. The way we solve problems depends on our thinking preferences and on the methods we have been taught.

2.3 Mountain Path Problem

Many people have trouble coming up with a solution. This is expected since the answer cannot be reasoned out with verbal, sequential thinking. Some people may use trial-and-error and make up a specific example with distances and times, but such a complicated approach is not necessary—we are seeking a general solution. The most common visual solution is some type of graph of height versus time, where varying slopes of the lines indicate the different speeds of going up and coming down. The slopes (and different starting and stopping points do not influence the essence of the answer—there will be a spot where the two lines intersect.

This visualization is still difficult, especially for those not familiar with graphing data. But when given another way to look at the problem, everyone immediately "sees" the answer. Imagine merging the two days, with two people on the path, one going up and one coming down. They will have to meet at some point on the path, at some time during the day. Through visualization and imagination, we can reframe problems to where it is much easier to see solutions.

2.4 The Fastball Problem

One solution is to place the ball in the center of a circle where the team members place their hands on it in sequence (and very quickly) while standing very close to each other. Another solution is for the team to form a path for the ball to roll across (or drop down) either by using outstretched arms or outstretched index fingers—this depends somewhat on the size of the ball being used.

2.5 Lateral Thinking Exercises

a. The details of age, height, and size are setting us up to think in the context of personal descriptions, and the question is interpreted to refer to body weight. But if we are trying to think creatively, we want to resist the given context—or at least go beyond it to consider other interpretations. Thinking of the question in terms of "what does he spend his time weighing?" leads you to another answer—meat. Or you can simply visualize Tony selling meat to a customer. What is he putting on the scales?

b. We can take 3 from 25 only once, because then it becomes 22.

c. To solve this problem, you have to break away from the obvious way of looking at things. Look at it in a new way—turn your book upside down, or hold the page up to a light and look at it from the backside. Did your mental blocks prevent you from trying these unfamiliar approaches?

d. You can draw a horizontal line through the IX. When you turn the page around, you have the Roman numeral VI on top of the line. But let's think in a new context—away from Roman numerals or straight lines. Add a curved "S" in front of the IX, and you have SIX.

e. In math, the scheme we are taught is to look at what remains. But, if you take two apples from five, what you have in your hand is two apples.

f. The way this problem is framed sets up one context (England, Holland, Spain, France—where?), but the solutions lies in being able to "see" that survivors are not buried!

g. Millions of letters are on desks and in file cabinets all over the State of Mississippi. The more easily you can slip from verbal thinking (letters in words) to visual thinking (envelopes with sheets of paper and a huge land area located in the Southern U.S., the more apt you are to solve problems like this one. Can you "see" another answer? What if you pictured all the letters of the alphabet in all the *writing* in Mississippi?

h. Beware of the context and the thinking pattern this exercise has set up—it can lead to false assumptions. You have probably assumed that there had to be a single, common answer. The answer to the question is quite simply: a chair, a bed, and a toothbrush.

2.6 Light Bulb Problem

In the office, turn on two of the lights. After a few minutes, turn one of them off. Then go to the warehouse and touch the two bulbs that are off. The one that is warm is connected to the switch that was turned on/off. Here, you needed to think beyond just seeing (light) to touching (heat). One of our creative problem solving students in the UK won two concert tickets with the answer. He heard the problem posed on a radio station—the DJ was astonished that someone got the solution so quickly.

2.7 Geometric Problems

The first four shapes take some thinking (and visualization) to solve, with various strategies like doodling and dividing into "lowest common denominators" and learning from the previous shapes. This, however, then creates a pitfall—to where we attempt to solve the last problem in a most complicated, instead of the easy way, by following previous patterns.

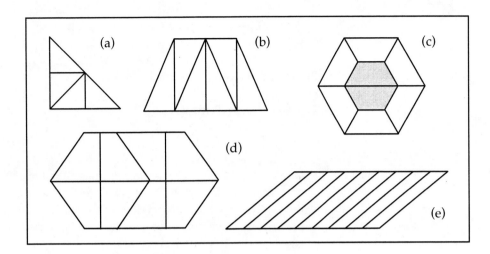

2.8 Sentence Problem

This problem has many different answers. You can start with *six* lower-case or *seven* (including the upper-case) or *eight* "t" letters, but then you need to think out of the box. The sentence has *English typewritten "t" letters, black letters, Times New Roman style letters, no crooked or broken letters*, and so on.

INVENTIVE THINKING EXERCISES

2.9 The Missing Baseball Problem

The boy invented a bat made out of a wide transparent front part with a screw-on lid. Three brightly colored balls can be stored in the handle for transport (and visibility).

2.10 The Hanging Chain Problem

Try reframing the problem—or what is the real problem? Depending on what you perceive to be the problem, your mind will find solutions in that direction. Here are three different solutions:

a. Are the chains too short? Tie your shoestrings or a piece of clothing to one of the chains; then pull that lengthened chain toward the other, which you are now able to reach.

b. Is the distance too far? Set the chains in motion toward each other to shorten the distance. If they are not heavy enough to move, tie your shoes to one or both of them to make a better pendulum. When the chains are close together, grab them quickly before they swing in the opposite direction.

c. Are your arms too short? If you have a flexible body and long legs (and good balance), you might be able to hook one chain with your foot.

2.11 Moving the Transformer Problem

The original problem and solution are embedded in the narrative of a true story, as told in the opening chapter about TRIZ (Ref. 4.10). The solution (by an inventive accountant) consisted of blocks of ice stacked up carefully and built into a platform even with the transformer's platform. The ice tower was covered with a strong flat board, and the transformer was slid from its original position onto the board by workers using pry bars. The sun and warm night temperatures did the rest—by the end of the second day, all the ice had melted and the transformer arrived at ground level.

2.12   The Chocolate Candy Problem

Freeze the syrup and dip the syrup icicle into melted chocolate. The brandy could alternately be injected into the upright molded bottles, and then capped or closed off with a chocolate plug.

2.17   Logic Puzzle

This is a problem that can be reasoned out, but it helps to use visual thinking. If we remove two lines (thus deleting the top right square), we have five squares, yes, but two excess lines (which could form a new square). So what we need is to look for the possibilities of subtracting a square by removing only one line. Can you see this? Take the top edge of the middle square in the top row, and the bottom line of the middle square in the bottom row, and presto: you have only four squares left. Now use the two lines to form a new square in the nook at either end of the figure.

2.18   Lateral Thinking, One More Time

This puzzle requires three-dimensional spacial thinking. The answer is a tetrahedron. You can construct it like this: Use three toothpicks to form the base. Attach a toothpick to one corner each, then raise the three toothpicks up to meet and form a pyramid. Again, just by having this problem follow the logic puzzle made it harder to make the lateral leap to 3-D space.

2.19   The Soup Spoon Problem

As long as you visualize a regular soup spoon, you soon realize this isn't going anywhere—it is impossible to feed that many people with one spoon at the same time. The key here is to think about the spoon laterally.

- What if this was a spoon made of solid gold? You could sell it and with the money donated to a large inner-city homeless shelter, a lot of people could be fed, all at the same time.
- What if an organization made a huge pizza in the shape of a spoon as a fund raiser? Then people could make a donation, line up, and at the sound of a gong help themselves to a slice.
- Or what if an entrepreneur built a restaurant—named "Rosie's Soup Spoon"—perhaps even in the shape of a spoon, with seating for 100?
- Now, can you think of additional ideas?

CHAPTER 3

3.7 Definition of Entrepreneurship

Quadrant A words: Identifying; developing; better way.
Quadrant B words: Process; to do something; end result.
Quadrant C words: None—there are no "people" or sensing words.
Quadrant D words: Vision; innovative idea; opportunity; creation; new; venture; risk; uncertainty.

CHAPTER 4

4.10 Check Your Assumptions

Most people assume Anthony and Cleopatra are people.
But what if they were fish?

Index

ISBN 142510472-X

9 781425 104726